GM
TIONS

MW01686958

Microsoft®

Outlook® 365

2019 Edition

Denise Seguin

PARADIGM
EDUCATION SOLUTIONS

Minneapolis

Vice President, Content and Digital Solutions: Christine Hurney
Developmental Editor: Katie Werdick
Director of Production: Timothy W. Larson
Associate Production Editor/Project Manager: Melora Pappas
Senior Digital Production Specialist: Julie Johnston
Copy Editor: Sweet Tea Editorial, LLC
Tester: Jeff Johnson
Vice President, Director of Digital Products: Chuck Bratton
Digital Projects Manager: Tom Modl
Senior Director of Digital Products and Onboarding: Christopher Johnson
Supervisor of Digital Products and Onboarding: Ryan Isdahl
Vice President, Marketing: Lara Weber McLellan
Marketing and Communications Manager: Selena Hicks

ISBN 978-0-76389-513-6 (print)
ISBN 978-0-76389-512-9 (digital)

7900 Xerxes Avenue S STE 310
Minneapolis, MN 55431-1118
Email: customerservice@ppij.com
Website: ParadigmEducation.com

Printed in the United States of America

28 27 26 25 24 23 22 21 20 19   1 2 3 4 5 6 7 8 9 10

Activity 5 Arranging Messages in Conversations

Note: To perform Steps 2 and 3 of this activity, you must have completed Chapter 1, Assessment 1 and Assessment 2.

1. With the Inbox folder active, group messages in the Sent Items folder into conversations by completing the following steps:
   a. Click *Sent Items* in the Folder pane.
   b. If necessary, click the View tab.
   c. Click to insert a check mark in the *Show as Conversations* check box in the Messages group.
   d. Click the This folder button in the Microsoft Outlook message box. Outlook arranges the Content pane to show messages that have threaded replies or forwards in groups. Each group has an Expand button next to the message header in the Content pane.

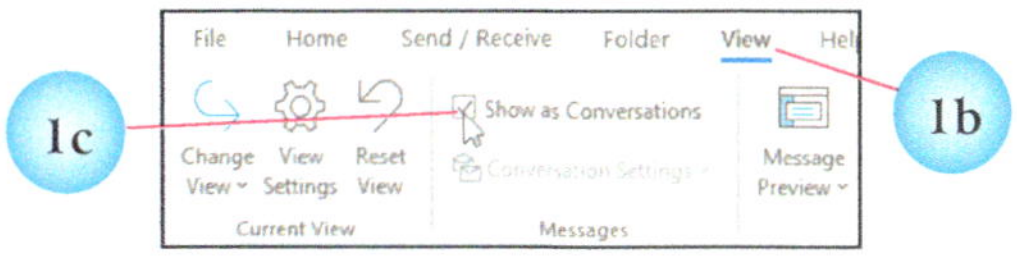

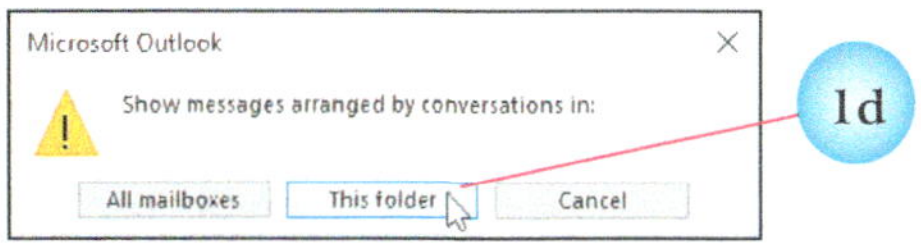

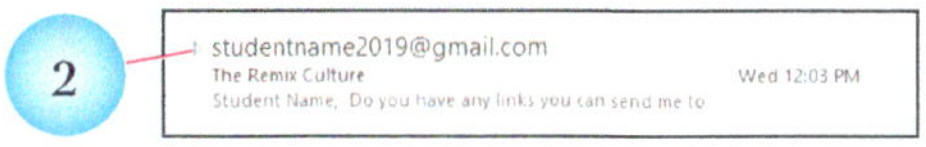

2. Locate the conversation with the subject *The Remix Culture*. The message with the conversation thread will have an Expand button (right-pointing arrow) next to it in the Content pane. Click the Expand button to view the threaded messages. You may need to click the Expand button a second time to expand the list. ***Note:** You will not have this conversation if you did not complete Assessments 1 and 2 in Chapter 1. In that case, skip to Step 4.*
3. Click each message in the conversation and then read the message in the Reading pane.
4. Click to remove the check mark from the *Show as Conversations* check box in the Messages group and then click the This folder button. The messages are no longer grouped by conversations.
5. Click *Inbox* in the Folder pane.

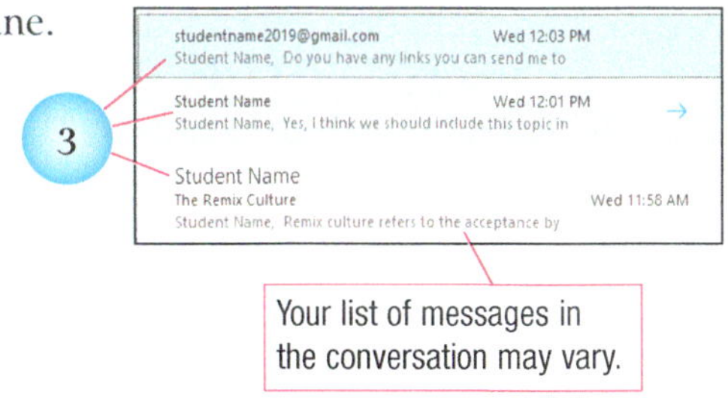

Modifying Conversation Settings

When Conversations view is active, clicking the Conversation Settings button in the Messages group on the View tab displays the drop-down list shown in Figure 2.7. Click *Show Messages from Other Folders* to toggle the view to group conversations in other folders or only in the active folder. Click *Show Senders Above the Subject* to turn on or off the display of the sender's name above the grouped conversation's subject line. Click *Always Expand Selected Conversation* to instruct Outlook to show threaded messages without having to expand the message with the conversation thread yourself. Select *Use Classic Indented View* to have messages indented in the expanded view to show the hierarchy of the messages (the order in which you received the messages).

Figure 2.7 Conversation Settings Drop-down List

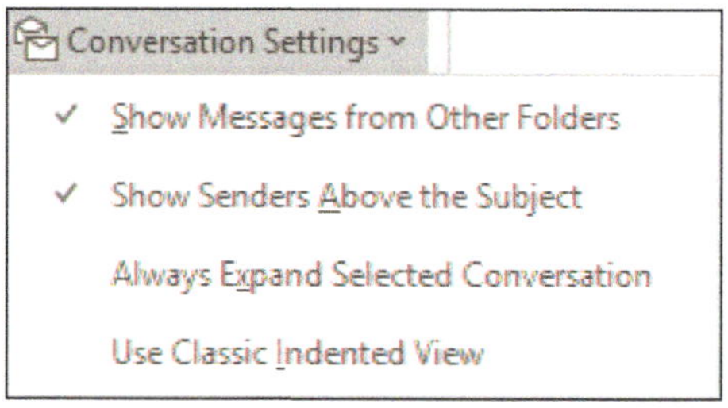

Ignoring and Deleting Messages in a Conversation

Ignore

Clean Up

Two buttons in the Delete group on the Home tab work with conversations: Ignore and Clean Up. The Ignore button moves messages in the selected conversation to the Deleted Items folder. Future messages that are threads of the selected conversation will also be automatically placed in the Deleted Items folder. Use the Ignore button if you are copied on a message by mistake and do not want to follow the thread.

TIP Use the Ignore button to disregard a message that someone accidentally sent to you as part of a group email when you do not need to follow the conversation as recipients respond.

The Clean Up button displays a drop-down list with the options *Clean Up Conversation*, *Clean Up Folder*, and *Clean Up Folder & Subfolders*. Use these options to instruct Outlook to search through the selected conversation(s) and delete the messages with duplicate content. For example, assume that you sent a message to a person and they replied to you. Next, you replied to the person's reply and then they replied to your reply. By default, each reply received contains all the message thread text. Since the last message received contains the original message and all the replies that were exchanged, you really need to save only the last message. Clicking the *Clean Up Conversation* option will automatically move messages with duplicated text to the Deleted Items folder.

Activity 6 Cleaning Up a Conversation

***Note:** To complete this activity, you must have completed Chapter 1, Assessment 1 and Assessment 2.*

1. With the Inbox folder active, group Sent Items by conversations and then clean up a conversation to remove the duplicated messages by completing the following steps:
   a. Click *Sent Items* in the Folder pane.
   b. If necessary, click the View tab.
   c. Click to insert a check mark in the *Show as Conversations* check box in the Messages group and then click the This folder button.
   d. Expand the conversation with the subject *The Remix Culture* (remember that you may need to click the Expand button two times to see all the messages in the conversation).

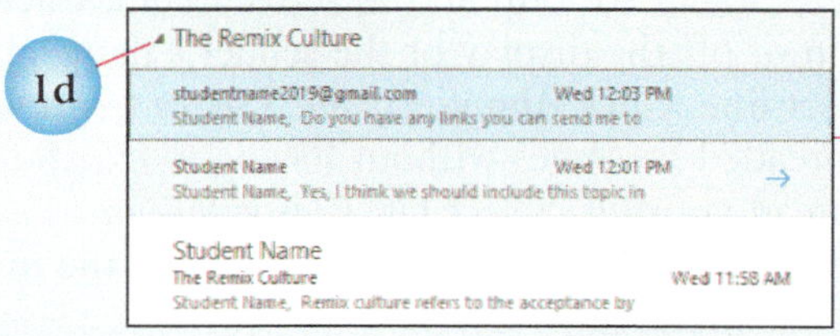

Your list of messages in the conversation may vary.

e. With the first message selected in *The Remix Culture* conversation, click the Home tab.

f. Click the Clean Up button in the Delete group.

g. Click *Clean Up Conversation* in the drop-down list.

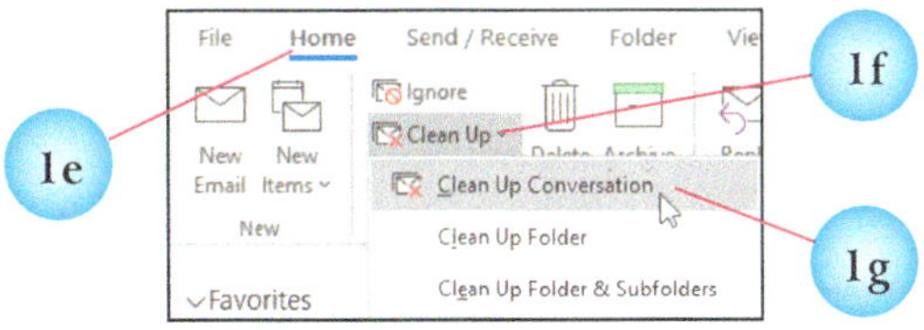

h. In the Clean Up Conversation message box, click the Clean Up button. Click OK if a second message box appears (see ***Note*** below). Outlook moves the messages with duplicated content in the conversation to the Deleted Items folder.
Note: *Click OK and then proceed to Step 3 if you receive the message informing you that no messages were cleaned up. You may or may not have duplicated content, depending on how you completed the assessments in the review and assessment for Chapter 1.*

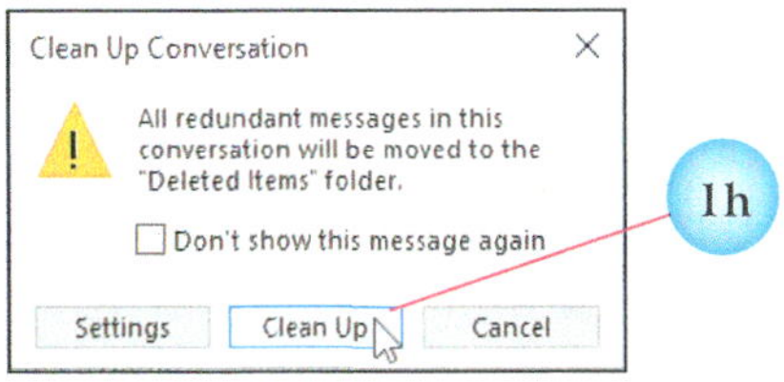

2. Click *Deleted Items* in the Folder pane. Notice the message(s) in the Conversation group with the subject *The Remix Culture* that was moved to the Deleted Items folder.

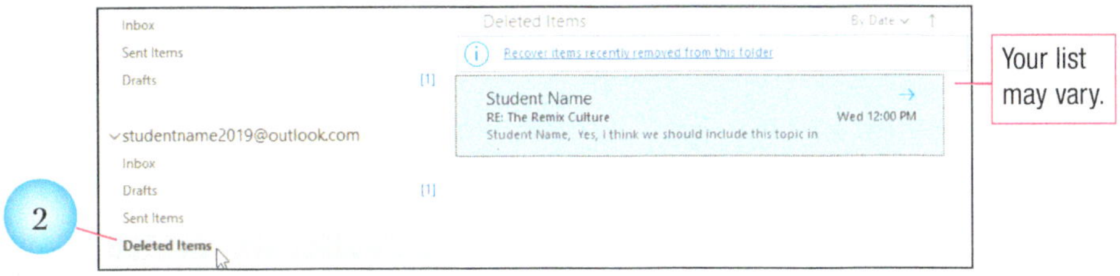

3. Click *Sent Items* in the Folder pane.
4. Click the View tab, click the *Show as Conversations* check box to remove the check mark, and then click the This folder button in the Microsoft Outlook message box.
5. Click *Inbox* in the Folder pane.

Tutorial

Applying Color Categories to Messages

Applying Color Categories to Messages

Organize messages by assigning categories to those messages that can be grouped by a common characteristic. You can arrange the Content pane to display messages grouped by category. This allows you to view a series of related messages together. For example, you can assign a category to all messages about a project and then view the messages by arranging the Content pane by Categories view.

Outlook provides six color categories. You can assign a category to existing messages or assign a category as you are creating a new message. A category color label can be edited to provide a description of the topic to which the category relates. For example, you can rename *Blue category* as *BEA Conference*. The same color category can be applied to other Outlook items so that related appointments, contacts, and tasks are easy to identify. The first time you apply a color category, Outlook prompts you to rename the category.

Categorize

In a Message window, open the Properties dialog box and assign a color category using the Categories button near the bottom left of the dialog box.

Activity 7 Applying Color Categories to Messages

1. With the Inbox folder active, apply color categories to message headers in the Content pane by completing the following steps:
   a. Click to select the message header for the message with the subject text *Outlook Signatures*.

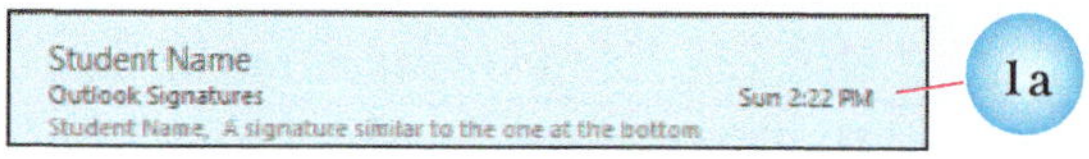

   b. If necessary, click the Home tab.
   c. Click the Categorize button in the Tags group.
   d. Click *Red category* in the drop-down list.
   e. Click the No button in the Rename Category dialog box with a message asking if you want to rename the category. The first time you use a color category, Outlook displays the Rename Category dialog box. (You will rename the categories in Step 2.) Outlook assigns Red category to the message and displays a *Red category* bar in the Reading pane and a red rectangle in the message header.

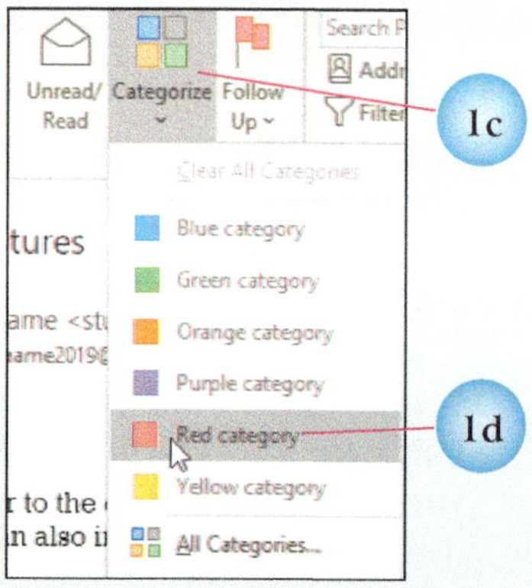

   f. Right-click any one of the message headers with the subject text *Social Media Essay*, point to *Categorize*, and then click *Blue category* on the shortcut menu. Click the No button in the Rename Category dialog box that displays.

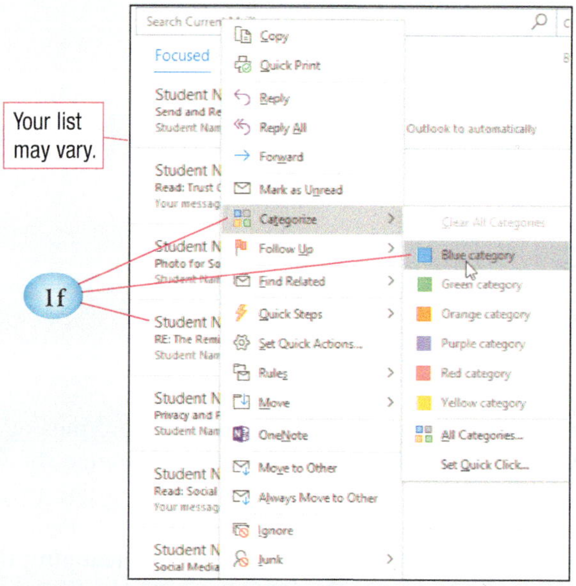

   g. Assign the Blue category to all the other messages with the subject text *Social Media Essay* by completing steps similar to Steps 1a through 1d or Step 1f. ***Note:*** *You will not be prompted to rename the category, since this is not the first time you are using the blue color category.*
2. Edit the labels to create descriptive titles for the color categories by completing the following steps:
   a. Click the Categorize button in the Tags group and then click *All Categories* in the drop-down list.

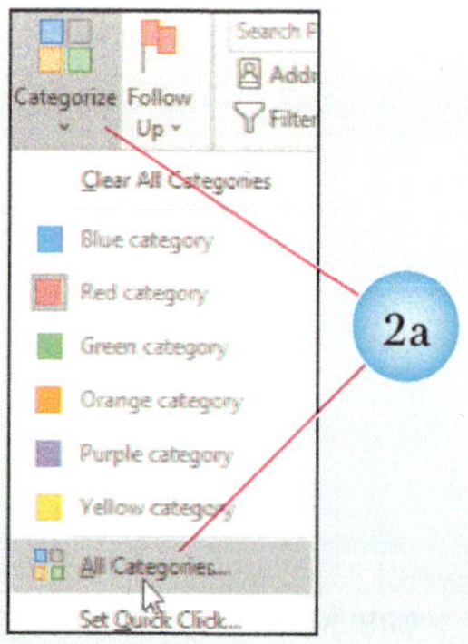

b. With *Blue category* selected in the *Name* list box, click the Rename button.
c. Type Social Media Essay and then press Enter.
d. Click *Red category* in the *Name* list box and then click the Rename button.
e. Type Outlook Tips and then press Enter.
f. Click OK. Notice that the colored category bar in the Reading pane for the selected message now displays the descriptive label for the color category.

3. Click the View tab and then click the *Categories* option in the Arrangement group option box.
4. Review the arrangement of messages in the Content pane. Notice that all the messages you assigned the blue color category are grouped in an expanded list with the heading *Social Media Essay* next to a blue rectangle. The message assigned the red color category is grouped and shown expanded below the heading *Outlook Tips*. Messages with no color category assigned are displayed at the top of the list.
5. Restore the messages back to the default date arrangement by clicking the *Date* option in the Arrangement group option box on the View tab.

A check mark displays next to a category if a message assigned a color category is active when the dialog box is opened.

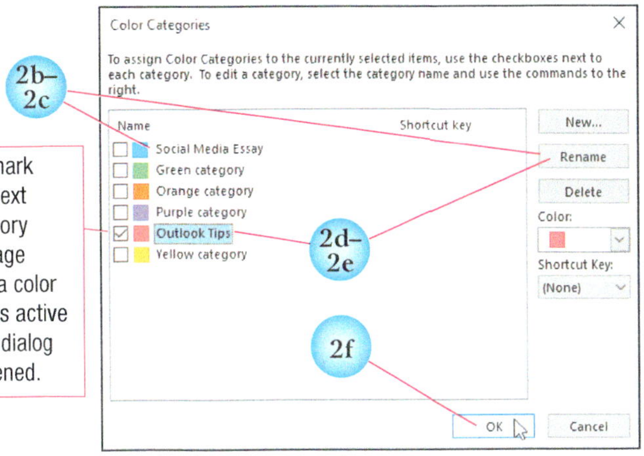

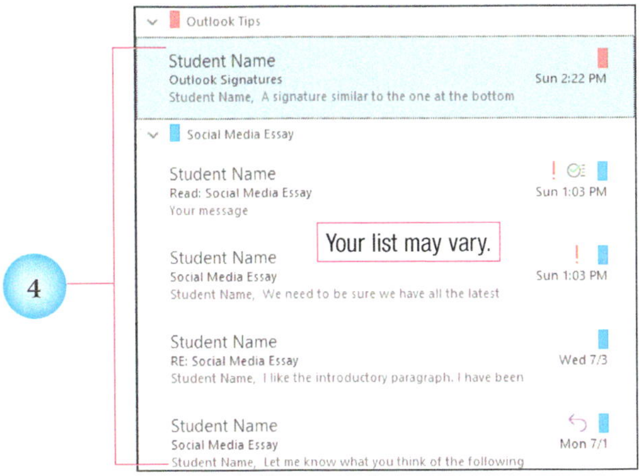

Applying Categories to Messages in Outlook.com

Click a message header to open the message and display message options on the Menu bar. Click the Categorize button on the Menu bar and then click the desired color category. Color categories assigned to messages and renamed in the desktop edition carry over to the same email account in Outlook.com.

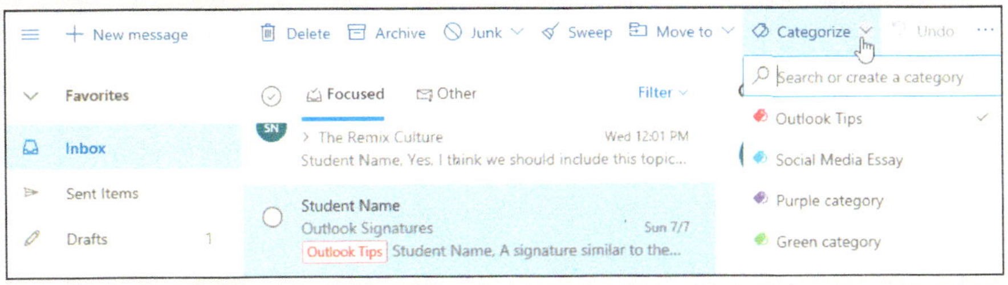

Tutorial

Creating a Folder and Moving Messages

Creating a Rule to Move Messages Automatically

Managing Mail Folders

So far, you have been working with five folders set up in Outlook to organize mail messages: Inbox for mail that has been received, Outbox for mail that has been created but not yet uploaded to the mail server, Sent Items for messages that have been uploaded to the server and delivered to recipients, Drafts for messages started but not finished, and Deleted Items for messages that have been deleted. Creating a new folder with a descriptive name allows you to manage messages by putting related items together in one place. For example, if you are working on a project and have been sending and receiving several messages about it, consider creating a folder in which to store those messages separately from other messages.

Think of creating a folder and then moving related messages to it as organizing messages in separate containers. Clicking the folder name in the Folder pane allows you to view the group or project messages independently from other messages.

Expanding Folders and Creating a New Folder

The folder list in the Folder pane displays the names of the Outlook mail folders in a hierarchical arrangement. A right-pointing arrow (Expand button) next to a folder name in the list indicates that the folder contains subfolders. Click the Expand button to show the names of the subfolders.

Complete the following steps to create a new folder or subfolder:

1. Right-click the name of the Outlook folder in the Folder pane in which you want the new folder created as a subfolder. For example, right-click *Inbox* if you want to create a new subfolder within the Inbox folder.
2. Click *New Folder* on the shortcut menu.
3. Type the name for the new folder and then press Enter.

New Folder

To create a new folder using the ribbon, click the Folder tab and then click the New Folder button in the New group. This opens the Create New Folder dialog box, as shown in Figure 2.8. Type the name for the new folder in the *Name* text box and then click the name of the folder in which the new folder should be placed. For example, to create a new folder as a subfolder in the Inbox, click *Inbox* in the *Select where to place the folder* list box and then click OK. To create the new folder at the same level in the folder hierarchy as Inbox, click the email account name at the top of the folder list.

Figure 2.8 Create New Folder Dialog Box

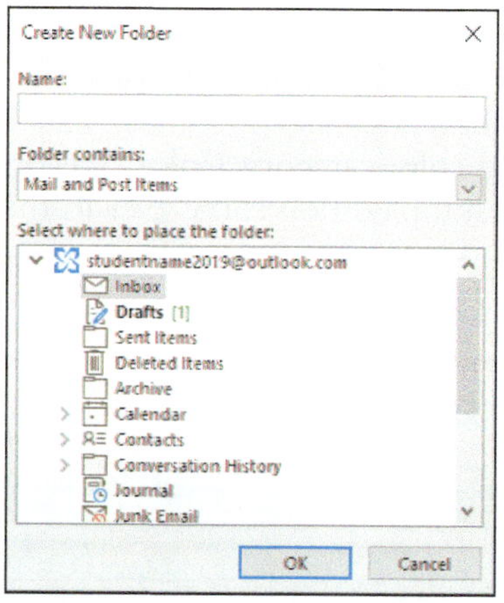

Moving Messages

Before you move messages, expand the folders in the Folder pane, if necessary. Once you have created new folders in which to organize messages, Outlook provides several methods for moving a message from one folder to another:

Move

- With the message header selected in the Content pane, drag the message header from the current folder to the desired folder name in the Folder pane.
- With the message header selected in the Content pane, click the Move button in the Move group on the Home tab and then click the desired folder name in the drop-down list.
- Right-click the message header in the Content pane, point to *Move* on the shortcut menu, and then click the desired folder name. Click the *Other Folder* option if the desired folder name does not appear in the list of folders. Then, in the Move Items dialog box, select the destination folder name in the *Move the selected items to* list box and click OK.
- Select the message header in the Content pane and then click the Move to button (first button) in the Quick Steps group on the Home tab. The Move to button displays a folder name if the button has already been assigned to a folder.

The first time the Move to button in the Quick Steps group is used, the First Time Setup dialog box opens. In the dialog box, click the *Move to folder* option box arrow (displays *Choose folder*), click the desired folder name, or click *Other Folder* and then double-click the desired folder name in the Select Folder dialog box. Click Save when finished. The Move to button displays the folder name. The next time you need to move a message to the same folder, select the message and then click the folder name button in the Quick Steps group.

To change the destination folder displayed on the Move to button in the Quick Steps group, display the shortcut menu for the button and then click the *Edit [folder name]* option. In the Edit Quick Step dialog box, click the current folder name option box, click the desired folder, or click *Other Folder* and then double-click the desired folder name in the Select Folder dialog box. Click the Save button when finished.

More than one message can be moved in one operation by selecting multiple message headers first. To do this, hold down either the Ctrl key or the Shift key on the keyboard while clicking with the mouse to select message headers. If the messages to be moved are not next to each other in the Content pane, hold down the Ctrl key while you click each message header. If the messages to be moved are in a continuous list in the Content pane, click the first message header at the top of the list, hold down the Shift key, and then click the last message header in the list. This action selects all messages from the first message header clicked to the second message header clicked.

Activity 8 Creating a New Folder and Moving Messages

1. With the Inbox folder active, create a subfolder within the Inbox folder by completing the following steps:
   a. Click the Folder tab and then click the New Folder button in the New group.

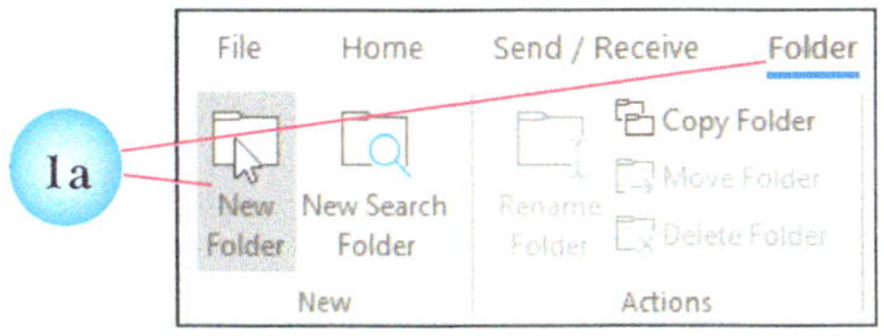

b. In the Create New Folder dialog box with the insertion point positioned in the *Name* text box, type Social Media.

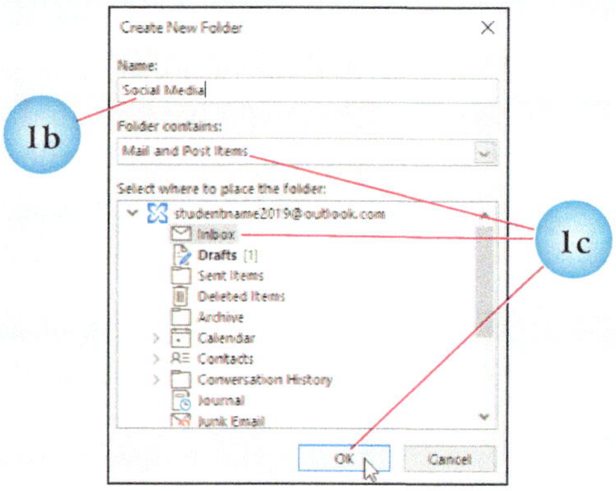

c. With *Folder contains* already set to *Mail and Post Items* and *Inbox* already selected in the *Select where to place the folder* list box, click OK.

2. Move messages from the Inbox folder to the Social Media folder by completing the following steps:
   a. Select the message header in the Content pane for the first message assigned the blue *Social Media Essay* category.
   b. Hold down the Ctrl key and then click each additional message header assigned the blue *Social Media Essay* category. If you click a message by mistake, click the message header a second time while holding down the Ctrl key and the message will be deselected. If you are using a tablet with a touchscreen and cannot select multiple messages, proceed to Step 2c and move each message individually.

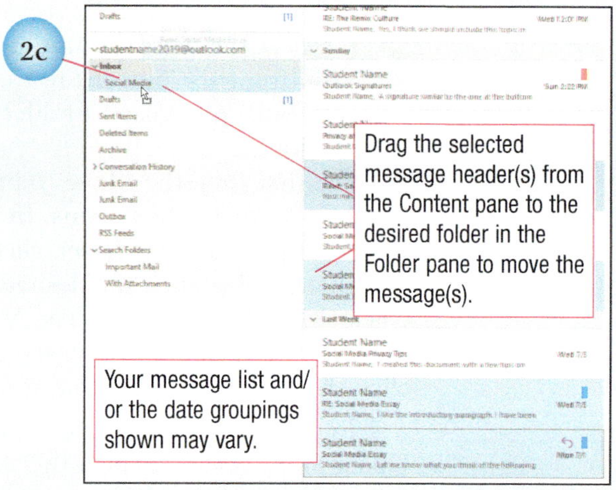

   c. Position the mouse pointer within any of the selected message headers, hold down the left mouse button, and then drag the selected message headers from the Content pane to the *Social Media* folder name in the Folder pane. If you are using a tablet with a touchscreen, you may need to slide each message header individually to the *Social Media* folder name.

3. Move a message to the Social Media folder using the Move button by completing the following steps:
   a. If necessary, select the message header for the message with the subject text *Social Media Privacy Tips* and then click the Home tab.

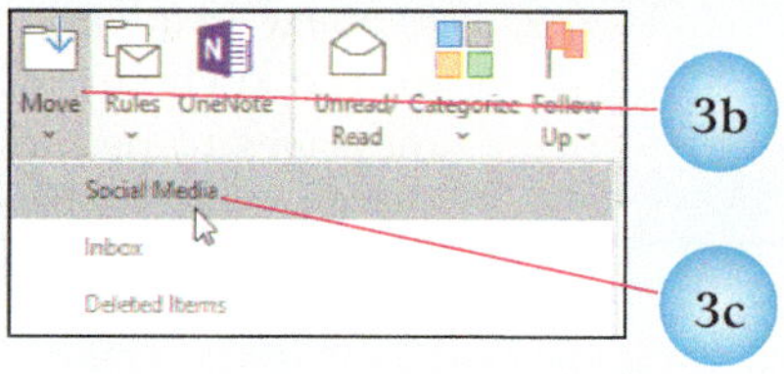

   b. Click the Move button in the Move group.
   c. Click *Social Media* in the drop-down folder list. The message is moved to the Social Media folder.

4. Click *Social Media* in the Folder pane to view the folder contents.

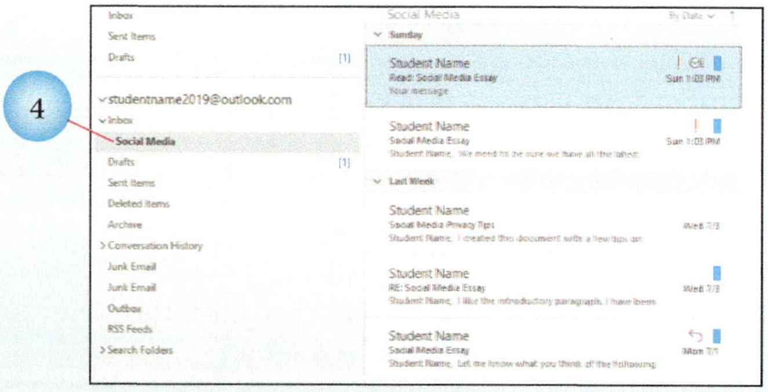

5. Click *Inbox* to make Inbox the active folder. Notice that the quantity of Inbox messages you need to manage is much smaller now that you have moved messages to a subfolder.

Managing Messages in Outlook.com

Right-click a folder to display the shortcut menu and then click *Create new subfolder* to create a new subfolder within an existing folder. To create a new folder at the same level as the Inbox folder, scroll to the bottom of the folder list, click *New folder*, type the name for the new folder, and then press Enter. Move messages by selecting message headers and using the *Move to* drop-down list on the Menu bar.

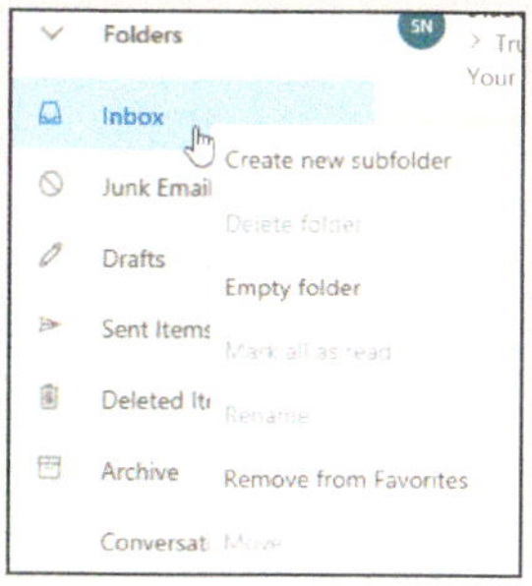

TIP Set aside a time on the same day each week to clean up your Inbox by deleting unneeded messages and moving messages to folders. Doing this will help to keep your Inbox a manageable size. If you receive several emails a day, you may need to do this more than once per week.

A common method used to manage mail messages is to organize messages in folders in a similar manner to how you organize documents on your hard disk or storage medium. Create folders and subfolders and routinely move related messages from the Inbox to these other folders. Use the buttons in the Actions group on the Folder tab to manage folders. Buttons in the Actions group include renaming, copying, moving, and deleting folders.

Make deleting messages when they are no longer needed and emptying the Deleted Items folder part of your message management routine. Consider that in a month's time (assuming a standard five-day workweek), the number of messages in your Inbox will grow to 200 if you receive 10 messages a day, and after five months, you will be trying to manage over 1,000 Inbox messages!

Creating a Rule to Move Messages to a Folder Automatically

A ***rule*** is an action that is performed on messages based on a condition that you specify. Rules can be created that instruct Outlook to move messages to specific folders automatically. The condition that makes the messages move can be based on a name, a subject, or a message setting such as the *Importance* option.

Rules

The easiest method for creating a rule based on a sender's name or subject is to select a message in the Content pane that meets the condition, click the Rules button in the Move group on the Home tab, and then click *Create Rule* in the drop-down list. Outlook opens the Create Rule dialog box, where you can choose the condition and the action you want performed. Information from the active message is inserted next to the appropriate condition options, as shown in Figure 2.9.

Figure 2.9 Create Rule Dialog Box

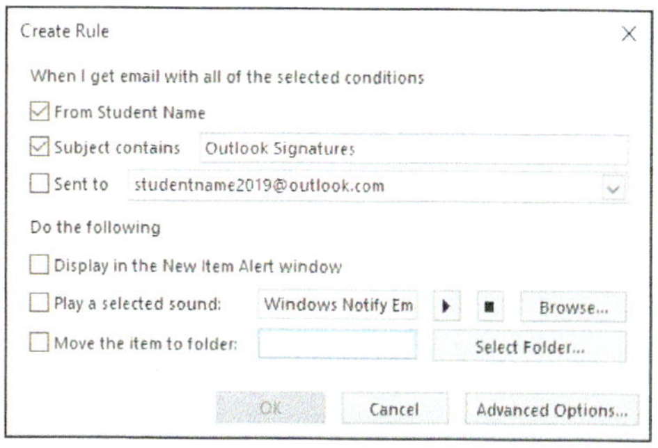

Activity 9 Creating a New Folder and Message Rule

1. With the Inbox folder active, create a new subfolder within the Inbox by completing the following steps:
   a. Right-click *Inbox* in the Folder pane and then click *New Folder* on the shortcut menu.
   b. Type Outlook Tips in the blank text box that appears below *Inbox* in the Folder pane and then press Enter.

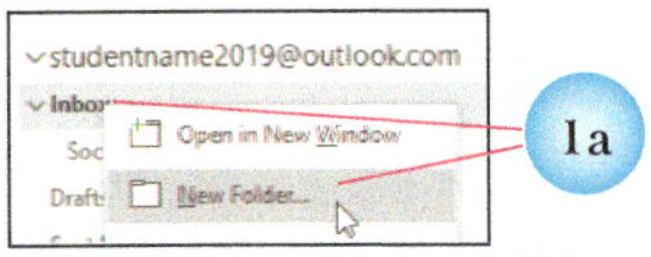

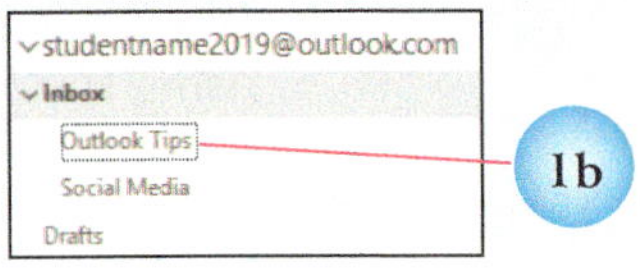

2. Create a rule to move messages received in the Inbox that have information about using the Outlook application to the Outlook Tips folder by completing the following steps:
   a. Select the message header in the Content pane with the subject *Outlook Signatures*.
   b. Click the Rules button in the Move group on the Home tab and then click *Create Rule* in the drop-down list.
   c. Click to insert a check mark in the *Subject contains* check box in the *When I get email with all of the selected conditions* section in the Create Rule dialog box.
   d. Click to place an insertion point in the *Subject contains* text box and then delete the word *Signatures* so that the entry in the text box consists of only the word *Outlook*.
   e. Click to insert a check mark in the *Move the item to folder* check box in the *Do the following* section. This causes the Rules and Alerts dialog box to open with the folder list.
   f. In the Rules and Alerts dialog box, click the Expand button next to *Inbox* in the *Choose a folder* list box, click *Outlook Tips*, and then click OK. This will place the text *Outlook Tips* in the *Move the item to folder* text box in the Create Rule dialog box.
   g. Click OK in the Create Rule dialog box to complete the rule.

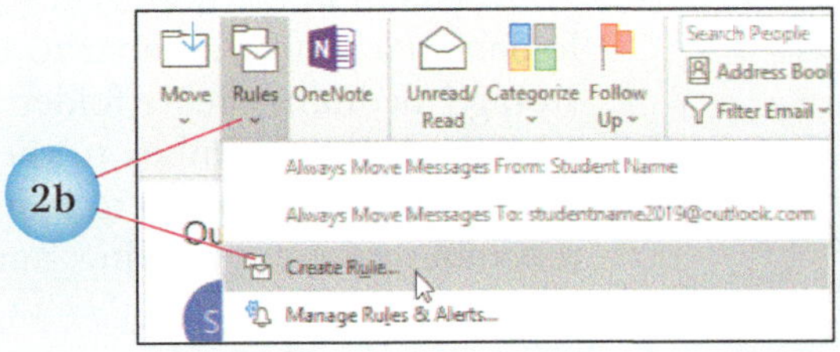

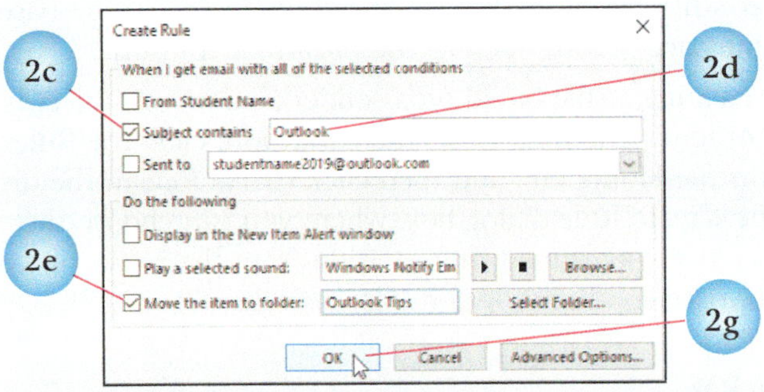

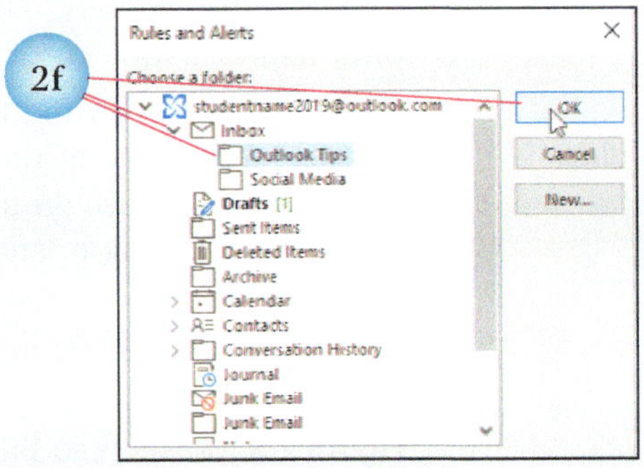

   h. Click OK in the Success message box indicating that the rule has been created.

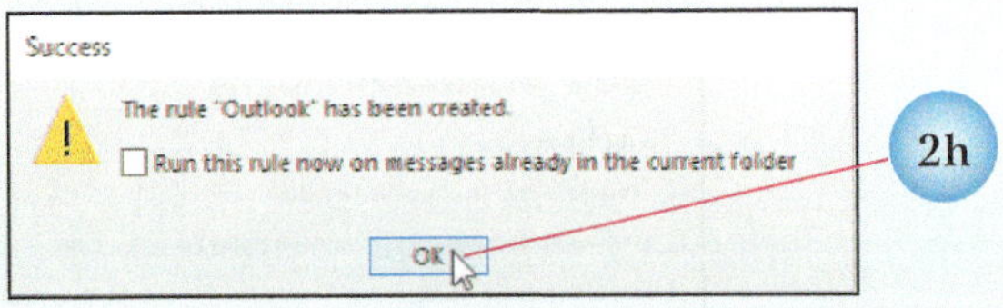

3. New rules that are created are applied automatically to messages as they are received. Manually apply the message rule created in Step 2 to existing messages in the Inbox by completing the following steps:
   a. Click the Rules button in the Move group and then click the *Manage Rules & Alerts* option in the drop-down list.
   b. In the Rules and Alerts dialog box with the Email Rules tab active, click the Run Rules Now button.

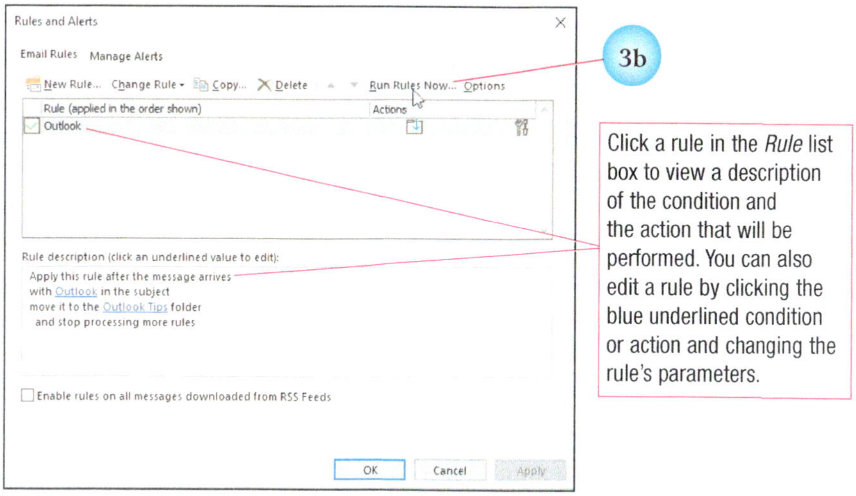

   c. In the Run Rules Now dialog box, click to insert a check mark in the *Outlook* check box in the *Select rules to run* list box and then click the Run Now button. Outlook applies the rule to the existing messages and moves messages that meet the specified condition.
   d. Click the Close button to close the Run Rules Now dialog box.
   e. Click OK to close the Rules and Alerts dialog box.

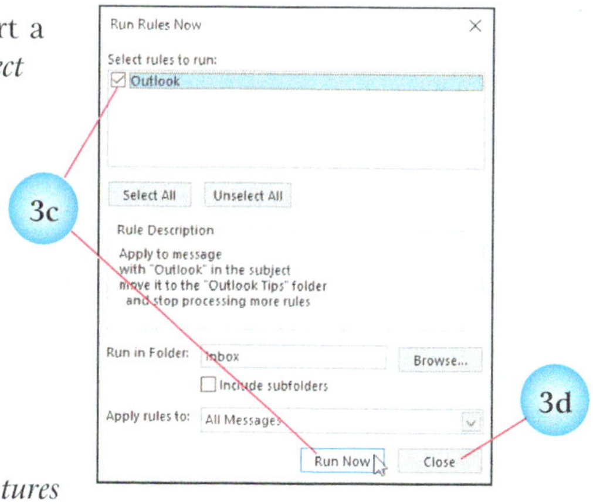

4. Click *Outlook Tips* in the Folder pane to view the folder contents. Notice that Outlook moved the message with the subject *Outlook Signatures* to the Outlook Tips folder. In the future, any message received with the word *Outlook* in the *Subject* field will be placed in the Outlook Tips folder automatically.
5. Click *Inbox* to make Inbox the active folder.

TIP Consider creating a rule that will move messages received from your manager to an Action folder so messages from him or her are automatically grouped together in your Inbox.

Creating rules is a powerful message management tool for controlling the size of your Inbox. If you receive many messages in a day and several that are related in some way, consider creating folders and rules to direct the messages to specific locations where you can easily view and manage the content. Outlook displays folder names that have new messages in bold and indicates a count of the unread emails in the folder list. When using rules to automatically direct messages to folders, periodically look at the folder list to see if you have new email that needs to be read.

Creating a Rule in Outlook.com

Display the Rules pane by clicking the Settings button (gear icon located near the right end of the blue Outlook banner) and then clicking the *View all Outlook settings* option at the bottom of the Settings panel. With *Mail* selected in the left pane in the Settings dialog box, click *Rules* in the center pane and then click the *Add new rule* option in the right pane (displays next to plus symbol).

Type a name for the new rule in the text box next to 1 (displays the text *Name your rule*) and then select the appropriate options in the *Add a condition* section and the *Add an action* section. Click the Save button when finished and then close the Settings dialog box.

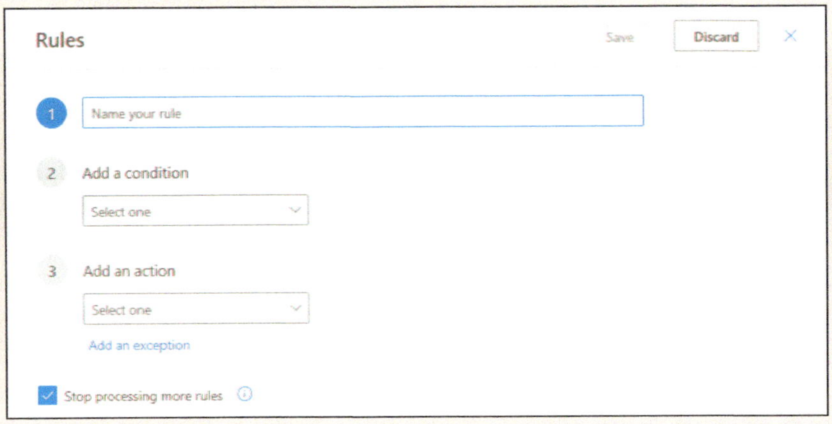

Creating a New Rule Using the Rules Wizard

Exchange Server

Click the File tab, click the Automatic Replies button, and then click *Send automatic replies* to set up a response message that will be sent automatically to the first email message you receive from each sender when you are away from work. Enter text that tells the reader when you will be back and provide alternative contact information for longer absences.

In Activity 9, the new rule was created by selecting a message header for a message that met the condition. In some cases, you may want to create a new rule from scratch. The Rules Wizard, shown in Figure 2.10, helps you to create a new rule based on templates for the most frequently used rules grouped into two types: organization and notification.

Templates in the *Stay Organized* section help you move messages to folders or follow up on messages that require further action. For example, if a message arrives in your Inbox with a certain project name in the subject text, you can have it automatically flagged for follow-up and moved to a project folder. Templates in the *Stay Up to Date* section prompt you with a notification alert when a certain type of message arrives in your Inbox. For example, a message can be automatically sent to your smartphone if a message from your manager arrives in your Inbox.

Complete the following steps to create a new rule using the Rules Wizard:

1. Click the File tab.
2. Click the Manage Rules & Alerts button in the Account Information backstage area.
3. Click the New Rule button in the Rules and Alerts dialog box with the Email Rules tab active.

TIP Users who are not connected to an Exchange account do not have access to the Automatic Replies feature; however, combining a reply template with a rule will produce the same result. Use the Tell Me feature to open the Help task pane and look up step-by-step instructions in the article titled *Use rules to create an out of office message.*

4. Select the rule template and customize the rule description in the Rules Wizard dialog box, as shown in Figure 2.10. Use the Next button in the Rules Wizard to specify multiple conditions and/or exceptions to the rule and to assign a name for the rule.
5. Click the Finish button in the Rules Wizard dialog box when you are done.

Figure 2.10 Rules Wizard Dialog Box

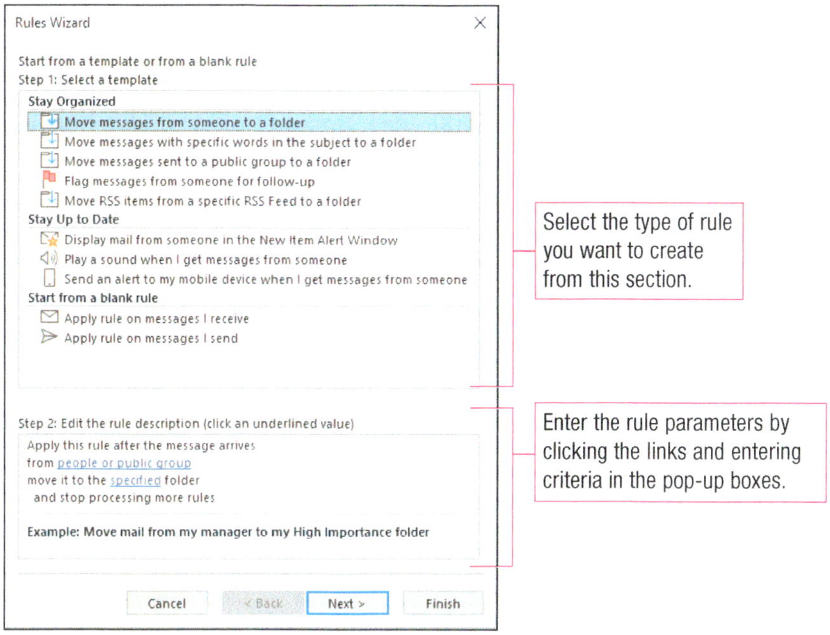

Understanding the Junk Email and Phishing Filters

TIP *Phishing* is the term used to describe messages that lure you to a disguised website where you are asked to enter passwords, credit card numbers, or other personal information, which identity thieves use to commit fraud.

You have probably noticed the Junk Email folder in the Folder pane. It is a good idea to check this folder periodically to review its contents and see if legitimate messages have been moved to Junk Email by mistake. In an attempt to protect you from spam and malicious phishing messages, Outlook automatically screens all new messages as they are received. Messages that are deemed to be spam are moved to the Junk Email folder. Messages that are deemed to be phishing are placed in the Inbox but have attachments, links, and Reply and Reply All buttons disabled.

Managing Messages That Junk Email Filters Mishandle

Junk

Messages that appear in your Inbox that are not screened correctly by the junk email filters can be marked as junk so that future messages from the same sender are moved to the Junk Email folder. To do this, select the message that was missed by the junk filters, click the Junk button in the Delete group on the Home tab, and then click the *Block Sender* option in the drop-down list.

At times, legitimate messages are routed to the Junk Email folder by mistake. When that happens, select the message in the Junk Email folder, click the Junk button in the Delete group on the Home tab, and then click the *Never Block Sender, Never Block Sender's Domain (@example.com)*, or *Never Block this Group or Mailing List* option in the drop-down list.

Modifying Junk Email Filter Settings

By default, junk email protection is set to *No Automatic Filtering*. This setting moves messages that are likely spam and messages from blocked senders to the Junk Email folder. You can increase the level of protection to *Low* or *High*. Changing the protection level will catch more junk messages; however, keep in mind that more legitimate messages will also be considered junk. Outlook junk filters identify spam by reviewing the following characteristics of a message: email address and internet domains, time sent, and keywords associated with spam.

To view and change the filter settings, click the Junk button in the Delete group on the Home tab and then click *Junk E-mail Options* in the drop-down list. This action opens the Junk Email Options dialog box, as shown in Figure 2.11.

With the Options tab active, you can change the protection level from *No Automatic Filtering* to *Low, High,* or *Safe Lists Only*. You can also choose to have messages identified as junk email permanently deleted instead of moved to the Junk Email folder.

Figure 2.11 Junk Email Options Dialog Box with Options Tab Selected

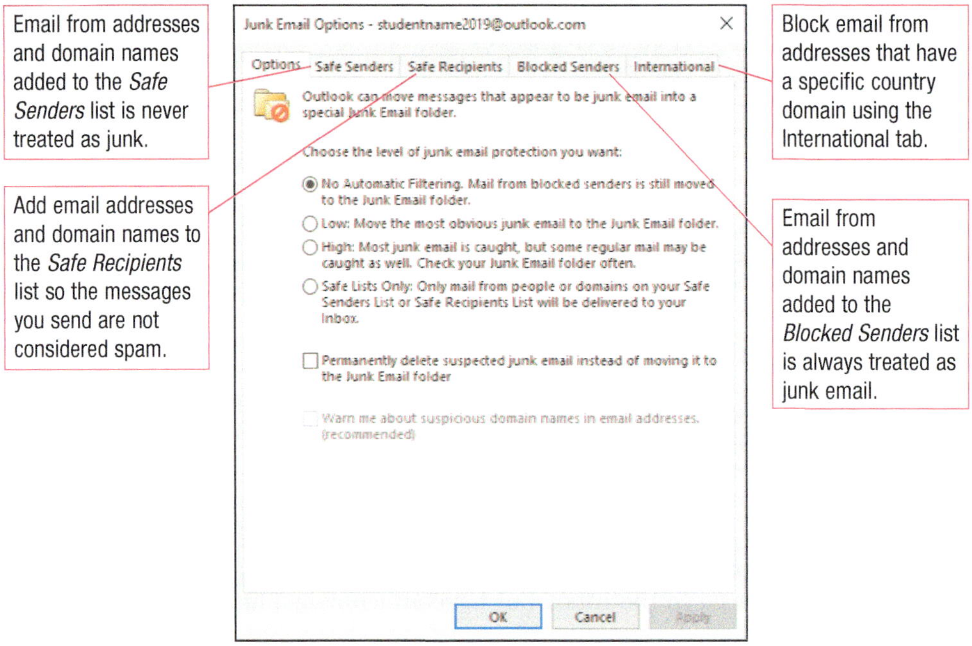

Archiving Folders

Over time, your mail folders grow larger in size due to the accumulation of stored messages. If you use email for essential records of transactions, agreements, plans, or other details, you should archive the messages instead of deleting them. An ***archive*** is a file containing old messages that have been purged (removed) from the mail folder. The archived messages can be retrieved, if necessary, by expanding the archive folder that displays in the Content pane when an archive file has been opened.

You can manually transfer old items to the archive file, or you can turn on and then allow the global AutoArchive feature to have Outlook transfer the items automatically. Items are considered for archiving when they reach a specified age. When active, the default setting is for AutoArchive to run every 14 days and clean out items that are older than six months. You can change the AutoArchive options for each Outlook folder. AutoArchive can either delete items or move old items to the storage file. The default setting moves old items to a file named *archive.pst*.

To change the default options for AutoArchive, click the File tab and then click *Options* in the left pane in the Account Information backstage area to display the Outlook Options dialog box. Click *Advanced* in the left pane in the dialog box and then click the AutoArchive Settings button in the *AutoArchive* section. In the AutoArchive dialog box, shown in Figure 2.12, change the options as required and then click OK.

TIP When activated, AutoArchive runs automatically. Every 14 days, Outlook displays a message asking if you want to run the archive process to remove older messages to the archive folder.

Figure 2.12 AutoArchive Dialog Box

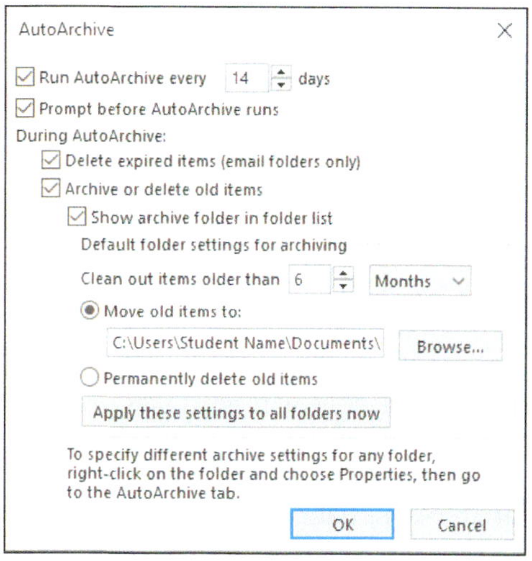

TIP Before archiving, clean out from mail folders any messages that do not need to be retained to avoid storing messages unnecessarily.

To set AutoArchive options for individual folders, right-click the folder name in the Folder pane, click *Properties* on the shortcut menu, and then click the AutoArchive tab in the Properties dialog box. Choose from the following three options: *Do not archive items in this folder, Archive items in this folder using the default settings*, and *Archive this folder using these settings*. Choosing *Archive this folder using these settings* makes active the options shown in Figure 2.13. Changes made to AutoArchive properties for individual folders override the global settings in the Outlook Options AutoArchive Settings.

Figure 2.13 Inbox Properties Dialog Box with AutoArchive Tab Selected

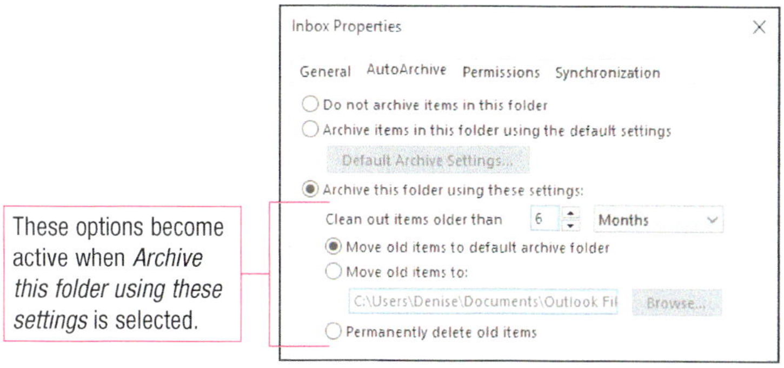

By default, the Outlook folders Calendar, Tasks, Sent Items, and Deleted Items have the option *Archive items in this folder using the default settings* selected. The folders Inbox, Junk Email, Notes, Drafts, and Outbox have the option *Do not archive items in this folder* selected. Contacts are not archived.

Manually Archiving Items

Archive

Tools

To move an individual message to the Archive folder, select the message header in the Content pane and then click the Archive button in the Delete group on the Home tab. You can also select multiple messages and move them in one step. Note that when you archive items manually, the size of your mailbox file is not reduced.

To have Outlook perform an archive by examining messages during a specified time frame, click the File tab, click the Tools button in the Account Information backstage area, and then click the *Clean Up Old Items* option in the drop-down list. This action opens the Archive dialog box, as shown in Figure 2.14. Click *Archive all folders according to their AutoArchive settings* to archive all folders based on each folder's AutoArchive properties, or click *Archive this folder and all subfolders* to choose the folder and time frame you want to process. For the latter option, you next click the folder name in the folders list box; change the date in the *Archive items older than* text box; and use the Browse button to specify the drive, folder, and file name for the archive file. Clicking OK starts the archive process. Click the Back button to close the backstage area.

The message *Archiving [folder name]* displays near the right end of the Status bar as messages are removed to the archive file. You will also see the messages in the folder being removed if the folder is active in the Content pane.

In a workplace, email messages are retained using the same rules as any other business document (such as a paper invoice or purchase order). Check with your manager before manually archiving your messages. A corporate archive system may be in place that operates on the company's mail server for all mailboxes. It is possible an individual archive might violate the organization's security policy.

Figure 2.14 Archive Dialog Box

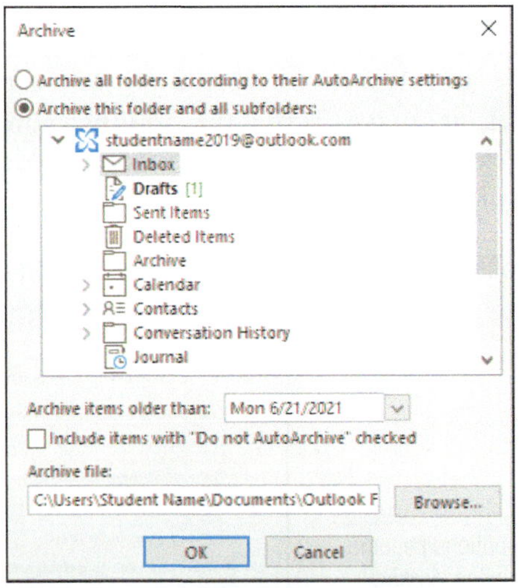

Activity 10 Turning On AutoArchive Settings and Manually Archiving Sent Items

1. With the Inbox folder active, check the global AutoArchive settings on the computer you are using by completing the following steps:
   a. Click the File tab and then click *Options* in the left pane in the backstage area.
   b. Click *Advanced* in the left pane in the Outlook Options dialog box.
   c. Click the AutoArchive Settings button in the *AutoArchive* section.

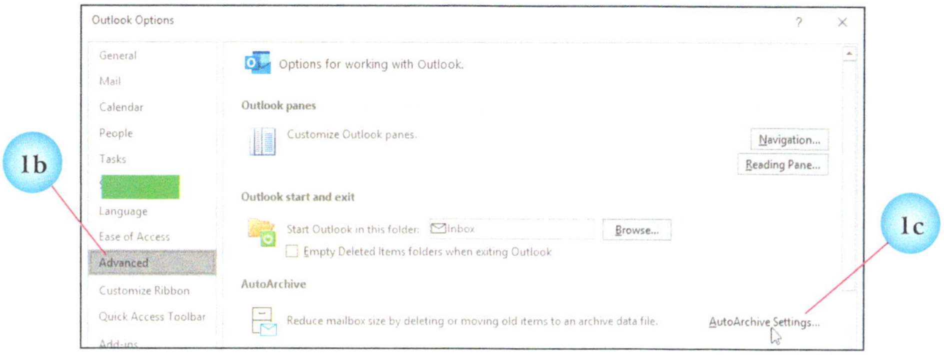

   d. If necessary, click to insert a check mark in the *Run AutoArchive every [ ] days* check box to turn AutoArchive on. ***Note:*** *Skip this step if the option is already active.*
   e. Review the default AutoArchive settings with AutoArchive active. For example, note that with the AutoArchive feature turned on, the default option prompts you before AutoArchive cleans out items that are older than six months.

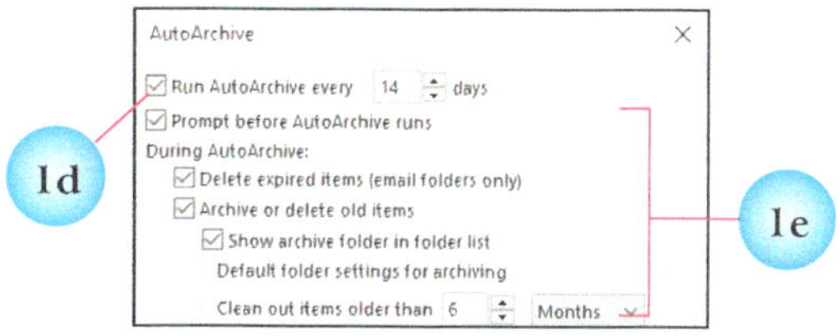

   f. Click OK to close the AutoArchive dialog box and then click OK to close the Outlook Options dialog box.
2. View and change AutoArchive settings for the Inbox folder by completing the following steps:
   a. Right-click *Inbox* in the Folder pane.
   b. Click *Properties* on the shortcut menu.
   c. Click the AutoArchive tab in the Inbox Properties dialog box. The default AutoArchive option for this folder is *Do not archive items in this folder*.
   d. Click *Archive this folder using these settings* to make it active. ***Note:*** *Skip this step if the option is already active.*

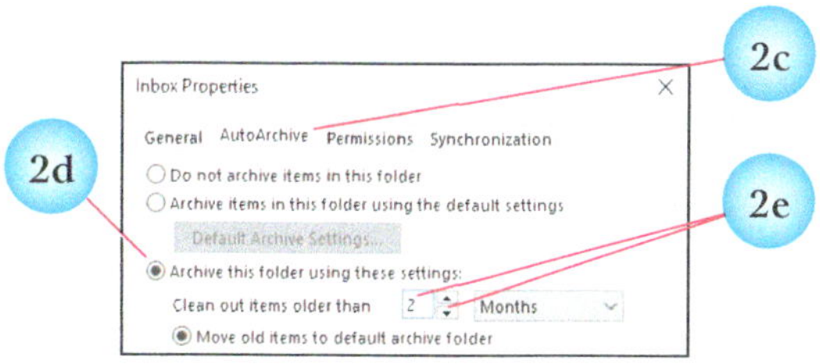

   e. Click the *Clean out items older than* measurement box increment (up) or decrement (down) arrow until the number *2* appears in the box.
   f. Click OK.
3. Manually archive the Sent Items folder by completing the following steps:
   a. Click the File tab.
   b. Click the Tools button and then click *Clean Up Old Items* in the drop-down list.

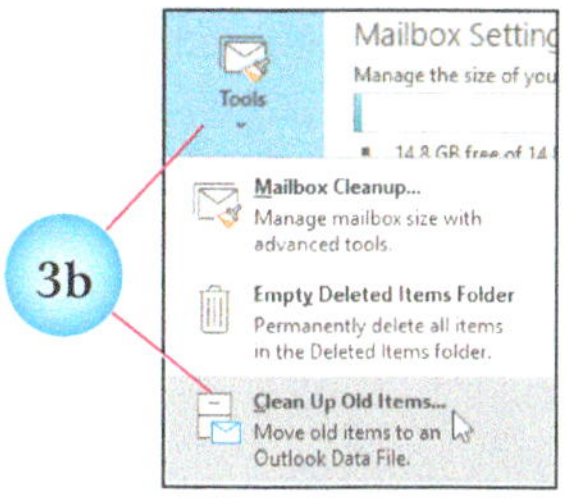

c. If necessary, click *Archive this folder and all subfolders* in the Archive dialog box to make that option active.
d. Click *Sent Items* in the folder list box.
e. Click the *Archive items older than* option box arrow and then click a date in the drop-down calendar that is two days before the current date.
f. Click the Browse button. In the Open Outlook Data Files dialog box, navigate to the drive for your storage medium, select and delete the current file name in the *File name* text box, and then type SentItemsArchive-YourName-[CurrentDate] where *[CurrentDate]* is replaced by today's date and your first and last names are substituted for *YourName*.
g. Click OK to close the Open Outlook Data Files dialog box.
h. Click OK to close the Archive dialog box. Depending on the number of messages in the Sent Items folder, archiving may take a few moments to complete.

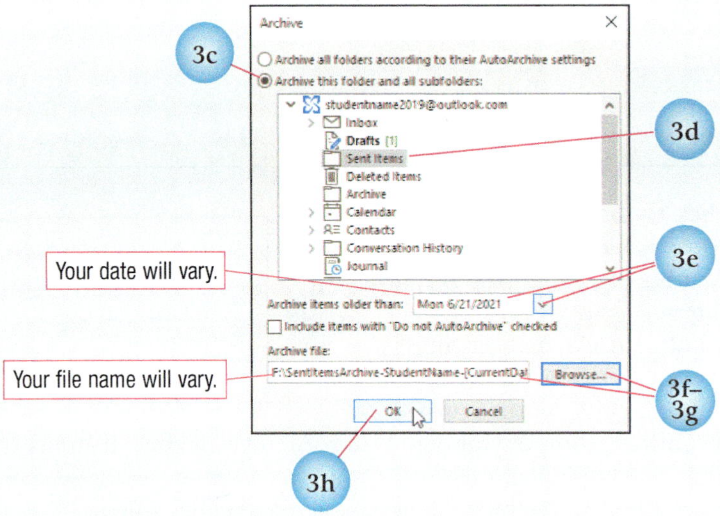

4. Click the Back button in the backstage area. Notice the new *Archives* entry in the Folder pane.
5. Click *Sent Items* in the Folder pane. Only messages sent in the last two days are shown; the list may be empty if you have not sent any messages in the last two days.
6. Click the Expand button next to *Archives* in the Folder pane. The list expands and displays a Sent Items folder. Notice also that Outlook added Deleted Items and Search Folders folders.
7. Click *Sent Items* in the expanded folder list below *Archives* in the Folder pane. Outlook displays in the Content pane the messages that were moved from the main Sent Items folder in Step 3. ***Note:*** *The Content pane may be empty if you do not have messages in your Sent Items folder that are more than two days old. If that is the case, return to Step 3 and redo the steps, changing the date in Step 3e to today's date.*
8. Make Inbox the active folder in the Content pane.

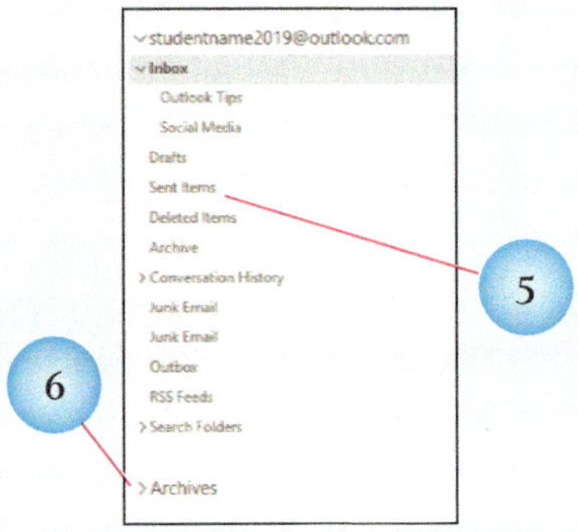

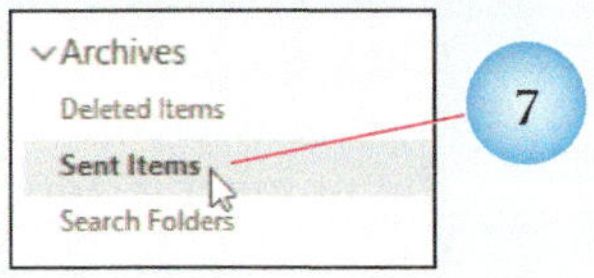

TIP In the Outlook for Office 365 enterprise edition, a feature called *Online Archive* moves old messages to an online archive set up and maintained by a company administrator.

If you create an archive file on your computer's hard drive, make a copy of the archive on a removable storage medium (such as an external hard drive or USB flash drive) for backup and record retention purposes. Alternatively, consider saving a copy of the archive in cloud storage (such as OneDrive), where the file can be accessed from any device with an internet connection. Email archiving and records management are critical functions in today's workplace, which relies on email for transactions, instructions, meeting notes, and other communications.

Using the Mailbox Cleanup Tool

Click the File tab, click the Tools button in the backstage area, and then click *Mailbox Cleanup* in the drop-down list to open the Mailbox Cleanup dialog box, as shown in Figure 2.15. From this dialog box, you can view the current sizes of your mailbox and individual folders, find old items, start an AutoArchive process, view and empty the Deleted Items folder, and delete all alternate versions of items in your mailbox. The advantage of using the Mailbox Cleanup feature is that you can access all the mail folder maintenance tools from one dialog box.

Figure 2.15 Mailbox Cleanup Dialog Box

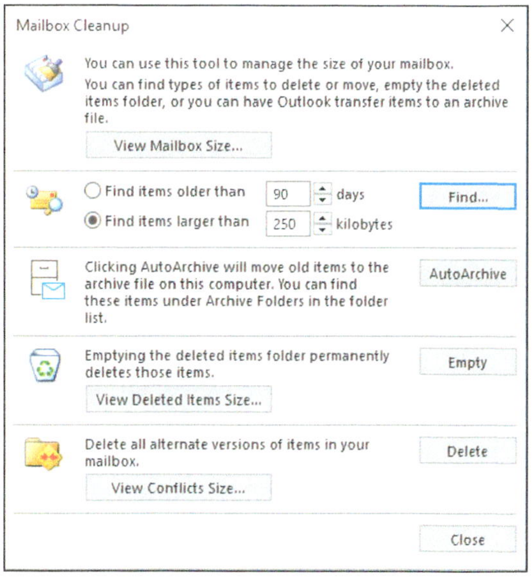

Restoring Archived Items

To retrieve items saved in an archive file, click the File tab, click *Open & Export* in the left pane in the backstage area, and then click the Open Outlook Data File button in the Open panel. Browse to the location of the archive file and then double-click the file name in the Open Outlook Data File dialog box. Expand *Archives* in the Folder pane and then click the name of the folder in the expanded list containing the archived messages. Open, read, and print messages as required. You can copy or move items from the archive folder to current folders, if necessary. When finished, right-click *Archives* in the Folder pane and then click *Close "Archives"* on the shortcut menu.

Chapter Summary

- Find messages by typing a keyword or phrase in the *Instant Search* box at the top of the Content pane. Buttons in the Scope and Refine groups on the Search tab are used to reduce the number of messages in the search results.
- A search folder stores search settings for searches that are often repeated. Create a new search folder using the New Search Folder button in the New group on the Folder tab.
- Click the Up arrow sort control at the top of the Content pane to change the sort order of messages from newest to oldest.
- Click the *By Date* group control at the top of the Content pane to change how messages are grouped, or select an option in the Arrangement group option box on the View tab.
- In Conversations view, Outlook groups a message with all its threaded replies and forwarded messages. Insert a check mark in the *Show as Conversations* check box on the View tab and then choose the current folder or all mailboxes to group messages by conversations.
- The Conversation Settings button in the Messages group on the View tab provides options for grouping and displaying conversations.
- Ignoring a conversation means that current and future messages in the thread are deleted.
- The Clean Up button in the Delete group on the Home tab automatically deletes duplicated messages in a conversation.
- Apply color categories to messages as a method of organizing related messages.
- Moving messages into folders is another way of organizing related messages. Create new folders or create subfolders within existing folders to store messages.
- Move messages by dragging the message headers from the Content pane to other folder names in the Folder pane.
- A *rule* stores conditions that move messages to a specific folder as soon as they are received. Create a new rule based on an existing message that meets the condition or by using the Rules Wizard.
- Outlook automatically screens new messages and moves messages considered spam to the Junk Email folder. Junk email filters work by comparing email addresses to lists of known spam or other message characteristics associated with spam and by using artificial intelligence to identify a message likely to be spam or phishing.
- Use options from the Junk button in the Delete group on the Home tab and modify options in the Junk Email Options dialog box to refine the junk email filtering in your Inbox.
- An archive is a file containing old items that have been purged from the active folder. Use the AutoArchive dialog box to set global archive options. Individual folders can have their own AutoArchive options.
- Perform a manual archive by selecting a message and then clicking the Archive button in the Delete group on the Home tab or by opening the Archive dialog box from the Tools button in the backstage area.
- The Mailbox Cleanup dialog box provides all folder maintenance features in one location.
- Open an Archive file to view, print, and/or restore an archived message.

Commands Review

FEATURE	BUTTON	RIBBON TAB AND GROUP, OR OTHER METHOD	SHORTCUT
Archive messages	OR	Home, Delete OR File, Tools	
Arrange messages		View, Arrangement OR click *By Date* at top of Content pane	
Assign color category		Home, Tags	
Change AutoArchive settings		File, *Options, Advanced*	
Clean up conversation		Home, Delete	
Create message rule		Home, Move OR File, Manage Rules & Alerts	
Create new folder		Folder, New Folder	Ctrl + Shift + E
Find message		Click in *Instant Search* box	Ctrl + E
Ignore conversation		Home, Delete	Ctrl + Delete
Modify junk email options		Home, Delete	
Move messages		Home, Move OR Home, Quick Steps	
Search folders		Folder, New Search Folder	
Use Conversations view		View, Messages	
Use search tools on Search tab		Click in *Instant Search* box	Ctrl + E

Quick Steps

Use Instant Search
1. Click in *Instant Search* box.
2. Type search word(s).
3. Review items in search results list.

Clear Search Results
Click Close Search button

Create a Search Folder
1. Click Folder tab.
2. Click New Search Folder button in New group.
3. Click desired search folder option.
4. If necessary, add criteria in *Customize Search Folder* section.
5. Click OK.

Arrange Messages
1. Click View tab.
2. Click desired option in Arrangement group option box.

OR

1. Click desired control at top of Content pane.
2. If necessary, click desired option in drop-down list.

Arrange Messages by Conversations
1. Click View tab.
2. Click *Show as Conversations* check box in Messages group.
3. Click All mailboxes or This folder button.

Clean Up a Conversation

1. Select conversation to be cleaned up.
2. Click Home tab.
3. Click Clean Up button in Delete group.
4. Click *Clean Up Conversation.*
5. Click *Clean Up.*

Apply a Color Category to a Message

1. Select message in Content pane.
2. Click Categorize button in Tags group on Home tab.
3. Click desired color category.
4. If prompted, type descriptive label for category and click OK.

Create a Folder

1. Right-click name of Outlook folder in which to create new subfolder.
2. Click *New Folder.*
3. Type name for new folder.
4. Press Enter.

OR

1. Click Folder tab.
2. Click New Folder button in New group.
3. Type name for new folder.
4. Select name of folder in which to place new folder.
5. Click OK.

Create a Rule

1. Select message header that meets condition.
2. Click Rules button in Move group on Home tab.
3. Click *Create Rule.*
4. Change condition options as required.
5. Click *Move the item to folder* check box.
6. If necessary, expand folder list.
7. Click desired folder name.
8. Click OK three times.

Change Junk Email Filter Settings

1. Click Junk button in Delete group on Home tab.
2. Click *Junk E-mail Options.*
3. Change options as required.
4. Click OK.

Change Global AutoArchive Settings

1. Click File tab.
2. Click *Options.*
3. Click *Advanced.*
4. Click AutoArchive Settings button.
5. Change settings as required.
6. Click OK two times.

Perform a Manual Archive

1. Click to select message(s).
2. Click Archive button in Delete group on Home tab.

OR

1. Click File tab.
2. Click Tools button.
3. Click *Clean Up Old Items.*
4. Click *Archive this folder and all subfolders.*
5. Click folder name to archive.
6. Enter date in *Archive items older than* text box.
7. Click Browse button.
8. Navigate to drive and folder and type archive file name.
9. Click OK two times.

CHAPTER 3

Using Calendar for Scheduling

Performance Objectives

Upon successful completion of Chapter 3, you will be able to:

1 Schedule, edit, move, and delete appointments and events
2 Schedule recurring appointments
3 View and print daily, weekly, and monthly calendars
4 Change the Calendar view to show only active appointments
5 Turn on the Reading pane and view appointment details
6 Apply color categories to appointments and view appointments by category
7 Create conditional formatting rules
8 Schedule meetings by sending meeting requests
9 Accept, decline, and update meeting requests
10 Change calendar options
11 Display and work with multiple calendars
12 Share a calendar
13 Delete a calendar

The Calendar module in Outlook is used to schedule appointments and events such as a dental checkup or a conference. An appointment can be created for any type of activity for which you want to set aside a block of time in your calendar. A meeting can also be created in the calendar on a day and time where you invite other people to join you for a set time. An appointment or meeting that occurs on a regular basis can be created as a recurring item that is entered only once. The Reminder feature sounds a chime and displays a reminder message at a set interval before the appointment, event, or meeting time.

Meetings are integrated with email so that an individual can send a meeting request to others as an email message. When the invitee responds to the message by accepting a meeting request, the details are automatically added to his or her calendar. In this chapter, you will use Calendar to schedule multiple appointments, events, and meetings and explore various methods of displaying, printing, and viewing calendar information.

The online course includes additional training and assessment resources.

Data Files

No student data files are required for this chapter.

Tutorial

Display the Calendar

Schedule an Appointment

Scheduling Appointments and Events

Click the Calendar text label or icon on the Navigation bar to display the contents of the Calendar module. The calendar opens for the current date in Day, Work Week, Week, or Month view depending on the view displayed when Outlook was closed in the prior session. Figure 3.1 displays the Calendar in Day view. The top section in the Folder pane is the Date Navigator, which shows the current month with directional arrows that allow you to browse backward and forward to previous and upcoming months. The current month or current date has the background shaded blue in the Date Navigator.

TIP The Peek feature shows you the current day's appointments in a pop-up balloon. Point to Calendar on the Navigation bar to peek at today's schedule from another module. Within Calendar, point to a scheduled appointment to view more appointment details.

Schedule a new appointment by first displaying the month, week, or day of the appointment in the Appointment area. To do this, click the appointment date in the Date Navigator or click the Back or Forward button (left- or right-pointing arrow) next to the date displayed at the top of the Appointment area and then scroll one month, week, or day at a time. (Alternatively, click the Go To dialog box launcher, type the date, and then press Enter or click OK.) Click within the date box for the date (Month view) or next to the appointment time (Day, Work Week, or Week view) in the Appointment area, type a short description of the appointment, and then press Enter or click outside the appointment box.

Display the Appointment window, shown in Figure 3.2 to enter more details about an appointment. To enter a new appointment using the Appointment window, click the desired day or time in the Appointment area and then perform one of the following actions:

New Appointment

- Click the New Appointment button in the New group on the Home tab.
- Double-click next to the appointment starting time in the Appointment area.
- Right-click next to the appointment starting time in the Appointment area and then click *New Appointment* on the shortcut menu.

Figure 3.1 Calendar Window in Day View

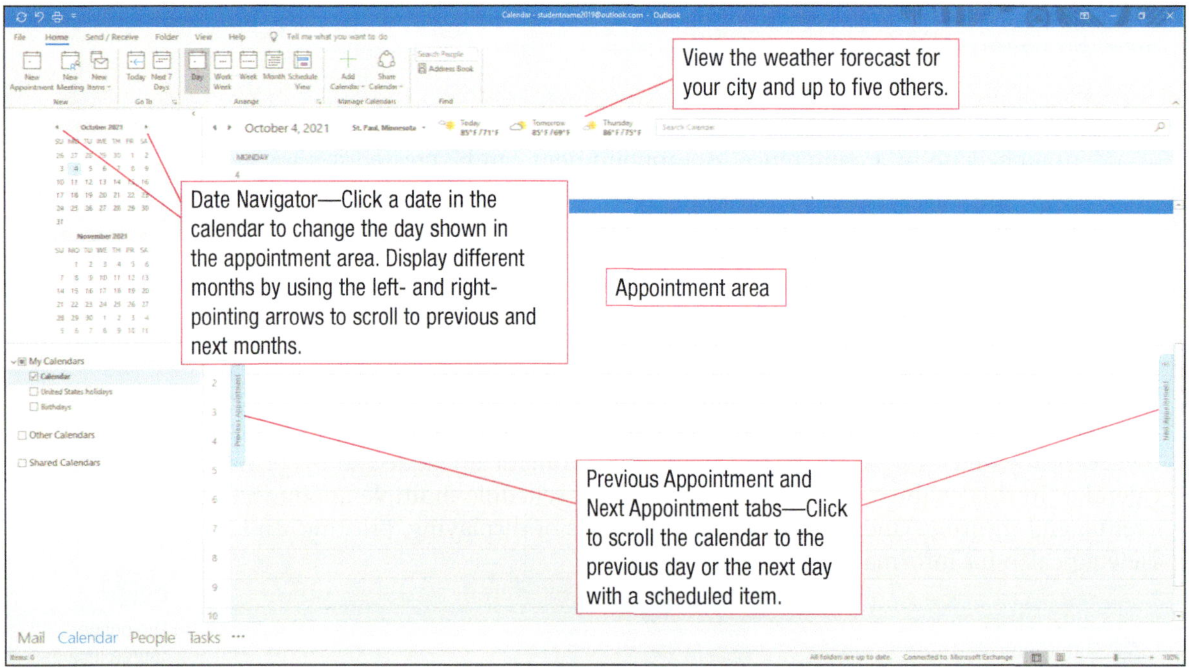

Figure 3.2 Appointment Window

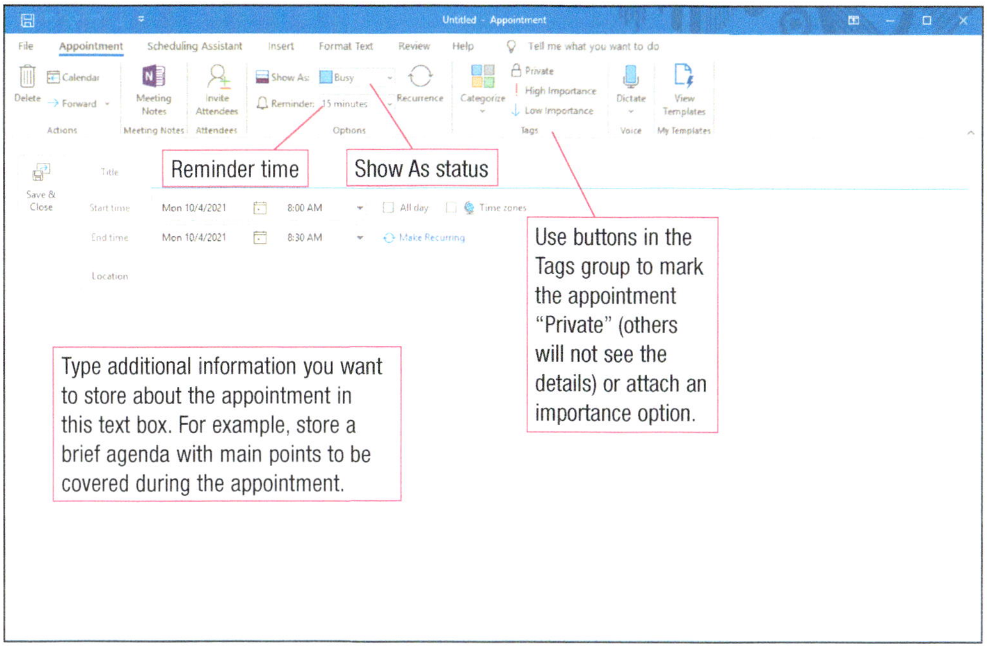

Type a description of the appointment in the *Title* text box. The *Start time* option box will display the day and time that you selected in Calendar before opening the Appointment window. Change the start day and time by clicking the *Start time* day or time option box calendar or arrow and then clicking the correct entry. If necessary, you can select the current time entry and type a specific time of your own, such as *10:50 AM*. Enter the end time for the appointment by clicking the *End time* day or time option box calendar or arrow and then clicking the correct day or time in the drop-down list. Click next to the Location button to open the *Location* text box and type information about where the appointment will take place.

By default, a reminder is set to display a reminder message and play a chime 15 minutes before the scheduled appointment. Click the *Reminder* option box arrow in the Options group on the Appointment tab to change the reminder time or select *None* in the drop-down list to turn off the Reminder feature.

Use the *Show As* option box arrow in the Options group on the Appointment tab to change the appointment status from the default option of *Busy* to *Free*, *Working Elsewhere*, *Tentative*, or *Out of Office* in the scheduled time slot. When other people view your calendar to plan a meeting, the time slot will appear as a colored or patterned bar, depending on the *Show As* setting.

Use the text box below *Location* to type additional information about the appointment that you want to store, such as driving directions, an agenda, reminders for items to take with you to the appointment, and background information on the person with whom you are meeting. When all the required entries have been made, click the Save & Close button in the Appointment window.

Activity 1 Scheduling Appointments and Navigating Using Go To Date

Note: The activities in this chapter instruct you to schedule appointments and meetings in October 2021. Check with your instructor, if necessary, for alternative instructions that schedule these items in the current month or in October of the current year.

1. With Outlook open, click the Calendar text label or icon on the Navigation bar. If necessary, change to Day view by clicking the Day button in the Arrange group on the Home tab.

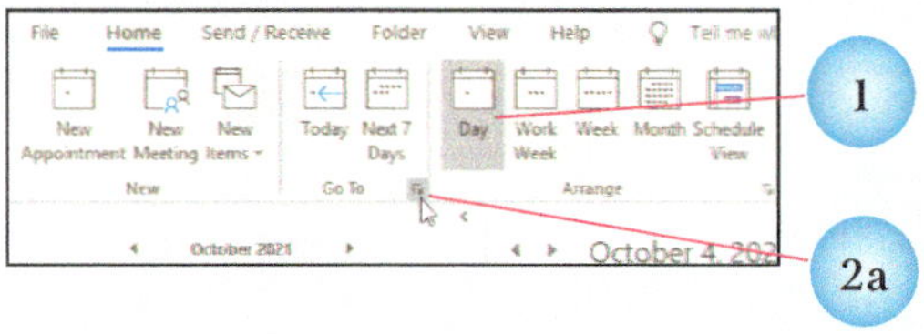

2. Add a new appointment to the calendar using the click-and-type method by completing the following steps:
   a. Click the Go to Date launcher button located at the bottom right in the Go To group on the Home tab.
   b. In the Go To Date dialog box, type 10/15/2021 and then press Enter or click OK.
   c. Click next to *10:00 AM* in the Appointment area. A blue shaded appointment box appears with a default duration set to one-half hour.
   d. Type Staff meeting for health and safety updates.
   e. Press Enter or click in the Appointment area outside the appointment box.

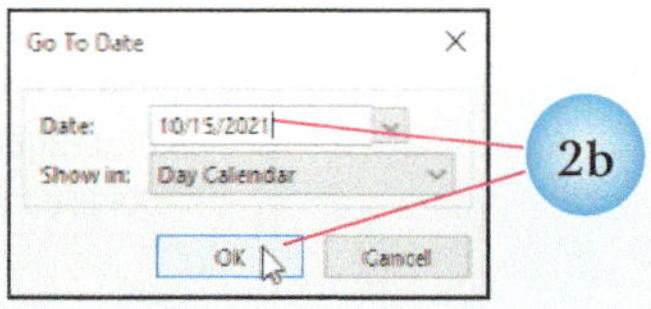

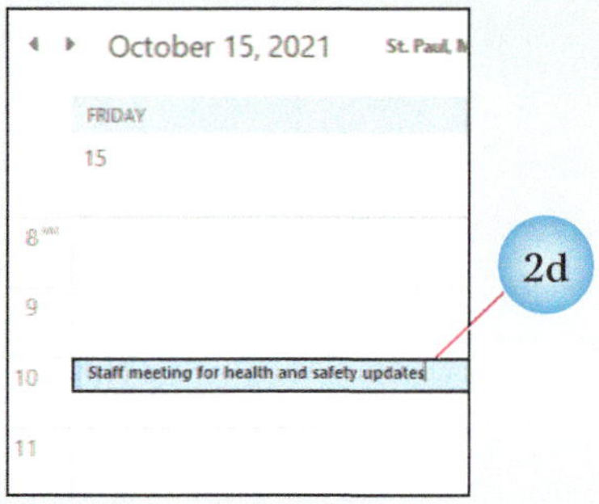

3. Add a new appointment using the Appointment window by completing the following steps:
   a. With *October 15, 2021* the active date, click next to *1:00 PM* in the Appointment area.
   b. Click the New Appointment button in the New group on the Home tab. An Untitled - Appointment window opens.
   c. With the insertion point positioned in the *Title* text box, type Lunch meeting with Leslie Taylor.
   d. Click the *End time* time option box arrow and then click *2:30 PM (1.5 hours)* in the drop-down list.
   e. Click next to the Location button to activate the *Location* text box and then type Kelly's Bistro.
   f. Click the *Show As* option box arrow in the Options group on the Appointment tab (currently displays *Busy*) and then click *Out of Office* in the drop-down list.
   g. Click the High Importance button in the Tags group on the Appointment tab.

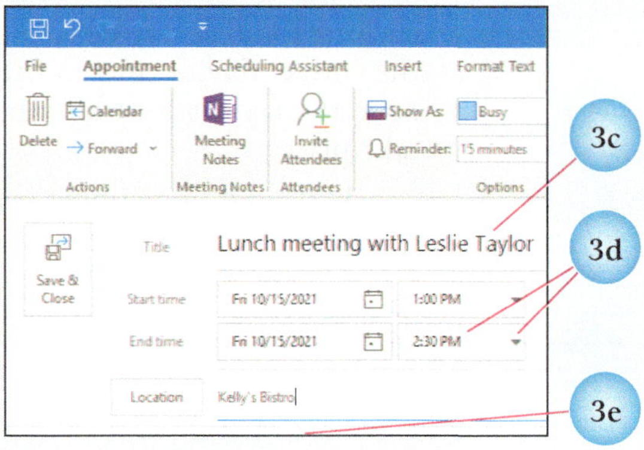

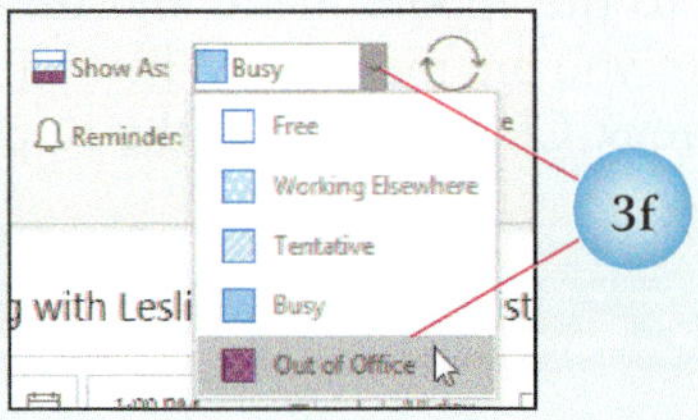

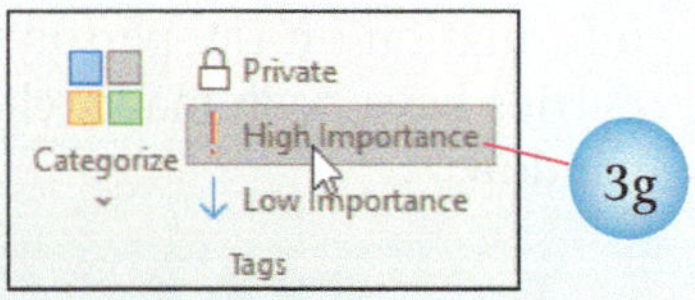

h. Click the *Reminder* option box arrow in the Options group (currently displays *15 minutes*) and then click *30 minutes* in the drop-down list.

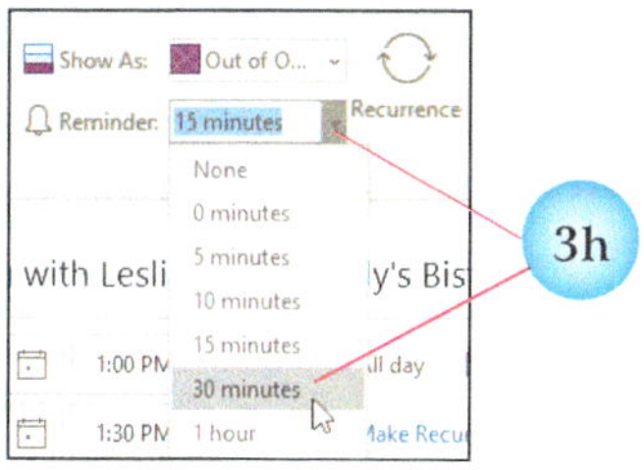

Right-click in the Time bar to display options for time increments.

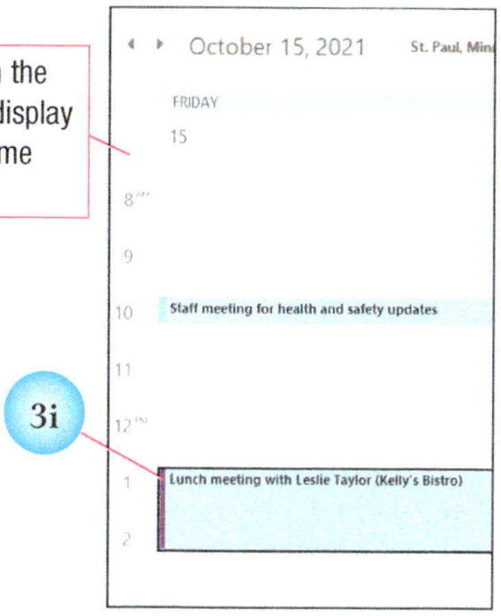

i. Click the Save & Close button in the Appointment window. The appointment appears in the Appointment area with a purple border at the left edge of the appointment box. Purple is the color displayed for times in the calendar that are *Out of Office*.

4. Click the File tab and then click *Print*. In the Print backstage area with *Daily Style* already selected in the *Settings* section, click the Print button or change the printer to the option that prints to a PDF and then click the Print button. You determine an appropriate file name if saving as a PDF.

Check Your Work

Scheduling Appointments in Outlook.com

To display the calendar, click the App launcher button in the upper left corner of the window next to Outlook, click *All apps*, and then click *Calendar* in the Apps pane, or click the Calendar icon on the Navigation bar at the bottom of the Folder pane.

Click the App launcher button to change to the Calendar module, or click the icon on the Navigation bar.

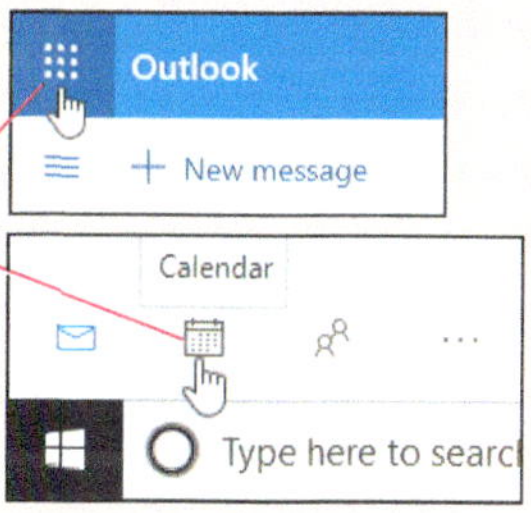

Click *Day*, *Work Week*, *Week*, or *Month* near the top right of the window to change the display by selecting another view in the drop-down list. Change the date by clicking a date in the current month in the Date Navigator. Use the Previous (Up arrow) and Next (Down arrow) buttons at the right of the current month to change to the previous or next month.

Add a new appointment in the Appointment area by clicking next to the appointment time and then entering the appointment details in the pop-out Calendar box that appears. Click *More options* in the bottom right corner of the box to display an expanded Calendar box with additional options, such as the *Show As* options and the *Categorize* options. Click the Save button in the Calendar box when finished.

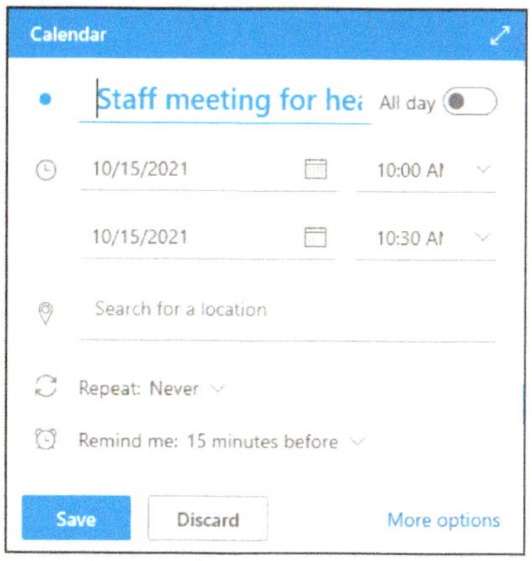

Tutorial

Scheduling a Recurring Appointment

Recurrence

TIP Meetings and events can also be set up as recurring items.

Scheduling Recurring Appointments

An appointment that occurs on a regular basis at fixed intervals needs to be entered only once, and Outlook automatically schedules the remainder of the occurrences within the recurrence pattern and range. To schedule a recurring appointment, open the Appointment window, enter the specifications for the first occurrence, and then click the Recurrence button in the Options group on the Appointment tab. The Appointment Recurrence dialog box shown in Figure 3.3 appears, in which you enter the recurring pattern details.

Figure 3.3 Appointment Recurrence Dialog Box

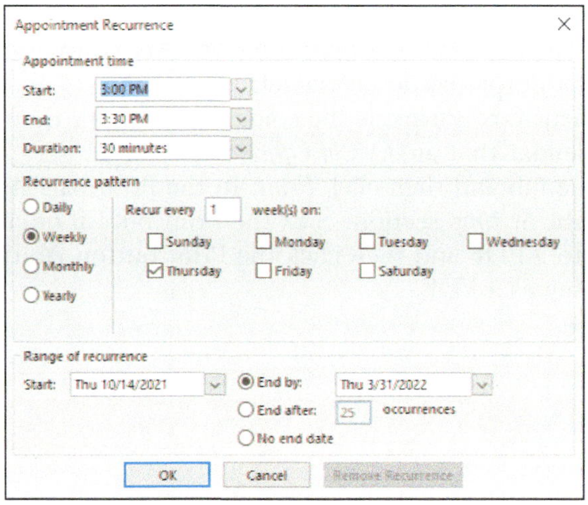

Activity 2 Scheduling a Recurring Appointment

1. With Calendar active and the date *October 15, 2021* displayed in the Appointment area, schedule a recurring appointment by completing the following steps:
   a. Click the Back button located next to *October 15, 2021* to display *October 14, 2021* in the Appointment area.
   b. Click next to *3:00 PM* in the Appointment area.
   c. Click the New Appointment button in the New group.
   d. With the insertion point positioned in the *Title* text box, type Project meeting.
   e. Click next to the Location button and then type Room 1A in the *Location* text box.
   f. Click the Recurrence button in the Options group on the Appointment tab.

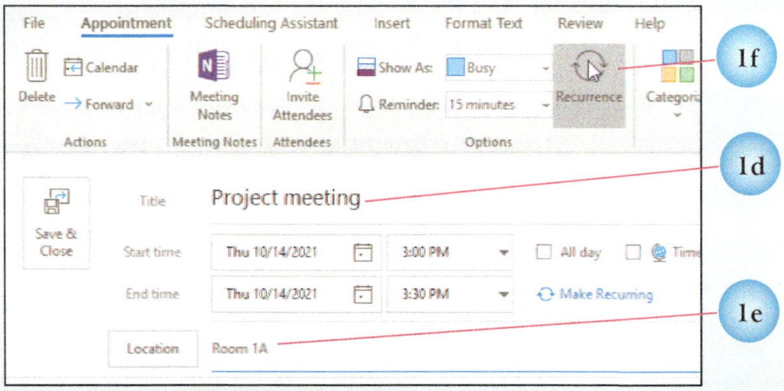

g. In the Appointment Recurrence dialog box, select the value *1* in the *Recur every* [ ] *week(s) on* text box in the *Recurrence pattern* section and then type 2.

h. Click OK to accept all the other settings and close the Appointment Recurrence dialog box. Outlook adds the recurrence details in the Appointment window below the *Title* text box.

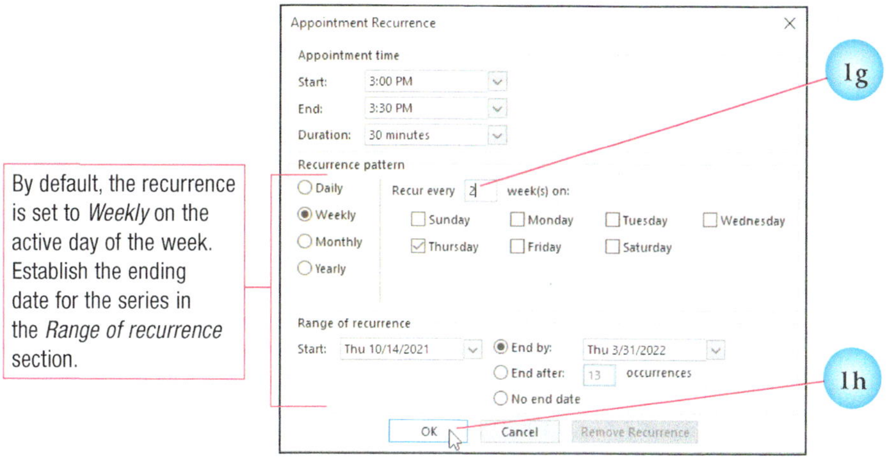

i. Click the Save & Close button in the Appointment window. The recurrence icon displays at the right end of the appointment box in the Appointment area to indicate the appointment is a recurring item.

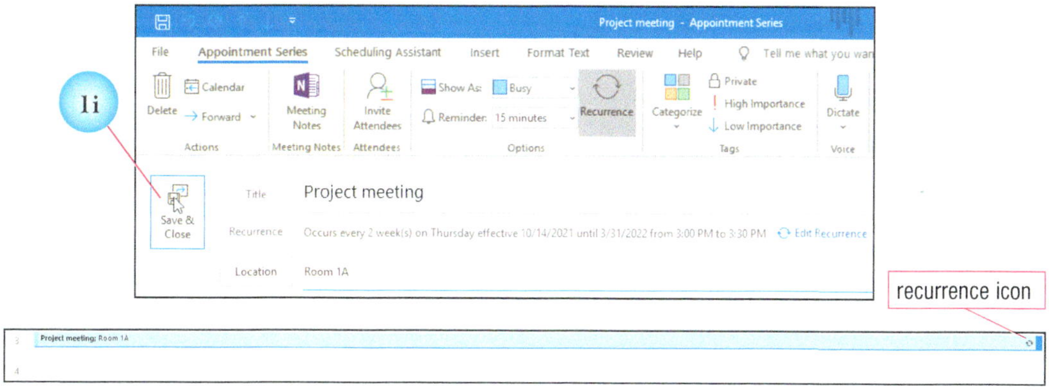

Scheduling Recurring Appointments in Outlook.com

Click the *Repeat* option arrow in the Calendar box and then choose a recurrence pattern in the drop-down list. Click the *Custom* option to make available additional options that allow you to specify the repeat pattern by choosing the number of days, weeks, months, or years between intervals; the day(s) of the week when the appointment recurs; and the end date for the appointment series.

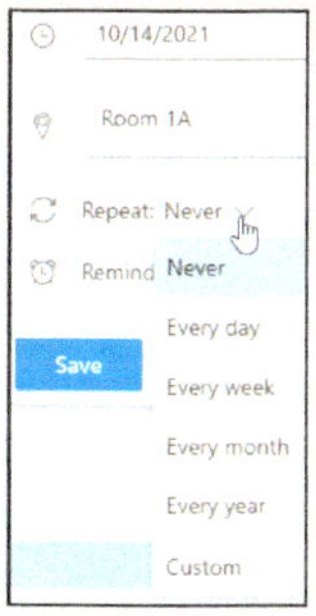

Tutorial

Scheduling Events in Calendar

Scheduling Events

An event differs from an appointment in that it is an activity that lasts an entire day or longer. Examples of an event include a seminar, training session, conference, trade show, and vacation. Other occasions that you might like to enter in the calendar as events are birthdays and anniversaries. An event does not occupy a time slot on the day it is scheduled. It appears in the banner for the scheduled day at the top of the Appointment area below the date.

TIP Create an event for any date for which you want to be reminded: birthday, anniversary, car maintenance, bill payment, and so on.

To schedule an event in Day view, double-click in the white text box below the colored bar for the day of the week at the top of the Appointment area to open an Untitled - Event window. The Event window is similar to the Appointment window, except that the *All day* check box at the right of the *Start time* day and time option boxes is automatically checked.

Each of these other methods also opens a new Event window:

New Items

- Right-click in the white text box below the colored bar with the day of the week at the top of the Appointment area and then click *New All Day Event* on the shortcut menu.
- Click the New Items button in the New group on the Home tab and then click *All Day Event* in the drop-down list.
- Click in the white text box below the colored bar with the day of the week at the top of the Appointment area, type the event description, and then press Enter.

Activity 3 Adding an Event

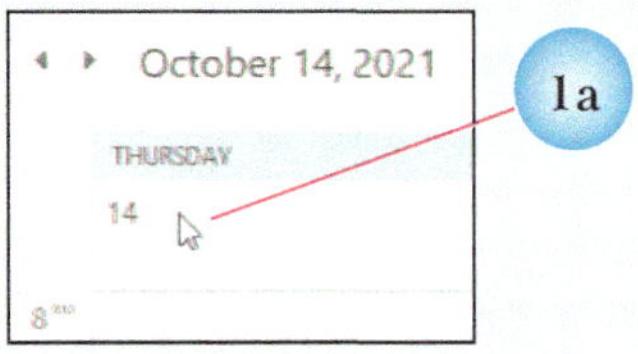

1. With Calendar active and the date *October 14, 2021* displayed in the Appointment area, schedule a one-day conference as an event by completing the following steps:
   a. Double-click in the white text box (displays *14*) below the colored bar for the day of the week (displays *THURSDAY*). An Untitled - Event window opens.
   b. With the insertion point positioned in the *Title* text box, type Social Media Conference.
   c. Click next to the Location button and then type Downtown Convention Center.
   d. Click the *Show As* option box arrow in the Options group on the Event tab (displays *Free*) and then click *Out of Office*.
   e. Click the High Importance button in the Tags group.
   f. Click the Save & Close button.

   The event title and location details appear below the date at the top of the Appointment area. In addition, the background color in the Appointment area for the day is shaded light purple because the event is defined as occurring out of the office.

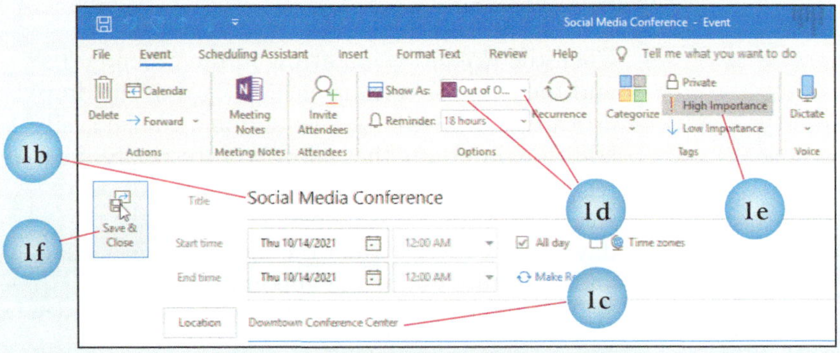

2. Click the Month button in the Arrange group on the Home tab. Notice that appointments appear in the calendar with times while events display the title entry only because an event does not occupy a time slot for the day.
3. Point to the entry for the Social Media Conference event on October 14 and read the event details in the pop-up balloon that appears.
4. Click the Day button in the Arrange group to restore the Appointment area to Thursday, October 14, 2021.

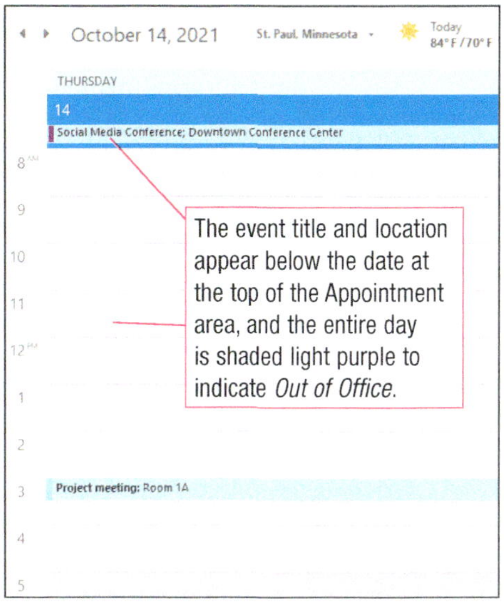

The event title and location appear below the date at the top of the Appointment area, and the entire day is shaded light purple to indicate *Out of Office*.

Scheduling Events in Outlook.com

In Day view, click in the white box next to the date at the top of the Appointment area to open a Calendar box set to a 1-day duration. Type the title and location and click *More options,* if necessary, to add more details. You can also click the New event button (displays with plus symbol) near the top left of the window to open a Calendar box. Click the *All day* switch to turn the feature on, removing the start time and end time options and displaying *1 day* as the duration.

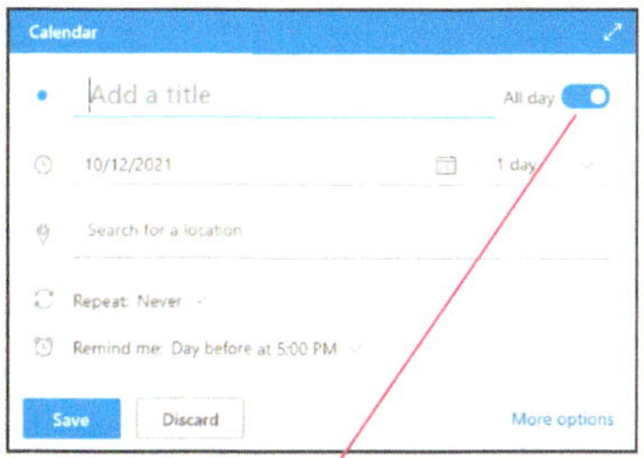

Click the *All day* switch to turn it on or off, which hides or displays the start and end time options.

Using Natural Language Phrases

In day or time text boxes within Appointment or Event windows, you can type natural language phrases, and Outlook will convert them to the appropriate entries. For example, in the *Start time* day text box, if you type *next Monday*, Outlook automatically calculates and enters the date for the Monday following the current day. In the time text box, type *ten o'clock am,* and Outlook converts the entry to *10:00 AM*.

Tutorial

Editing an Appointment

Editing, Deleting, and Moving Appointments

Double-click an existing appointment or event in the Appointment area to open the Appointment or Event window and then change the details. To delete an appointment or event, select the appointment or event box and then press the Delete key or click the Delete button in the Actions group on the Appointment tab.

Delete

To move an appointment, open the Appointment window and change the *Start time* and *End time* settings. You can also drag an appointment box to a new time or a new day. Display the calendar in Work Week, Week, or Month view to drag an appointment box to another day in the current week or month.

Activity 4 Editing, Deleting, and Moving Appointments

1. With Calendar active and *October 14, 2021* displayed in the Appointment area, change the starting time for the project status meeting (which you scheduled in Activity 2) by completing the following steps:
   a. Double-click the appointment box for *Project meeting* at 3:00 p.m.
   b. Since the appointment is one of a recurring series of appointments, Outlook displays the Open Recurring Item dialog box, asking if you want to open just this one occurrence or the entire series. Click to select *The entire series* option and then click OK.
   c. Click the Recurrence button in the Options group on the Appointment Series tab or click *Edit Recurrence* next to the Recurrence information.
   d. Click the *Start* option box arrow in the *Appointment time* section in the Appointment Recurrence dialog box and then click *4:30 PM* in the drop-down list. The *End* time automatically changes to *5:00 PM* because *Duration* is set to *30 minutes*.
   e. Click OK to close the Appointment Recurrence dialog box.
   f. Click the Save & Close button.

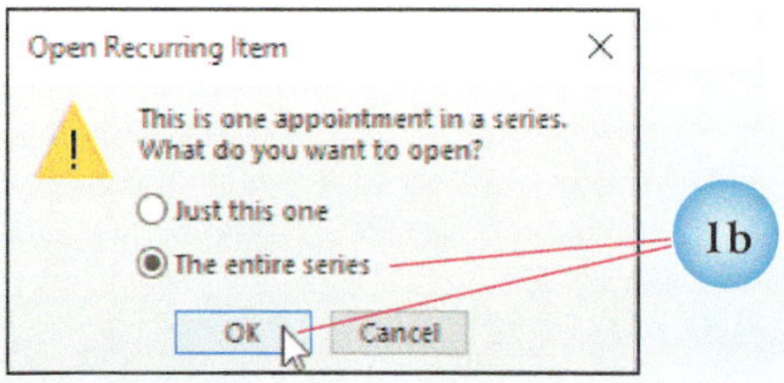

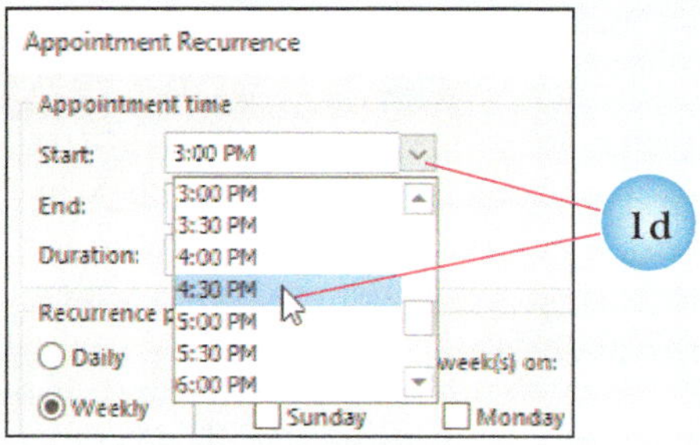

2. Delete the lunch appointment on October 15 by completing the following steps:
   a. Click *October 15* in the Date Navigator or click the Forward button at the top of the Appointment area.
   b. Click to select the appointment *Lunch meeting with Leslie Taylor* in the Appointment area. When the appointment is selected, a black border surrounds the appointment box and the appointment details appear in a pop-out balloon.
   c. Click the Delete button in the Actions group on the Appointment tab.

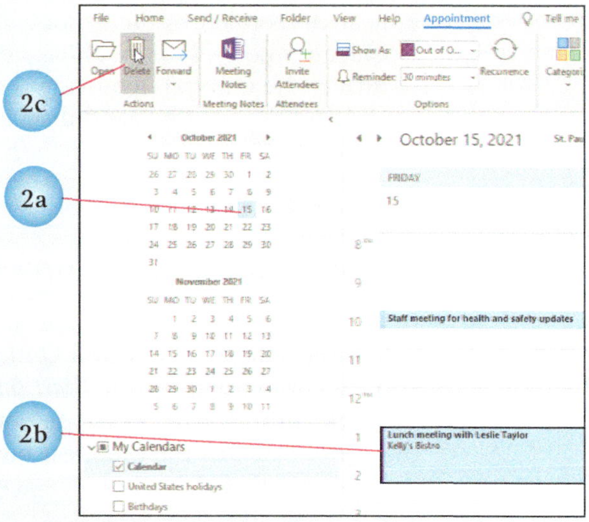

3. Double-click the appointment box for *Staff meeting for health and safety updates* to open the Appointment window.
4. Change the *Start time* to *1:00 PM* and then click the Save & Close button.
5. Display the Print backstage area and then click *Weekly Calendar Style* in the *Settings* section. Print or save the calendar as a PDF file. You determine an appropriate file name if saving as a PDF.

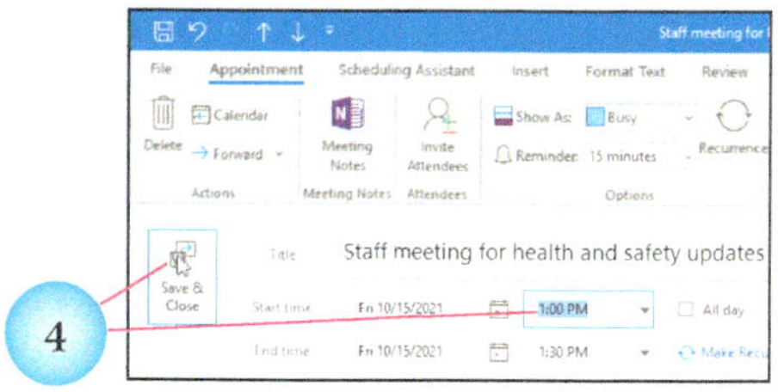

Check Your Work

Editing, Deleting, and Moving Items in Outlook.com

Click an existing appointment to open a pop-up box with the appointment or event details that includes Edit and Delete buttons. Click the Edit button to open the Calendar box to make changes to the details, or click the Delete button to remove the appointment or event from your calendar.

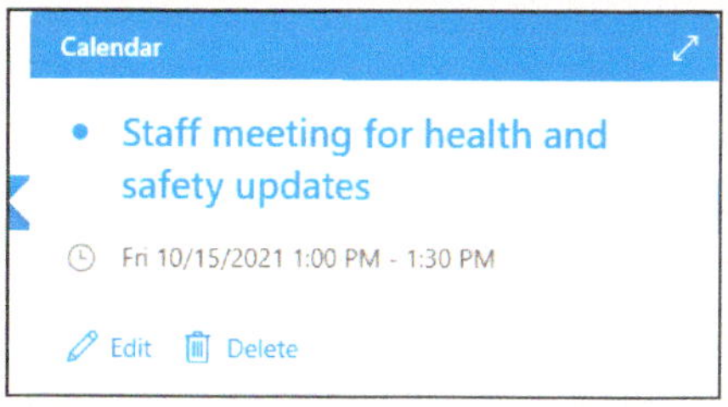

Changing the Calendar View

The Arrange group on the Home tab contains buttons that allow you to change the view for the calendar to Day, Work Week, Week, or Month, as shown and described in Figure 3.4.

TIP Before printing your calendar, change to the view you want to see in the printout, because Outlook automatically changes the print setting style to match the view.

Figure 3.4 Arrange Group on the Home Tab

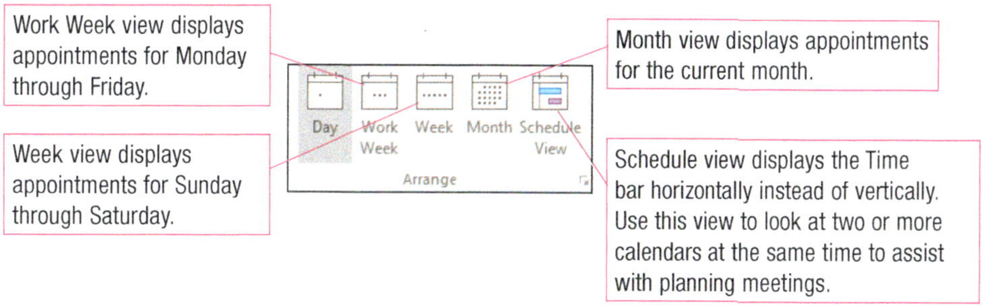

Displaying the Calendar in Table Format

Change View

Click the View tab and then click the Change View button in the Current View group to choose *List* or *Active*, which displays appointments in a table format. List view shows all the appointments that have been scheduled in the calendar, whereas Active view displays only those appointments that have not yet occurred.

Appointments and events are arranged in table format sorted by the start date in ascending order and grouped by recurrence option. Change the sort order to sort the list by subject or location by clicking the *Subject* or *Location* column heading. The list reorders in ascending order. Click the column heading a second time to change the sort order to descending order.

Displaying the Reading Pane

Reading Pane

Click the View tab, click the Reading Pane button in the Layout group, and then click *Right* or *Bottom* in the drop-down list to turn on the Reading pane at the right edge or bottom of the Calendar window. Select an appointment to view the details within the Reading pane. Figure 3.5 shows the Reading pane at the bottom of the window with the details displayed for the recurring project status meeting on October 14, 2021.

Figure 3.5 Calendar Window with Reading Pane at Bottom of Window

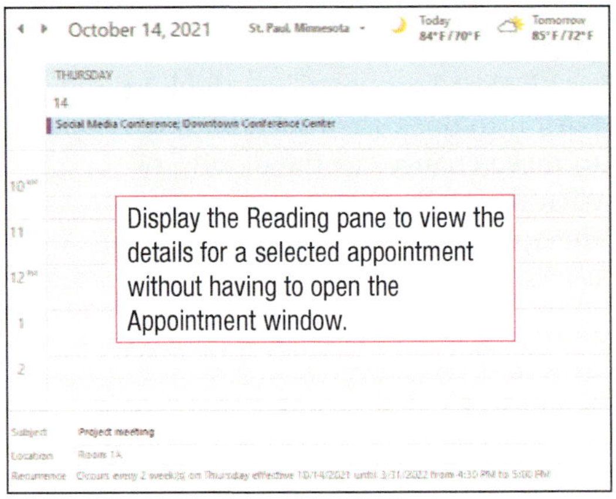

Activity 5 Changing the View and Displaying the Reading Pane

1. With Calendar active and *October 15, 2021* displayed in the Appointment area, change the current view to display only active appointments and increase the column width, and print by completing the following steps:
   a. Click the View tab, click the Change View button in the Current View group, and then click *Active* in the drop-down list. The calendar displays in a table format with the appointments grouped by the recurrence pattern. Information in some columns may not be entirely visible.
   b. If necessary, drag the column boundary at the right of *Subject* to the right to expand the column width if the entire subject text for each appointment is not currently visible. Dragging a column boundary right or left increases or decreases the column width. A black, vertical line indicates the new right column boundary position as you drag the mouse.

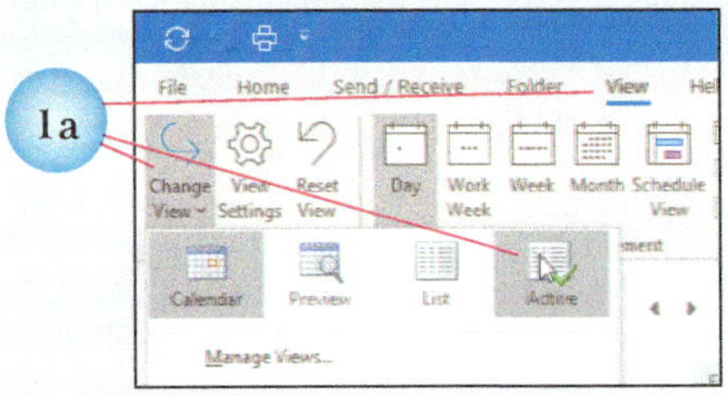

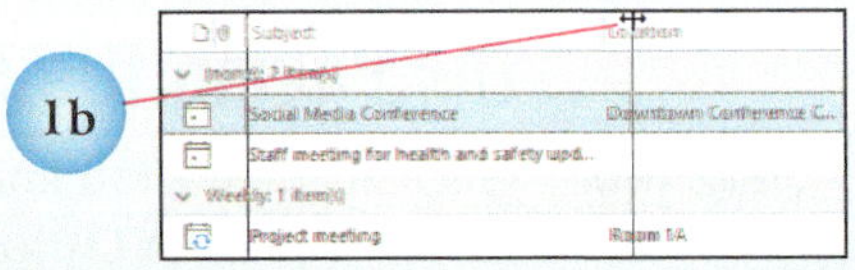

c. Double-click the right column boundary for the *Location* column. Double-clicking adjusts the column width to the length of the longest entry. If necessary, double-click the *Subject* right column boundary if the entire subject text is still not visible after completing Step 1b.

d. Double-click the *Start, End,* and *Recurrence Pattern* right column boundaries, if necessary, to display all the text in those columns.

2. Print the current view in landscape orientation by completing the following steps:

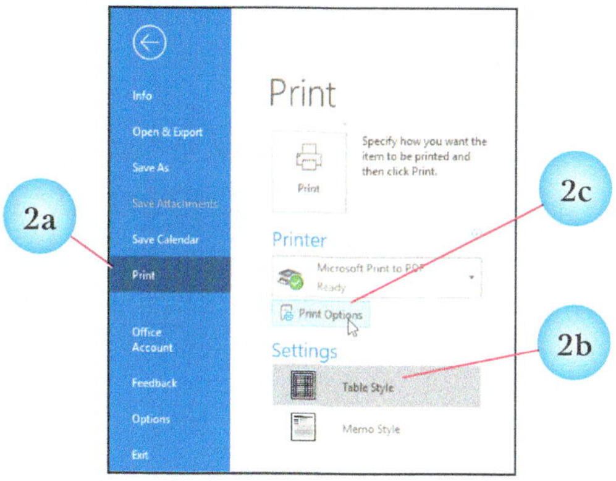

a. Click the File tab and then click *Print*.

b. Click *Table Style* in the *Settings* section in the Print backstage area.

c. Click the Print Options button.

d. Click the Page Setup button in the *Print style* section in the Print dialog box.

e. Click the Paper tab in the Page Setup: Table Style dialog box, click *Landscape* in the *Orientation* section, and then click OK.

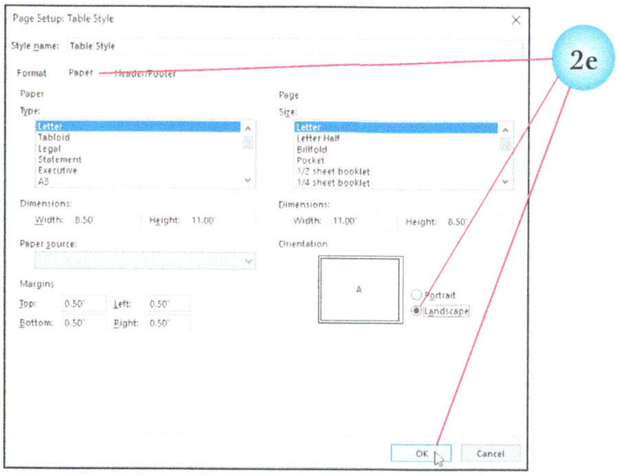

f. Click the Print button in the Print dialog box. Enter an appropriate file name if saving as a PDF. Some columns in your printout may not display all the text even though you resized the columns. Resizing the columns improves the display but not always the printout.

3. Click the Change View button in the Current View group and then click *Calendar* in the drop-down list to return to the regular calendar display.

4. Display *October 15, 2021* in the Appointment area, click the Home tab, and then click the Month button in the Arrange group to view the month October 2021.

5. Turn on the display of the Reading pane, view appointment details, and resize the pane by completing the following steps:

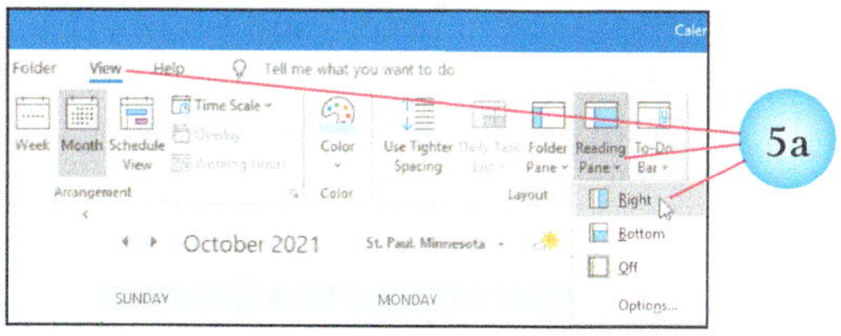

a. Click the View tab, click the Reading Pane button in the Layout group, and then click *Right* in the drop-down list.

b. Click to select the appointment on October 15 to display the appointment details in the Reading pane.

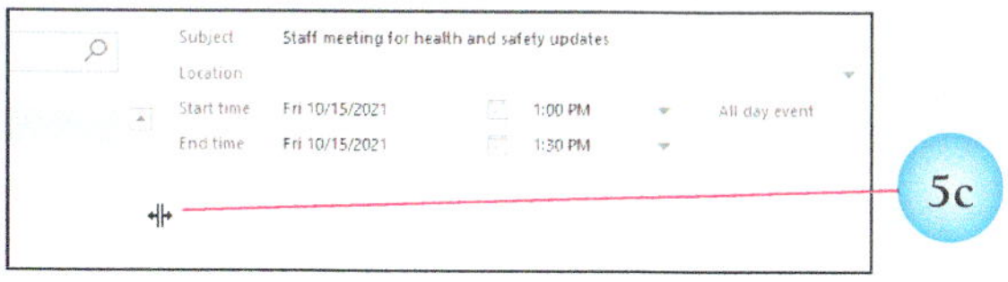

c. Drag the boundary line between the Content pane and the Reading pane to the left or right as needed when the pointer displays with the double vertical line and left- and right-pointing arrows to resize the pane until the Reading pane occupies approximately one-third of the window.

d. Click to select the appointment on October 28 and then read the appointment details in the Reading pane.

e. Click the View tab and then click the Week button in the Arrangement group. Review the layout of the Appointment area in Weekly Calendar style.

6. If necessary, click the View tab. Click the Reading Pane button and then click *Off* in the drop-down list.
7. Click the Home tab and then click the Day button in the Arrange group.
8. Click *October 15, 2021* in the Date Navigator.

Check Your Work

Applying Color Categories to Appointments

The same six color categories that can be assigned to messages can be assigned to appointments. By using the same categories in all the Outlook modules, you can assign a common color to all items related to the same project or task. An appointment that has been assigned a color category has the appointment box shaded the associated color in the Appointment area.

Categorize

When an appointment is selected in the Appointment area, the Appointment tab appears with the Categorize button located in the Tags group. Click the button and then click a color category to assign it to the selected appointment. You can also right-click an appointment box and choose *Categorize* on the shortcut menu to assign a category. Edit the color category titles by opening the Color Categories dialog box using the same technique you learned in Chapter 2.

More than one color category can be applied to an appointment. In that case, the last color category assigned to the appointment is displayed in the appointment box, and the appointment box includes a color category icon for each of the other assigned color categories at the right end of the box.

Activity 6 Applying Color Categories to Appointments, Renaming a Color Category, and Viewing Appointments by Category

1. With Calendar active and *October 15, 2021* displayed in the Appointment area, apply a color category to an existing appointment and event by completing the following steps:
   a. Display *October 14, 2021* in the Appointment area.
   b. Right-click *Social Media Conference* in the date banner at the top of the Appointment area, point to *Categorize*, and then click *Social Media Essay* (blue category) on the shortcut menu.
   c. Click to select the appointment box at *4:30 PM* for the *Project meeting*.

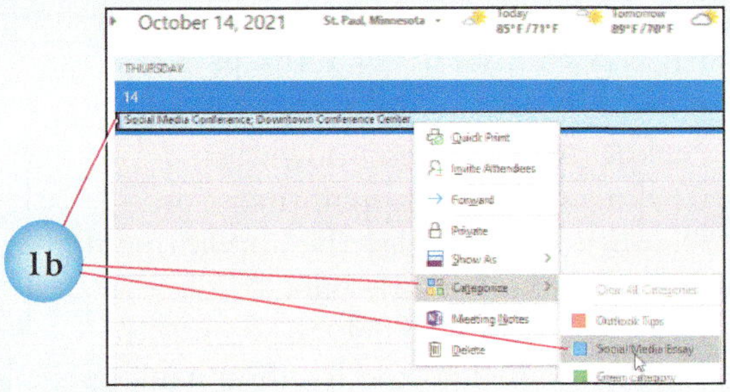

d. Click the Categorize button in the Tags group on the Appointment Series tab.
e. Click *Green category* in the drop-down list. Click the No button in the Rename Category dialog box informing you that this is the first time you have used the green color category and asking if you want to rename it. You will rename the category in the next step.

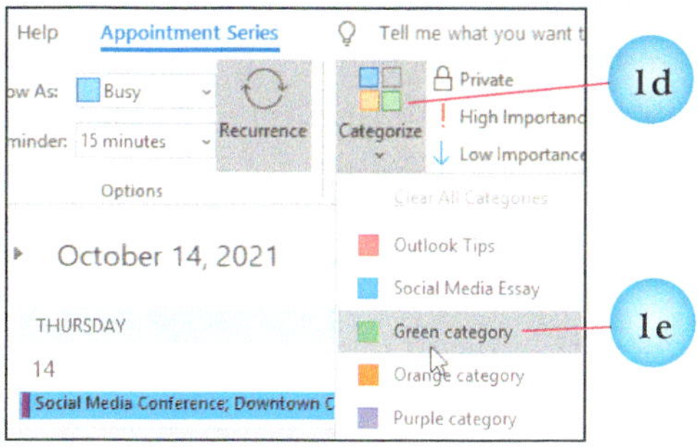

2. Rename the green color category by completing the following steps:
   a. Right-click the green-shaded *Project meeting* appointment box, point to *Categorize*, and then click *All Categories* on the shortcut menu.
   b. In the Color Categories dialog box with *Green category* already selected, click the Rename button.
   c. Type Conference Project and then press Enter.
   d. Click OK to close the Color Categories dialog box.

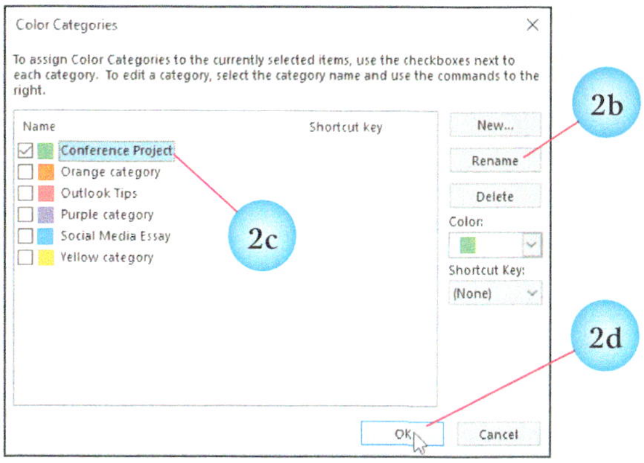

3. Schedule a new appointment and assign a category by completing the following steps:
   a. Display *October 15, 2021* in the Appointment area.
   b. Click next to *11:00 AM* in the Appointment area and then click the New Appointment button.
   c. Type Conference venue selection in the *Title* text box.
   d. Click next to the Location button and then type My office in the *Location* text box.
   e. Click the Categorize button in the Tags group on the Appointment tab and then click *Conference Project* (green category) in the drop-down list.
   f. Change the *End time* to *1:00 PM (2 hours)*.
   g. Click the Save & Close button.

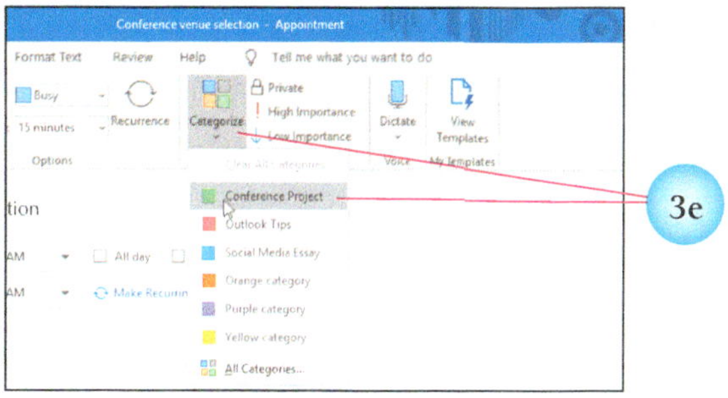

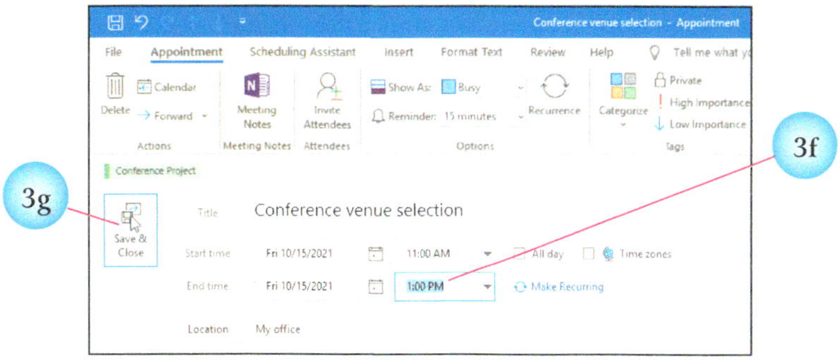

4. Display the active appointments grouped by color category by completing the following steps:
   a. Click the View tab, click the Change View button in the Current View group, and then click *Active* in the drop-down list.
   b. Click the Categories button in the Arrangement group option box. Outlook displays the appointments arranged in groups by assigned color category with each category automatically expanded to display all items.

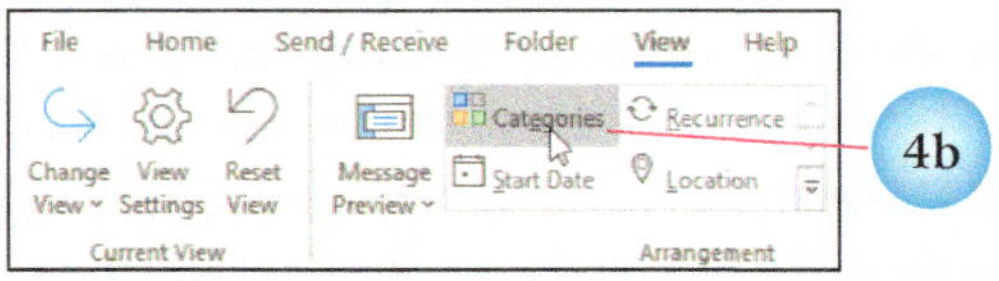

   c. If necessary, double-click the right column boundary for the *Subject*, *Location*, *Start*, and *End* columns to adjust the width of each to the length of the column's longest entry if the entries are not entirely visible.

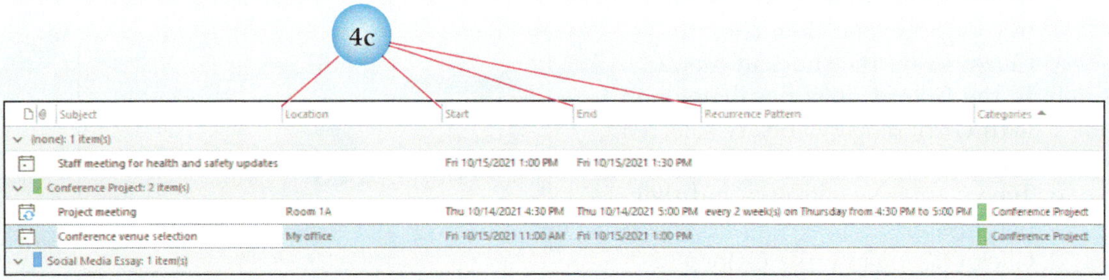

   d. Print the calendar in Table style and with landscape orientation. You determine an appropriate file name if saving as a PDF. Note that some columns in your printout may not display the full text.
5. Click the Change View button and then click *Calendar* in the drop-down list.
6. Display *October 15, 2021* in the Appointment area.

Check Your Work

Applying Color Categories to Appointments in Outlook.com

Apply a color category to an existing appointment by clicking to select the appointment, clicking the Edit button in the pop-out box, and then clicking *More options* at the bottom right in the Calendar box. Click the Categorize button on the Menu bar and then choose the desired color category in the drop-down list.

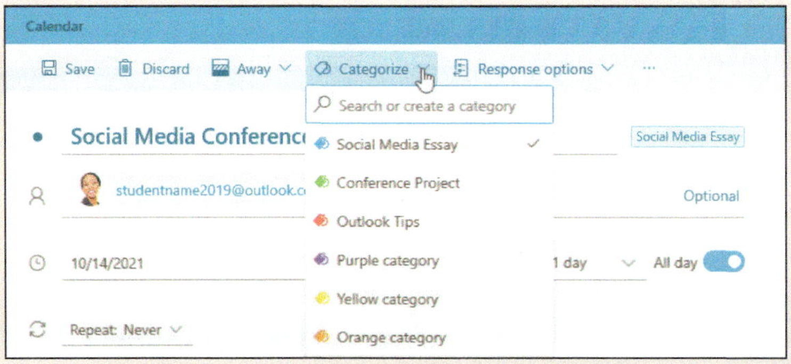

Tutorial

Creating an Appointment Rule

Creating a Conditional Formatting Rule with Color

You can create an appointment rule (similar to a message rule) that automatically applies a color to an appointment box based on a keyword that is typed in the *Title* field. For example, if you use Outlook to enter your personal appointments as well as your business appointments, you may wish to apply a color to all of your personal appointments to make them easily identifiable in the calendar.

View Settings

As you learned in Chapter 2, a rule performs an action on an item based on a condition you specify. Following the example, you would create the condition that the word *personal* exists in the *Title* field for the color to be applied automatically to the appointment. To create a conditional formatting rule, click the View Settings button in the Current View group on the View tab. In the Advanced View Settings: Calendar dialog box, click the Conditional Formatting button to open the Conditional Formatting dialog box, shown in Figure 3.6.

Click the Add button to create a new rule. Outlook displays the name *Untitled* in the *Name* text box in the *Properties of selected rule* section. Type a name to identify the rule and choose the color to apply in the *Color* list. Click the Condition button to open the Filter dialog box and set the criteria on which the appointment is to be formatted. When finished, click OK to close each dialog box.

Figure 3.6 Conditional Formatting Dialog Box

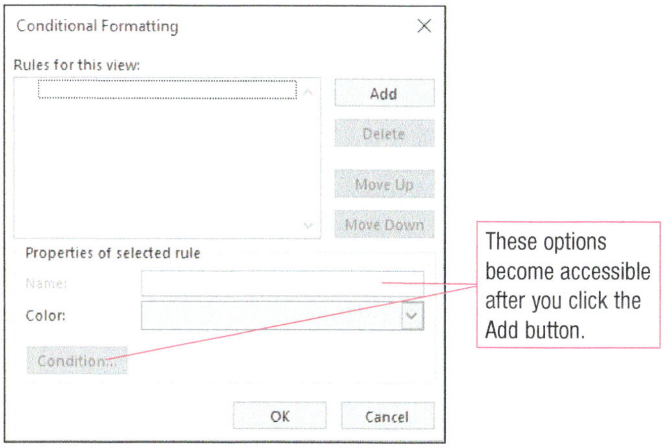

Activity 7 Creating a Conditional Formatting Rule Using Color

1. With Calendar active in Day view and the date *October 15, 2021* displayed in the Appointment area, rename the *Orange category* to *Personal* by completing the following steps:
   a. Right-click the *Staff meeting* appointment box at *1:00 PM*, point to *Categorize*, and then click *All Categories* on the shortcut menu.
   b. Click *Orange category* in the *Name* list and then click the Rename button. Do *not* click the check box to insert a check mark.
   c. Type Personal and then press Enter.
   d. Click OK.

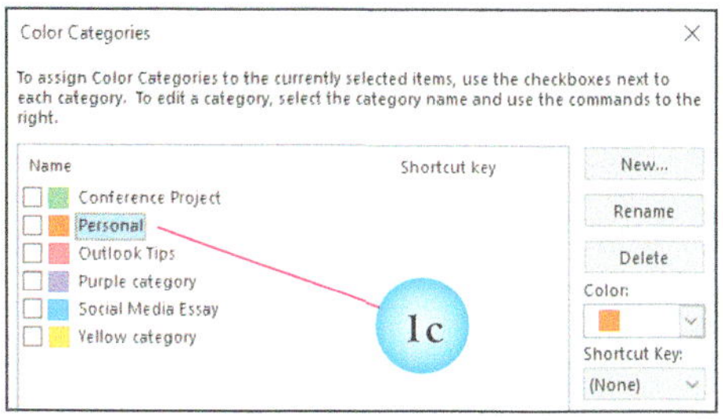

2. Create a conditional formatting rule to automatically format personal appointments with the orange color by completing the following steps:
   a. Click the View tab and then click the View Settings button in the Current View group.
   b. In the Advanced View Settings: Calendar dialog box, click the Conditional Formatting button.
   c. In the Conditional Formatting dialog box, click the Add button. A new rule named *Untitled* appears checked in the *Rules for this view* list box and in the *Name* text box in the *Properties of selected rule* section.
   d. With the text *Untitled* already selected in the *Name* text box, type Personal Appointments.
   e. Click the *Color* option box arrow and then click *Orange* (second color box).
   f. Click the Condition button.
   g. In the Filter dialog box, type personal in the *Search for the word(s)* text box.
   h. With *subject field only* already selected in the *In* text box, click OK to close the Filter dialog box.
   i. Click OK to close the Conditional Formatting dialog box.
   j. Click OK to close the Advanced View Settings: Calendar dialog box.

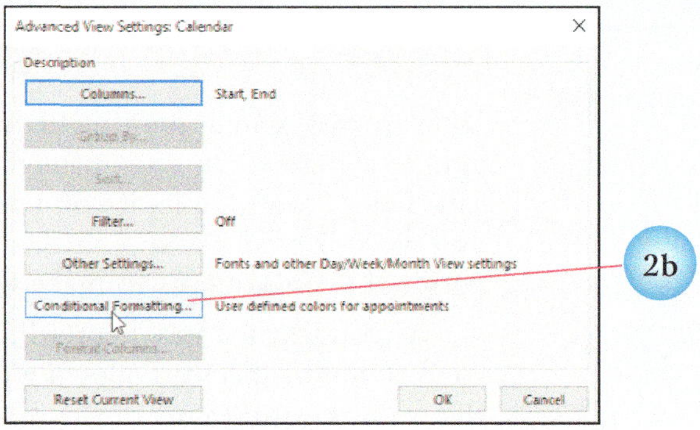

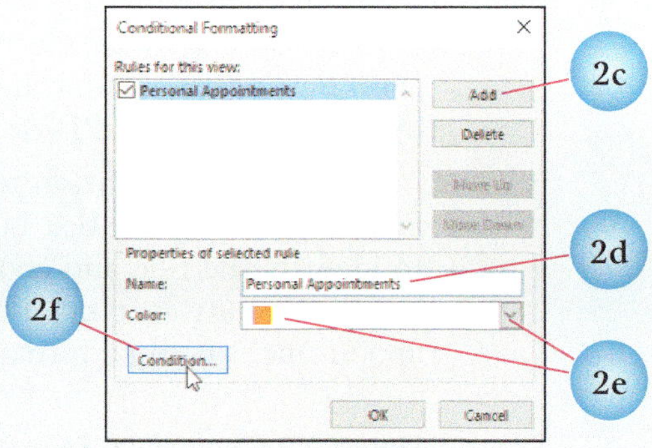

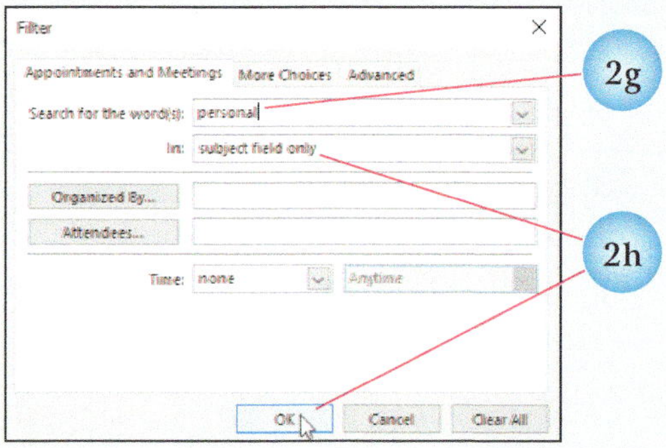

3. Schedule a new personal appointment on October 15, 2021, and see the rule applied to the appointment by completing the following steps:
   a. Click next to *9:00 AM* in the Appointment area.
   b. Type Personal appointment (doctor) and then press Enter. As soon as you press Enter, Outlook applies the orange color to the appointment box.

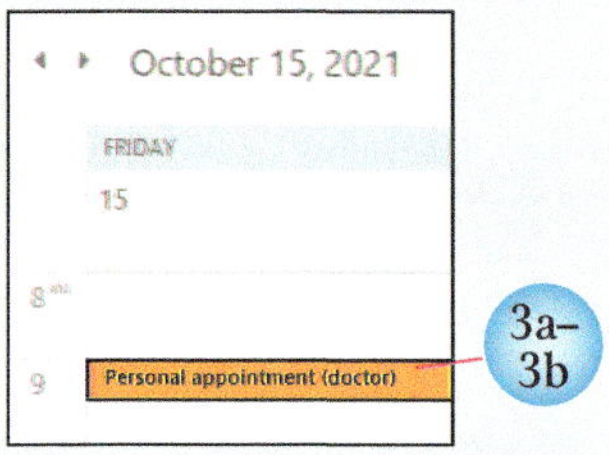

4. Click the File tab and then click *Print*. With *Daily Style* selected in the *Settings* section in the Print backstage area, print or save as a PDF the calendar, choosing an appropriate file name if saving as a PDF.

Check Your Work

Tutorial

Schedule a Meeting

Scheduling Meetings

Scheduling a meeting involves selecting the meeting day and time and opening a Meeting window in which you identify the title or subject of the meeting, the individuals you want to attend the meeting, the location, the meeting duration, and other options as required. Individuals are notified of the meeting via an email message once you click the Send button.

New Meeting

To begin creating a new meeting request, perform one of the following actions to open a Meeting window (see Figure 3.7):

- Click the New Meeting button in the New group on the Home tab.
- Click the New Items button in the New group on the Home tab and then click *Meeting* in the drop-down list.
- Open a new Appointment window and then click the Invite Attendees button in the Attendees group on the Appointment tab.
- Right-click in the Appointment area at the meeting start time and then click *New Meeting Request* on the shortcut menu.

Type the names or email addresses for the people you want to invite to the meeting in the *Required* text box separated by semicolons. If you are using an internal Exchange Server, you can use the Scheduling Assistant tab to help you find a day and time when most people are available. The Scheduling Assistant tab shows you the free and busy times for each individual added to the meeting request. Drag the vertical colored bar for the start or end time to adjust the meeting when you see a time slot that is available for everyone.

Exchange Server

Use the Room Finder button at the right of the *Location* text box to reserve a meeting room. Consider also using the Room Finder pane (see Figure 3.7), which shows suggested best times and available rooms. For example, click a suggestion in the Room Finder pane when most people and a room are available at the same time.

Figure 3.7 Meeting Window

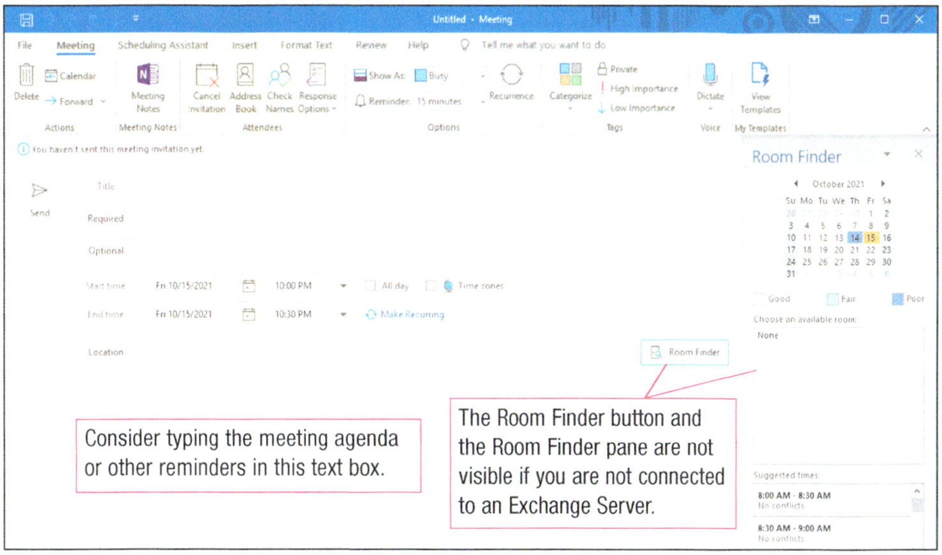

Activity 8 Scheduling a Meeting and Viewing Tracking Details

Note: In the rest of this chapter, you will be sending email messages for meeting requests to the student with whom you have been exchanging emails. Outlook does not allow you to send a meeting request to yourself. Check with your instructor, if necessary, for alternative instructions. One option is to use an email address for yourself that is not the same as the one you are using for these activities.

1. With Calendar active and the date *October 15, 2021* displayed in the Appointment area, schedule a meeting by completing the following steps:
   a. Click next to *3:00 PM* in the Appointment area.
   b. Click the New Meeting button in the New group on the Home tab.
   c. Type Keynote speaker planning meeting in the *Title* text box.
   d. Click next to the Required button and then type the email address for the person you are inviting to the meeting in the *Required* text box.
   e. Click next to the Location button and then type Meeting Room 1B in the *Location* text box.
   f. Click the *End time* time option box arrow and then click *4:00 PM (1 hour)* in the drop-down list.
   g. Click the Send button. The meeting is scheduled in your calendar, and an email message is sent to the student who was invited to the meeting.

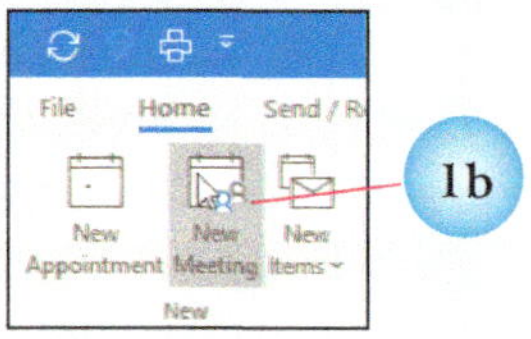

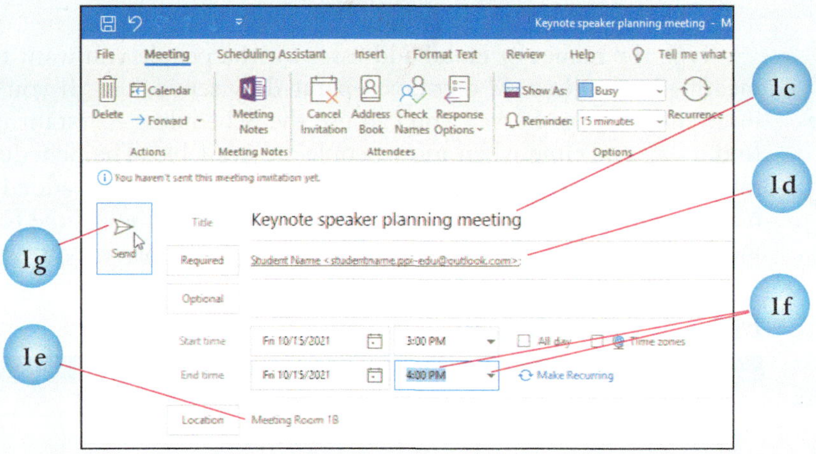

2. View the Scheduling and Tracking information in the Meeting window by completing the following steps:
   a. Double-click the *Keynote speaker planning meeting* appointment box at *3:00 PM*.
   b. Click the Scheduling Assistant tab. The Meeting window shows the *All Attendees* list and calendar entries for each attendee. On the tab and in the window are options to add more attendees, change the meeting day and time, or add a room.

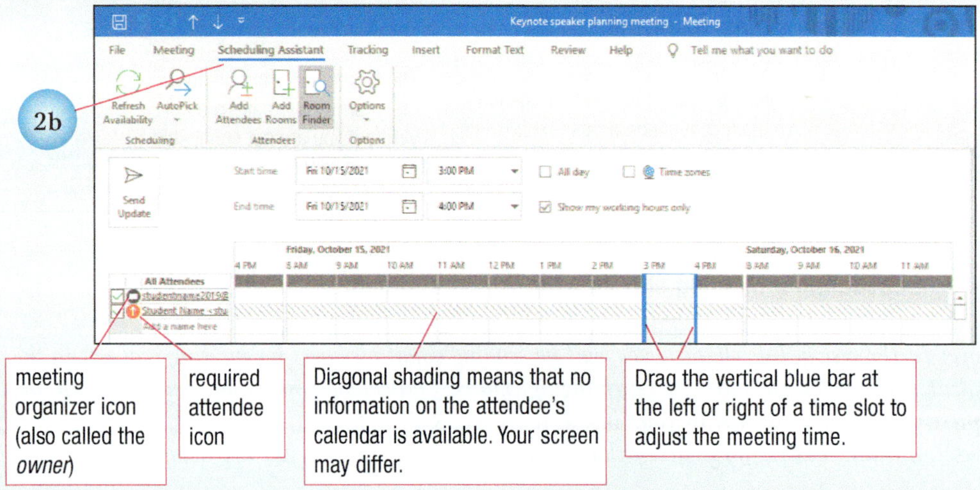

c. Click the Tracking tab. Notice the Response column where Outlook logs responses received from each attendee.

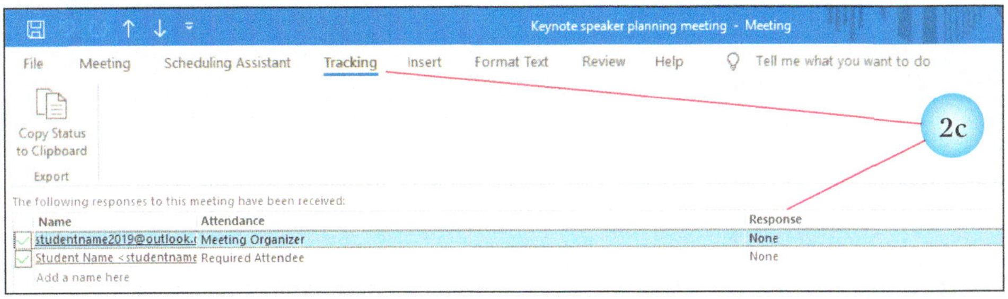

d. Click the Close button on the Meeting window Title bar.

3. View the meeting request email message sent by completing the following steps:
   a. Click the Mail text label or icon on the Navigation bar.
   b. Click *Sent Items* in the Folder pane.
   c. Double-click the message header for the meeting request sent in Step 1. Read the information sent to the required attendee in the meeting request message.
   d. Click the File tab within the message window, click *Print*, and then print or save as a PDF the message, choosing an appropriate file name if saving as a PDF.
   e. Close the message window.
4. Click *Inbox* in the Folder pane.

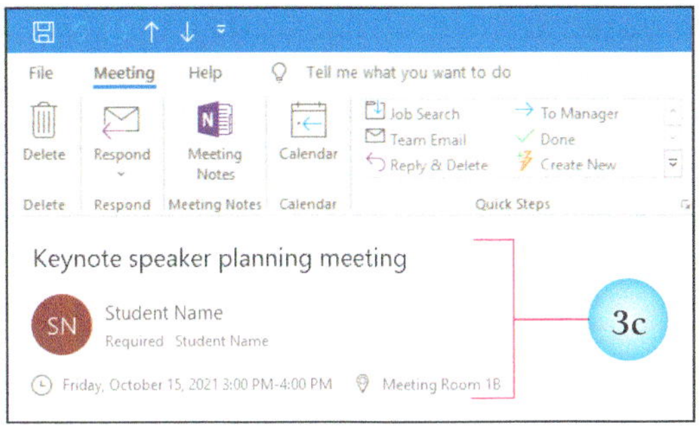

Check Your Work

Exchange Server

Resources such as meeting rooms and equipment can be automatically scheduled by including the resource as an invitee in the meeting request. The Exchange Server administrator sets up a mailbox for each resource and room allowing calendar entries for authorized schedulers. Outlook automatically sends an accept or decline message to the meeting organizer, depending on the resource or room availability.

Scheduling Meetings in Outlook.com

Create a meeting request in a Calendar box by clicking *More options* at the bottom right to display the expanded Calendar box. Add the email address of the person you want to attend the meeting in the *Invite attendees* text box. Add other entries or change options as required and then click the Send button. (The Save button on the Menu bar changes to the Send button as soon as an email address is added to the *Invite attendees* text box.)

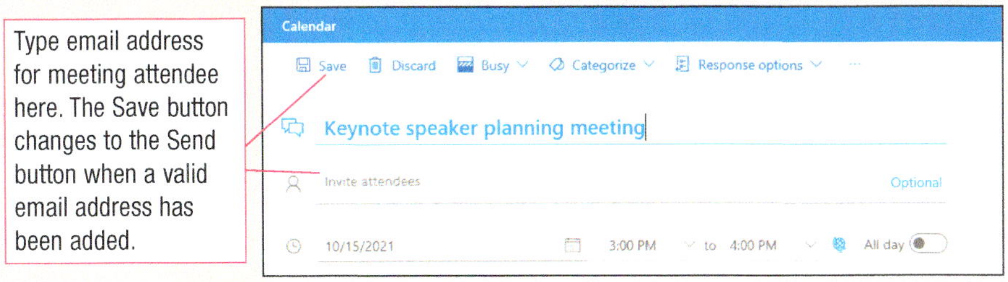

Tutorial

Accepting a Meeting Request

Responding to Meeting Requests

A meeting request message has buttons for responding to the meeting organizer in the Respond group on the Meeting tab (see Figure 3.8). Respond buttons are also included at the top right of the message in the Reading pane. The invitee can choose to click Accept, Tentative, Decline, or Propose New Time. Click the desired Respond button to send a reply message to the meeting organizer. Outlook also includes a preview of your calendar for the meeting day and time within the message so that you can easily determine if you have a conflicting appointment.

When the invitee chooses Accept, Tentative, or Decline, a drop-down list appears below the button with three options: *Edit the Response before Sending*, so that a few words of explanation can be provided; *Send the Response Now*, so that the meeting organizer receives the default response message of *User name has accepted*; and *Do Not Send a Response*. Accept or Tentative responses schedule the meeting in your calendar. If you choose Decline, the message is moved to the Deleted Items folder, and the meeting is not scheduled.

TIP Always respond promptly to meeting requests as a courtesy to the meeting organizer. If the meeting organizer is already aware you will attend the meeting, accept the meeting request and choose the *Do Not Send a Response* option.

The meeting organizer receives the responses by means of email messages. In addition, Outlook updates the Tracking page in the Meeting window so that the organizer can view all the invitation responses in one place.

If an invitee is unavailable at the meeting day and time, she can propose a new time for the meeting rather than decline the invitation. In this case, she clicks the Propose New Time button and chooses *Tentative and Propose New Time* or *Decline and Propose New Time*. In the Propose New Time dialog box, she enters a new start time and end time for the meeting and then clicks the Propose Time button. Adding a brief explanation in the message window before sending the reply is a good idea. The meeting organizer sees the original day and time and the proposed new day and time particulars in the response message.

Figure 3.8 Respond Buttons in Meeting Request Message

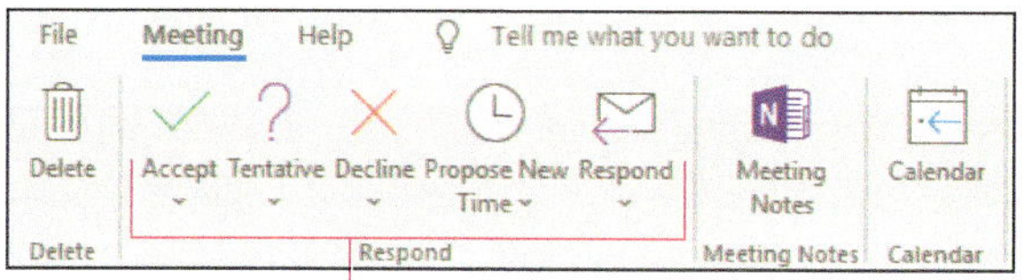

Activity 9 Accepting a Meeting Request

Note: *To complete this activity, you must have received a meeting request from another student for Activity 8. If you sent the request to yourself at a secondary email address, sign in to your other email account to complete this activity.*

1. With the Inbox folder active, accept a meeting request by completing the following steps:
   a. Double-click the message header in the Content pane for the message with the subject *Keynote speaker planning meeting*.
   b. Click the Accept button in the Respond group on the Meeting tab.
   c. Click *Edit the Response before Sending* in the drop-down list.

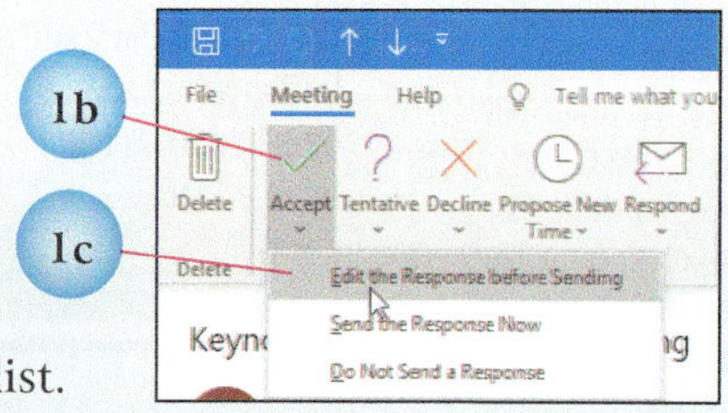

d. Type the following text in the message window:

The latest budget for the conference provides $5,000 to cover keynote speaker costs.

e. Print or save as a PDF the response message, choosing an appropriate file name if saving as a PDF.

f. Click the Send button. A message is sent to the meeting organizer with the subject text *Accepted: Keynote speaker planning meeting* below the attendee's name. Outlook also deletes the meeting request message from the Inbox once you have responded.

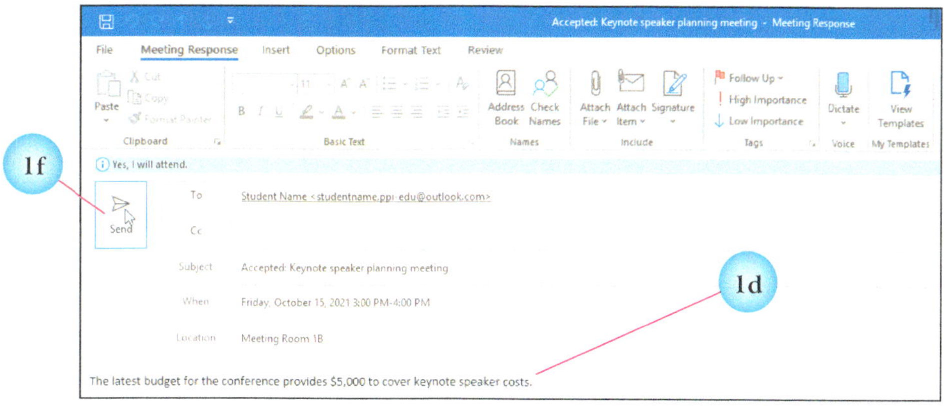

2. Display the calendar with the active date *October 15, 2021*. Outlook added the meeting to your calendar. ***Note:*** *You will have two meetings scheduled for 3:00 p.m. on October 15 if you have completed both Activities 8 and 9—one as a meeting organizer and the other as a meeting attendee. If you completed this activity from a secondary email account, sign out and return to the account you normally use for this course.*

Check Your Work

TIP You can forward a calendar item via an email message. Select the calendar item and then click the Forward button in the Actions group on the Appointment tab. A message window opens with the item details in a file attachment.

If you send a meeting request to someone who does not use Outlook and whose email program does not process Outlook requests, Outlook sends an email invitation message that includes the meeting details and attaches to the message an iCalendar text file (*.ics* file). The individual can use the file attachment to import the meeting into his or her scheduling program. For example, an *.ics* file can be imported into Google Calendar. An invitee who receives this type of request does not see the meeting respond buttons. He will use the Reply button to send an email back to the meeting organizer indicating his attendance.

Accepting a Meeting Request in Outlook.com

Outlook.com displays buttons to respond to a meeting invitation that are different than those shown in the desktop version. First, type a message to the meeting organizer in the text box above the respond buttons, if desired. Next, click the Yes button to accept, click the Maybe button to indicate tentative acceptance, or click the No button to decline the meeting invitation. The reply message sends immediately.

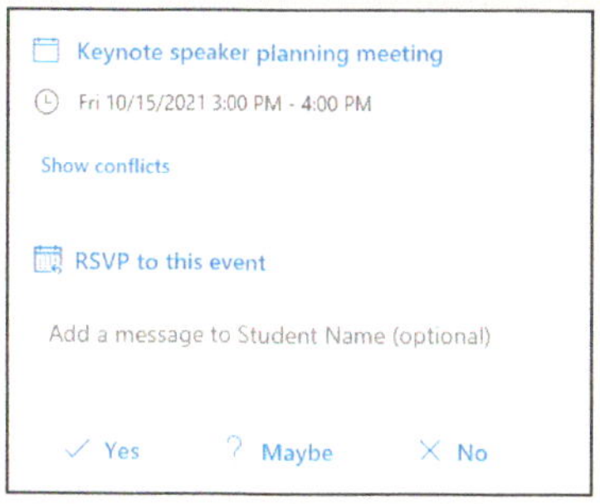

Updating and Canceling a Meeting

Periodically, meetings need to be rescheduled or canceled, or the list of individuals attending a meeting needs to be revised. Only the organizer of the meeting request can update or cancel a meeting.

Select the meeting in your calendar and use the buttons on the Meeting tab to make the required changes. You can also open the meeting window to make the required changes and then click the Send Update button when finished to send an email message with the changes to each attendee. Each attendee can then choose to accept or decline the revised meeting request.

Cancel Meeting

TIP Canceled meeting messages are sent as *High Importance* items.

To cancel a meeting, use the Cancel Meeting button in the Actions group on the Meeting tab or within the meeting window. Click the Send Cancellation button to instruct Outlook to send each attendee an email message with the word *Canceled* in the subject line. Each attendee can open the message and remove the meeting from his or her calendar using the Remove from Calendar button in the Respond group on the Meeting tab.

If you are an attendee to a previously accepted meeting and you delete the meeting from your calendar, Outlook prompts you to send a message to the meeting organizer.

Activity 10 Scheduling and Updating a Meeting

1. With Calendar active and *October 15, 2021* displayed in the Appointment area, click *October 18, 2021* in the Date Navigator.
2. Schedule a new meeting by completing the following steps:
   a. Click next to *1:00 PM* in the Appointment area.
   b. Click the New Meeting button in the New group.
   c. Type Volunteer planning meeting in the *Title* text box.
   d. Click next to the Required button and then type the email address for the person you are inviting to the meeting in the *Required* text box.
   e. Change the *End time* to *2:00 PM (1 hour)*.
   f. Click next to the Location button and then type Meeting Room 1B in the *Location* text box.
   g. Click the High Importance button in the Tags group on the Meeting tab.
   h. Click in the white text box below the *Location* text box and then type Please bring the names of volunteers you have confirmed to the meeting.
   i. Click the Send button.

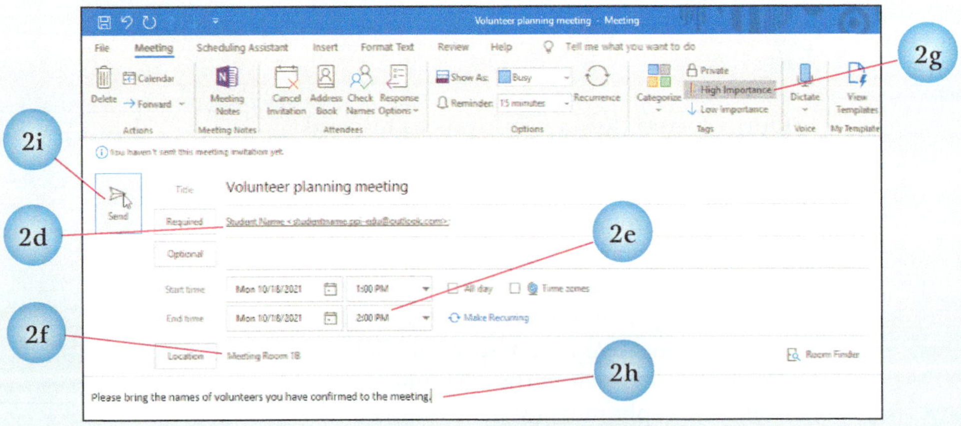

3. Update the meeting request sent in Step 2 to change the duration of the meeting by completing the following steps:
   a. Double-click the *Volunteer planning meeting* meeting box to open the Meeting window.
   b. Change the *End time* to *3:00 PM (2 hours)*.
   c. Click the Send Update button. Outlook updates the meeting specifications via email message to the attendee(s) and adjusts the appointment within your calendar.

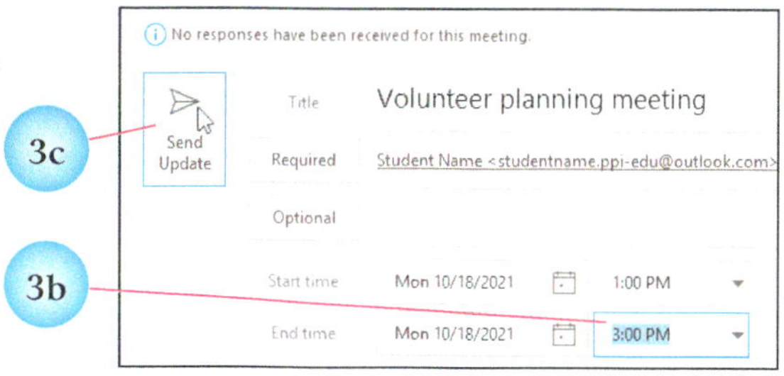

4. Read the updated meeting request by completing the following steps:
   a. Click the Mail text label or icon on the Navigation bar. If necessary, click the Send/Receive All Folders button on the Quick Access Toolbar. If you are using a secondary email address for yourself, make sure you have signed in to the other account.
   b. With the Inbox folder active, click the message header for the updated meeting request sent from Step 3. Notice in the Reading pane that the updated meeting time displays in color with the original meeting time shown in dimmed text with a line drawn through the text. If you signed in to a secondary email account, sign out and return to the account you normally use for this textbook.

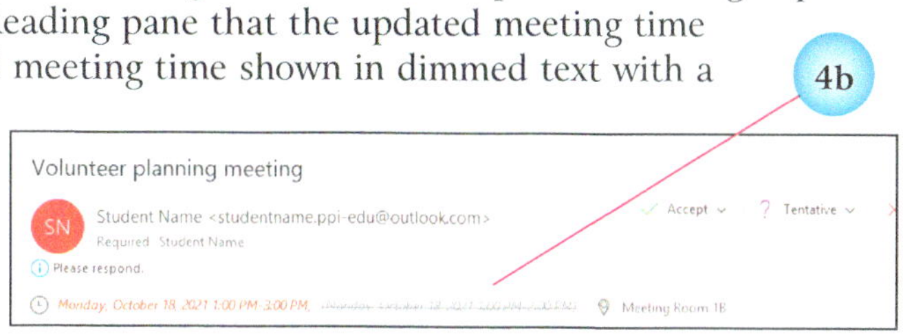

5. Click the Calendar text label or icon on the Navigation bar and display *October 18, 2021* in the Appointment area.
6. Display the Print backstage area. Print or save as a PDF the calendar with *Daily Style* selected in the *Settings* section, choosing an appropriate file name if saving as PDF. ***Note:*** *You will have two meetings scheduled for 1:00 p.m. on October 18 if you sent a meeting request and received a meeting request from another student for this activity. You are the meeting organizer for one and a meeting attendee for the other meeting.*

Check Your Work

Updating Meeting Attendees and Manually Tracking Responses

Exchange Server

Outlook tracks and updates meeting responses automatically when all attendees are connected to a Microsoft Exchange Server.

If after you send a meeting request a new attendee is to be invited to the meeting, open the Meeting window and type the email address of the new attendee in the *Required* text box. You can also click the Scheduling Assistant or Tracking tab, click *Add a name here* in the attendee list, and then type the name or email address of the person being added to the meeting. To remove an attendee from the meeting, right-click the attendee's name in the *Required* text box and then click *Cut* on the shortcut menu. The meeting organizer can choose to send an update message only to the individuals who have been added to or deleted from the meeting or to all the meeting participants.

Outlook tracks the responses received from attendees when they open the message and choose one of the Respond buttons. The replies can be viewed by the meeting organizer in the *Response* column on the Tracking tab. If, however, an attendee contacts the meeting organizer by telephone or a subsequent email with a change in his or her status, the meeting organizer can manually change the response status. To do this, open the Meeting window and click the Tracking tab.

TIP The Meeting Notes feature integrates Outlook with OneNote. OneNote can be used to store notes related to a meeting. The meeting organizer can opt to share the notes with the attendees by distributing the notes via a link to the OneNote workbook. To store notes, open the Meeting window, then click the Meeting Notes button on the Meeting tab.

Click in the *Response* column next to the attendee's name, and a drop-down list opens. Click the new status for the attendee, as shown in Figure 3.9.

Figure 3.9 Tracking Response Options on the Tracking Page

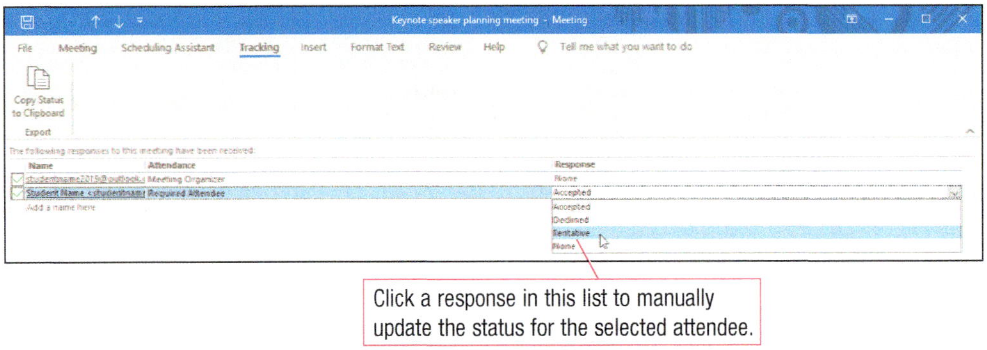

Changing Calendar Options

You can customize Calendar in Outlook by changing options in the Outlook Options dialog box. For example, if you work a nonstandard work week, select the days that apply to you in the *Work time* section in the Outlook Options dialog box with Calendar active. Click the Calendar Options dialog box launcher at the bottom right of the Arrange group on the Home tab, or click the File tab and then click *Options* to open the Outlook Options dialog box. With *Calendar* selected in the left pane, the Outlook Options dialog box appears, as shown in Figure 3.10.

Change the way the calendar displays in the Date Navigator with options in the *Work time* section. For example, if you change the *First day of week* entry from

Figure 3.10 Outlook Options Dialog Box with Calendar Options

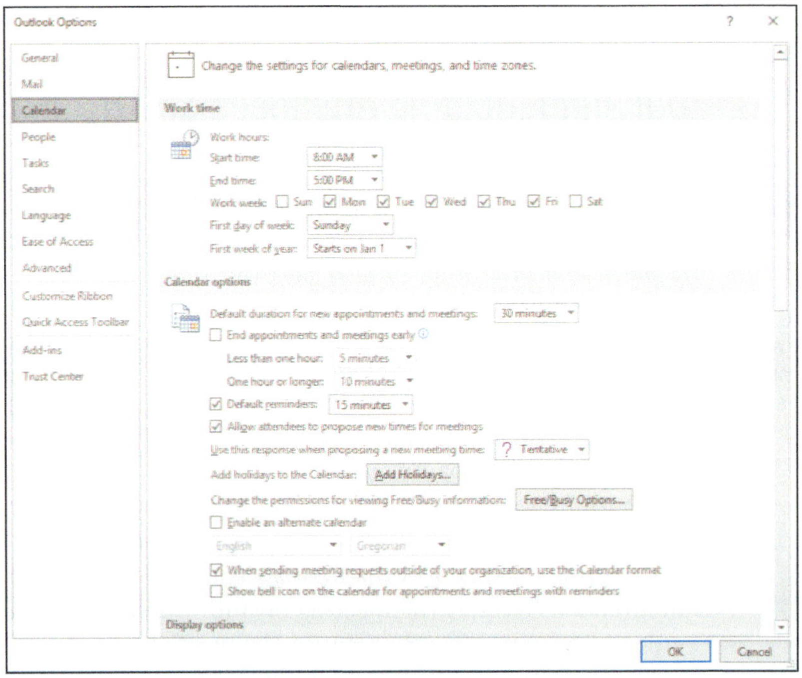

Sunday to *Saturday*, the Date Navigator displays with the first day in each week as *Saturday*. The columns are labeled *S S M T W T F*. Changing the *Start time* and *End time* entries makes the Appointment area background color for work day hours shorten or lengthen to reflect the length of the new work day.

Buttons or check boxes in the *Calendar options* section set default times for reminders, allow attendees to propose alternative meeting times to your meeting requests, set default responses when proposing new meeting times, add holidays for specific countries, and control calendar information sent via the internet.

The *Display options* section includes buttons or check box options to change the default calendar color, turn on week numbers in Month view and in the Date Navigator, show free appointments in Schedule view, and set the number of calendars that, when opened, cause the layout to adjust in Schedule view.

Add a text label at the top of the Time bar in the Appointment area for your time zone by typing the label in the *Time zones* section. Add a second time zone to the Time bar by inserting a check mark in the *Show a second time zone* check box. Type a label for the additional time zone and choose the time zone in the *Time zone* list box. Outlook adds a second column to the Time bar in the Appointment area to show appointments at the correct time for each time zone, as shown in Figure 3.11. You can add a third time zone if needed.

Use options in the *Scheduling assistant* and *Automatic accept or decline* sections to specify how to show calendar details in meeting requests or turn on automatic replies to requests. Turn off the display of the weather in the Appointment area, or change the temperature display from Fahrenheit to Celsius in the *Weather* section.

Figure 3.11 Appointment Area with Two Time Zones on Time Bar

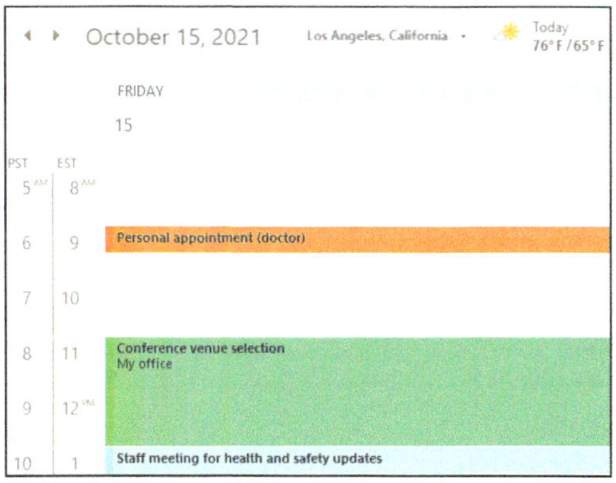

Activity 11 Customizing the Calendar Appearance

1. With Calendar active and *October 18, 2021* displayed in the Appointment area, change the start and end times for the work day, show week numbers in Month view and in the Date Navigator, and change the calendar's color scheme by completing the following steps:
   a. Click the Calendar Options dialog box launcher located at the bottom right of the Arrange group on the Home tab.

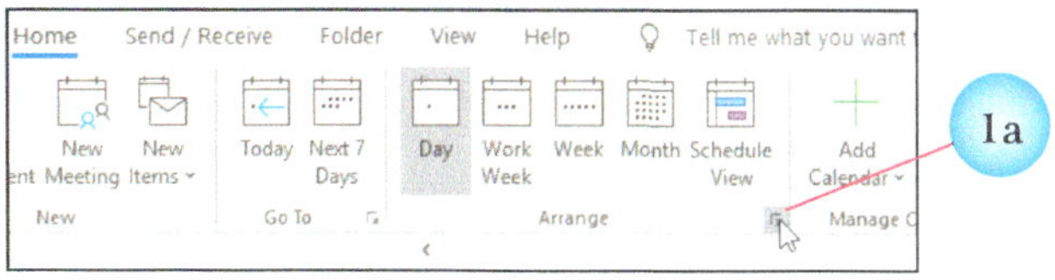

b. Click the *Start time* option box arrow in the *Work time* section and then click *9:00 AM* in the drop-down list.
c. Click the *End time* option box arrow in the *Work time* section, scroll down, and then click *6:00 PM* in the drop-down list.
d. Scroll down the dialog box, if necessary, to the *Display options* section, click the Default calendar color button, and then click the second color option in the first row (*Green*) in the drop-down color palette.
e. Click to insert a check mark in the *Show week numbers in the month view and in the Date Navigator* check box in the *Display options* section.
f. Click OK to close the Outlook Options dialog box.

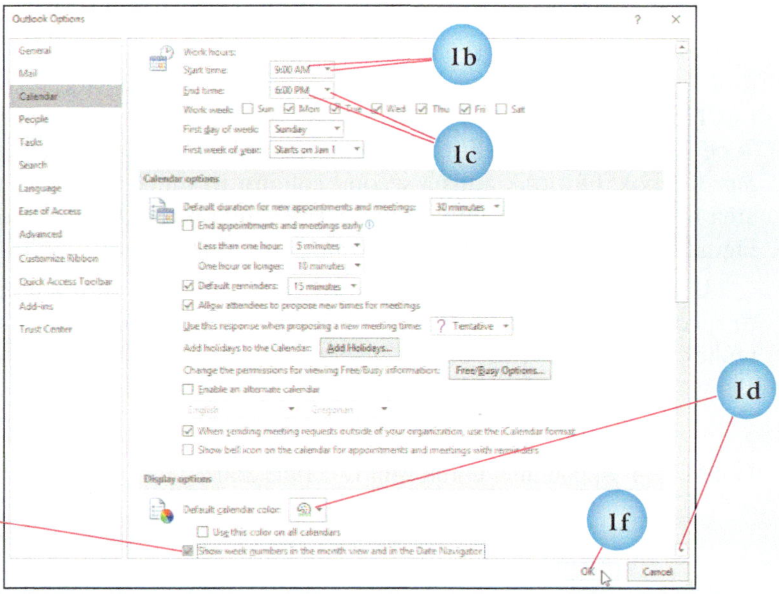

2. Review the appearance of the calendar with the new options applied. The Appointment area is shaded white for the new work day times between 9:00 a.m. and 6:00 p.m. Week numbers are added to the months displayed in the Date Navigator, and the color scheme is green.
3. Click the Month button in the Arrange group and review the options shown in this view. Notice the week numbers along the left edge of the calendar.

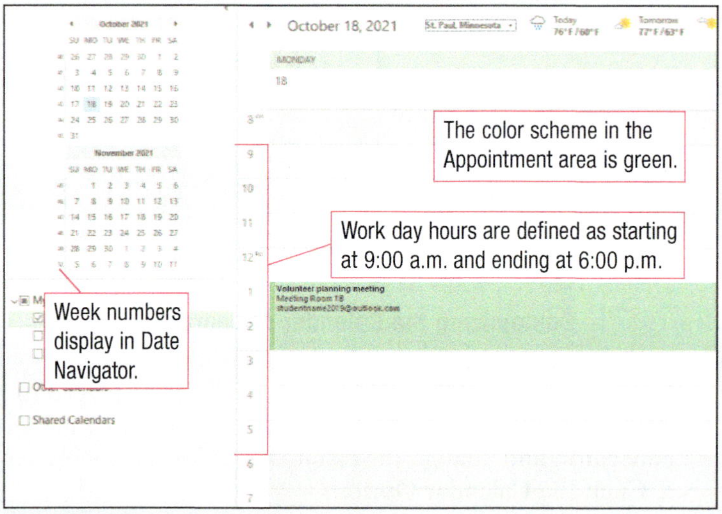

4. Click the Day button in the Arrange group and then print or save as a PDF the calendar with *Daily Style* selected in the *Settings* section in the Print backstage area. You choose an appropriate file name if saving as a PDF.

Check Your Work

Changing Calendar Options in Outlook.com

Customize the calendar by clicking the Settings button (gear icon near your name at top right of screen) to open the Settings panel. Choose a new theme, enable dark mode, turn on bold for event colors, change the time zone, date format, time format, and first day of week, or click the *View all Outlook settings* option to open the expanded Settings window with the Calendar options shown below. Click the Save button at the top of the Settings window when finished.

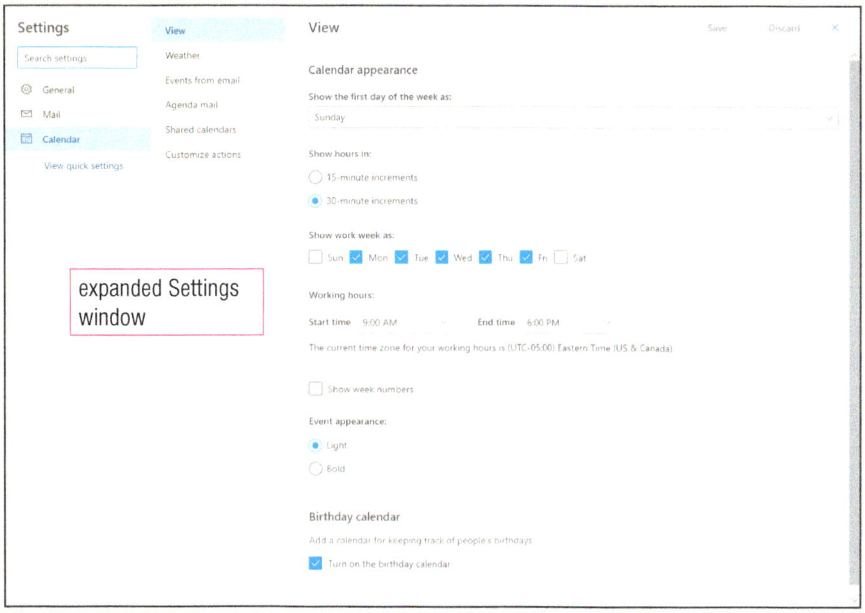

Working with More than One Calendar

You can view more than one calendar at the same time. Outlook displays multiple calendars side by side in the Appointment area, and all the calendars are synchronized to the same day or time period. For example, you may want to maintain a separate calendar for a special project that you are working on to keep the project activities separate from those of your main job. Another example might be that you want to maintain personal appointments separate from your business appointments.

To add a new calendar, create a new folder in which to store the new calendar items. Outlook adds the name of the new calendar in the *My Calendars* section of the Folder pane. Click to insert a check mark in the check box next to the calendar name in the *My Calendars* section of the Folder pane to display the new calendar beside the existing calendar.

You can lay one calendar over another to better see conflicts in scheduling. To do this, right-click one of the calendars in the Folder pane and then click *Overlay* on the shortcut menu. You can also click the left-pointing arrow next to the calendar name in the Calendar tab in the Appointment area to turn on Overlay mode.

Some older Microsoft email accounts are created as an Exchange ActiveSync account. Exchange ActiveSync account types cannot create a new calendar, contact, or task folder in the desktop edition of Outlook. Check the account type by clicking the File tab and then looking in the account information box at the top of the Account Information backstage area. The account type is shown below your email address. If you have multiple accounts, click the list box arrow to view other email account types. If the type is Exchange ActiveSync, you will not be able to add a second calendar.

Activity 12 **Displaying and Working with Two Calendars**

1. With Calendar active and *October 18, 2021* displayed in the Appointment area, create a new calendar folder by completing the following steps:
   a. Right-click *Calendar* below *My Calendars* in the Folder pane and then click *New Calendar* on the shortcut menu.
   b. In the Create New Folder dialog box with the insertion point positioned in the *Name* text box, type Volunteer Schedule.
   c. With *Calendar Items* selected in the *Folder contains* list box and *Calendar* selected in the *Select where to place the folder* list box, click OK.

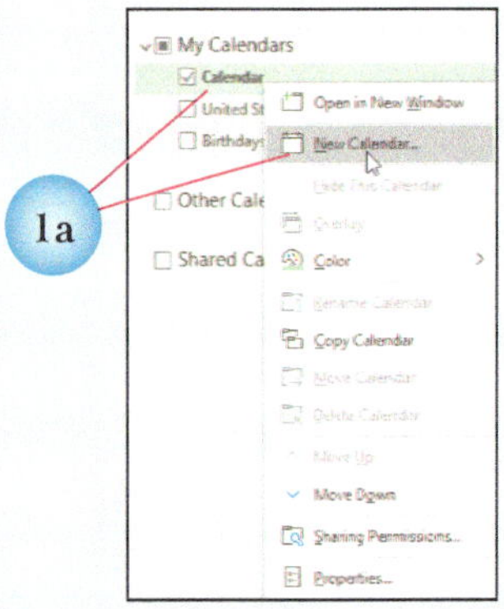

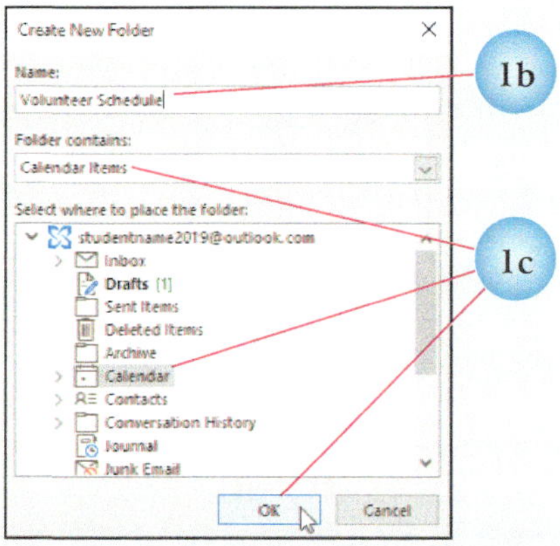

2. Click to insert a check mark in the *Volunteer Schedule* check box in the *My Calendars* section in the Folder pane. Outlook displays each calendar in a tab with the calendar folder name in the tab. Each calendar displays appointments for the same day and time.
3. Click *October 15, 2021* in the Date Navigator. Notice that both calendars display the same day simultaneously.

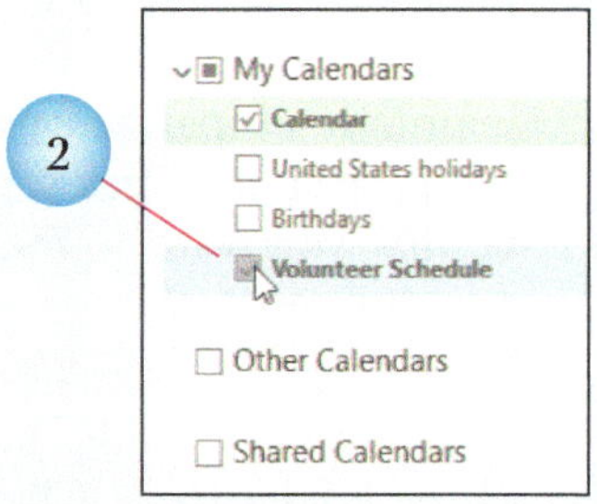

4. Schedule an appointment in the Volunteer Schedule calendar by completing the following steps:
   a. With *October 15, 2021* the active date, click next to *10:00 AM* within the Volunteer Schedule tab in the Appointment area.
   b. Type Ronald McDonald House and then press Enter.
   c. Double-click to open the Appointment window, change the *End time* to *12:00 PM (2 hours)*, and then click the Save & Close button.

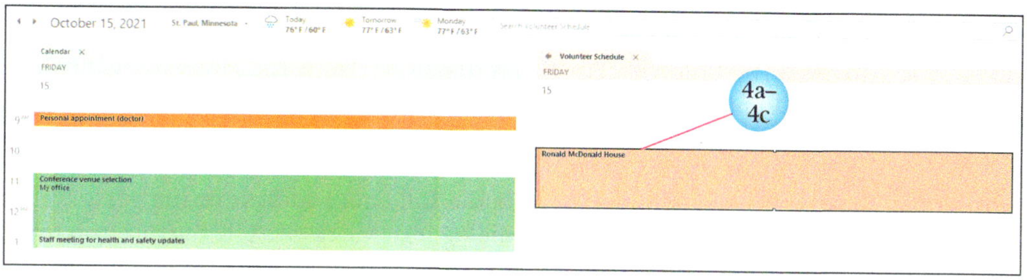

5. Click the left-pointing arrow on the Volunteer Schedule tab to select the option *View in Overlay Mode*. Overlay mode displays appointments for the same day in both calendars in one tab. The main calendar's appointments are shown at the right of the Volunteer Schedule appointments, allowing you to easily see scheduling conflicts, such as the one-hour overlap in the Ronald McDonald House and Conference venue selection appointments.

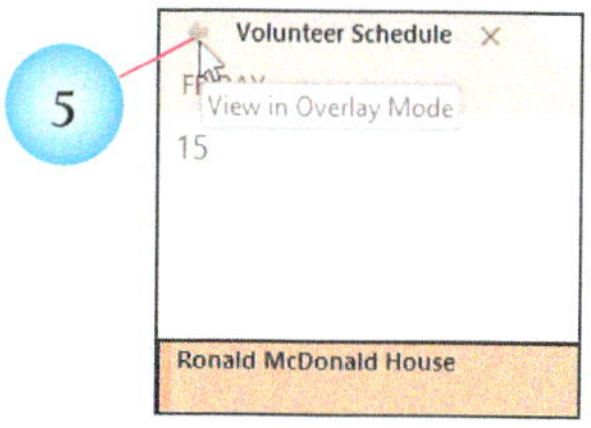

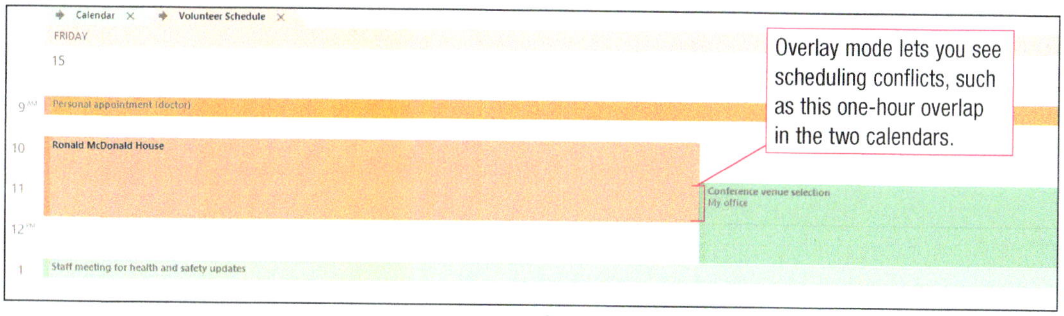

6. Click the right-pointing arrow in the Volunteer Schedule tab to select the option *View in Side-By-Side Mode*.

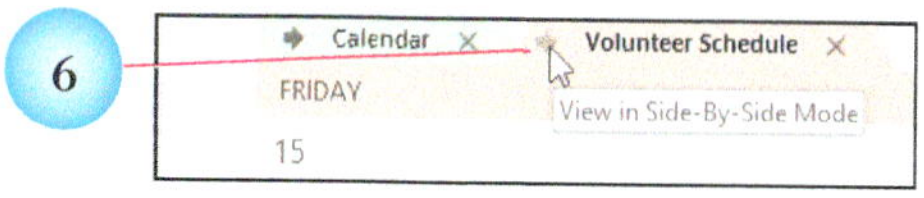

7. If necessary, click to select the Ronald McDonald House appointment box within the Volunteer Schedule tab and then print or save as a PDF the calendar in Daily style, choosing an appropriate file name if saving as a PDF.
8. Click the *Volunteer Schedule* check box in the *My Calendars* section in the Folder pane to clear the check box. Only the main calendar displays in the Appointment area.

Check Your Work

Tutorial

Sharing a Calendar

Sharing a Calendar

You can share your calendar with someone else, allowing the other person to view your appointments only or edit the appointments. A common practice in the workplace is for a manager to share her calendar with an assistant so that the assistant can book meetings and appointments on the manager's behalf. Another common practice is for a project manager to create a separate project calendar and share the calendar with all the team members assigned to the project.

Share Calendar

To share a calendar, click the Share Calendar button in the Manage Calendars group on the Home tab. Click the desired calendar to share in the drop-down list to open the Calendar Properties dialog box with the Permissions tab active. Click the Add button. Select the name in the list of users in the Add Users dialog box if the person is on the same Exchange Server as you. Alternatively, click the *Address Book* option box arrow and click *Contacts* in the drop-down list to choose someone in your Contacts folder, or type the full email address of the person in the *Add* text box at the bottom of the dialog box. Click the OK button to return to the Calendar Properties dialog box with the person's name shown in the *Currently sharing with* list box, as shown in Figure 3.12. Change the permission level from *Can view* to *Can edit* in the *Permissions* section if you want to allow the person to be able to add new appointments or edit appointments in your calendar. Click OK when finished to send the person an email message inviting him or her to view the shared calendar.

Figure 3.12 Calendar Properties Dialog Box with Permissions Tab Active

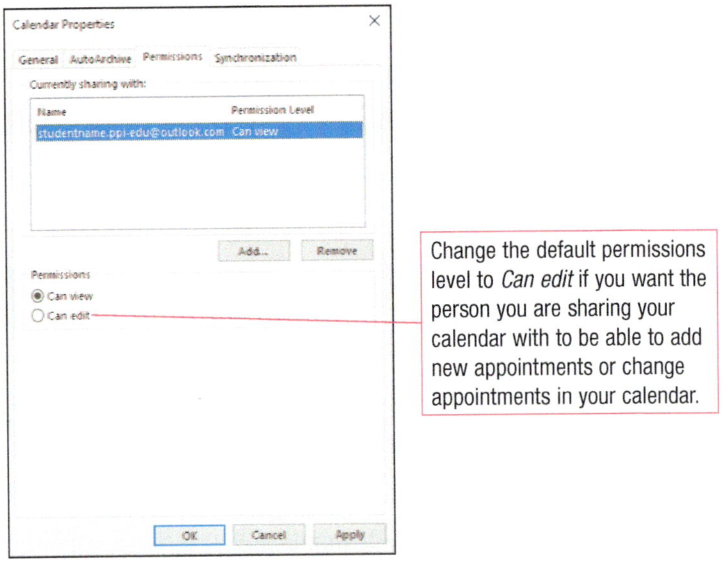

Deleting a Calendar

Outlook does not let you delete the primary calendar for your account. Any other calendar that you have created can be deleted by right-clicking the name of the calendar you want to remove in the Folder pane and then clicking *Delete Calendar* on the shortcut menu. Click the Yes button in the message box that asks if you want to move the calendar to your Deleted Items folder.

Chapter Summary

- Create a new appointment using the click-and-type method or with the New Appointment button in the New group on the Home tab.
- An appointment that occurs on an ongoing basis can be set up as a recurring appointment.
- An event is an activity that lasts an entire day or longer.
- Edit or delete an appointment by double-clicking the appointment box to open the Appointment window, or select the appointment box and use the buttons on the Appointment tab.
- Change the calendar view using the Day, Work Week, Week, and Month buttons in the Arrange group on the Home tab.
- Display appointments in a table format using the *List* or *Active* option in the Change View button drop-down list in the Current View group on the View tab.
- Display the Reading pane to view appointment details at the right or bottom of the window.
- Assign color categories to appointments to group related items.
- View appointments in a table format grouped by color categories using the Categories button in the Arrangement group option box on the View tab.
- Outlook can automatically apply color formatting to appointments based on criteria specified in a rule in the Conditional Formatting dialog box.
- Scheduling a meeting in Outlook is similar to creating an appointment, except that you invite people to the meeting by sending a meeting request email.
- The invitee responds to the meeting organizer using the Accept, Tentative, Decline, or Propose New Time button in the meeting request message.
- Responses to the organizer's meeting request are automatically tracked by Outlook for users connected to a Microsoft Exchange Server.
- Open the Meeting window to edit the details or change attendees. Click the Send Update button to send an email to meeting participants with details about the changes made to the day, time, location, or attendee list.
- Cancel a meeting with the Cancel Meeting button in the Actions group on the Meeting tab.
- Use the Tracking tab to manually change a response from a meeting attendee.
- Customize Calendar by changing options in the Outlook Options dialog box.
- Create a new calendar to store items separately from the main calendar.
- Click the check boxes for the calendars you want to display in the *My Calendars* section in the Folder pane. Outlook displays the same day and time in each open calendar.
- Display calendars in Overlay mode to view two calendars on the same tab, allowing you to see scheduling conflicts easily.
- Share your calendar information with someone else using the Share Calendar button in the Manage Calendars group on the Home tab.
- A calendar you have created can be deleted by right-clicking the calendar name in the Folder pane and then choosing *Delete Calendar* on the shortcut menu.

Commands Review

FEATURE	BUTTON	RIBBON TAB AND GROUP, OR OTHER METHOD	SHORTCUT
Apply conditional formatting		View, Current View	
Assign color category		Appointment, Event OR Meeting, Tags	
Cancel meeting		Meeting, Actions	
Change calendar options		Home, Arrange OR File, *Options*, *Calendar*	
Change current view		Home, Arrange OR View, Current View	
Create appointment		Home, New	Ctrl + N OR Ctrl + Shift + A
Create event		Home, New OR double-click in white text box below day of week colored bar at top of Appointment area	
Create meeting request		Home, New	Ctrl + Shift + Q
Create new calendar folder		Right-click Calendar folder, *New Calendar*	Ctrl + Shift + E
Create recurring appointment or meeting		Appointment, Event OR Meeting, Options	
Delete appointment or event		Appointment OR Event, Actions	Ctrl + D
Display Reading pane		View, Layout	
Go to date		Home, Go To	Ctrl + G
Share Calendar		Home, Manage Calendars	

Quick Steps

Schedule an Appointment Using Click and Type

1. Click appointment date in Date Navigator.
2. Click next to appointment time in Appointment area.
3. Type description of appointment.
4. Press Enter.

Schedule an Appointment Using the Appointment Window

1. Click appointment date in Date Navigator.
2. Click next to appointment time in Appointment area.
3. Click New Appointment button in New group on Home tab.
4. Type description in *Title* text box.
5. Change other options as required.
6. Click Save & Close button.

Schedule an Event

1. Display event date.
2. Double-click in date banner below day of week at top of Appointment area.
3. Type event description in *Title* text box.
4. Change other options as required.
5. Click Save & Close button.

Change the Current View

1. Click View tab.
2. Click Change View button in Current View group.
3. Click desired view.

Display the Reading Pane

1. Click View tab.
2. Click Reading Pane button in Layout group.
3. Click *Bottom* or *Right*.

Apply a Color Category to an Appointment

1. Select appointment.
2. Click Categorize button in Tags group on Appointment tab.
3. Click desired color category.

Create a Conditional Formatting Rule with Color

1. Click View tab.
2. Click View Settings button in Current View group.
3. Click Conditional Formatting button.
4. Click Add button.
5. Type name for new rule in *Name* text box.
6. Choose desired color in *Color* list box.
7. Click Condition button.
8. Choose filter criteria.
9. Click OK two times.

Schedule a Meeting

1. Display meeting date.
2. Click appointment time in Appointment area.
3. Click New Meeting button in New group on Home tab.
4. Type meeting description in *Title* text box.
5. Add invitees' names or email addresses in *Required* text box.
6. Type location in *Location* text box.
7. Change other options as required.
8. Click Send button.

Accept a Meeting Request

1. Display Inbox.
2. Select or open meeting request message.
3. Click Accept button.
4. Click *Edit the Response before Sending* or *Send the Response Now.*
5. If editing response, type message and then click the Send button.

Update a Meeting

1. Select meeting or open Meeting window.
2. Change attendees or otherwise edit meeting details.
3. Click Send Update.

Change Calendar Options

1. Click Calendar Options dialog box launcher in Arrange group on Home tab.
2. Change options as desired.
3. Click OK.

OR

1. Click File tab.
2. Click *Options*.
3. Click *Calendar*.
4. Change options as desired.
5. Click OK.

Create a New Calendar Folder

1. Right-click *Calendar* in Folder pane.
2. Click *New Calendar*.
3. Type new folder name.
4. Click OK.

CHAPTER 4

Managing Contacts and Creating Tasks

Performance Objectives

Upon successful completion of Chapter 4, you will be able to:

1. Add, edit, and delete contacts
2. Add a photo of a contact in the Contact window
3. Flag a contact for a follow-up activity
4. Sort and filter contacts
5. Apply a color category to a contact
6. Find a contact using search tools
7. Send an email message or schedule a meeting from the Contacts module
8. Create and use a contact group
9. Create, update, print, and delete tasks
10. Display a task list in Simple List view and Detailed List view

The People module is used to maintain all the information you need about the individuals or companies with whom you regularly communicate. The information you store about an individual or company, called a ***contact***, can include detailed information such as a manager's name, spouse's name, children's names, birthday, and anniversary. You can also store the person's photograph with the form. Outlook provides several methods for viewing contact data by sorting, filtering, and grouping related records. When you activate the People module, the Contacts folder becomes active, and then you can add, edit, delete, and view contacts.

Working in the Tasks module is similar to maintaining a to-do list. You can track information about a task, such as how much of it has been completed, the priority it has been assigned, and its due date. Tasks can be displayed in To-Do list view or in a table format with additional columns of information about each task, such as the due date and current status.

Data Files

Before beginning the chapter activities and assessments, download the files from your Cirrus course or from your ebook by going to the Table of Contents, clicking the Student Data Files link, and saving the files to your storage medium (such as a USB flash drive).

The online course includes additional training and assessment resources.

Tutorial

Add People

Adding a New Contact

Data saved in the People module is like an electronic address book with the names, addresses, telephone numbers, email addresses, and other information for individuals whom you want to call, text, or email. Data stored about each person is structured like a database, with each contact occupying a ***record*** in a folder. Each unit of information about an individual within the record, such as a telephone number, is referred to as a ***field***. Approximately 140 fields are available for storing information about a contact, including three addresses, three email addresses, and up to 19 telephone numbers. This information can be viewed or printed in a variety of formats and orders.

When you activate the People module, the Contacts folder displays in the Folder pane below *My Contacts*. More than one contacts folder may display in the Folder pane if you have created additional folders to maintain separate lists of people with whom you communicate. For example, you could create a folder to store personal contacts separately from your work-related contacts.

The default view for the Contacts folder is People view, as shown in Figure 4.1. The first contact you will add to the Contacts folder in Activity 1 is shown in Figure 4.1, with the Reading pane displaying the People card for the selected contact (Ms. Kayla McAllister).

New Contact

To open the Contact window with the General page active (see Figure 4.2), click the New Contact button in the New group on the Home tab. The General page displays the most frequently used fields, such as job title, company name, business address, and telephone numbers, as well as email, web, and instant messaging addresses.

Use the *Notes* text box at the right side of the window to type information about the contact that you want to remember. For example, type the person's favorite color, a memorable vacation the person has mentioned, or a reminder about how you know the person.

Figure 4.1 People View for Contacts Folder with First Record Added in Activity 1

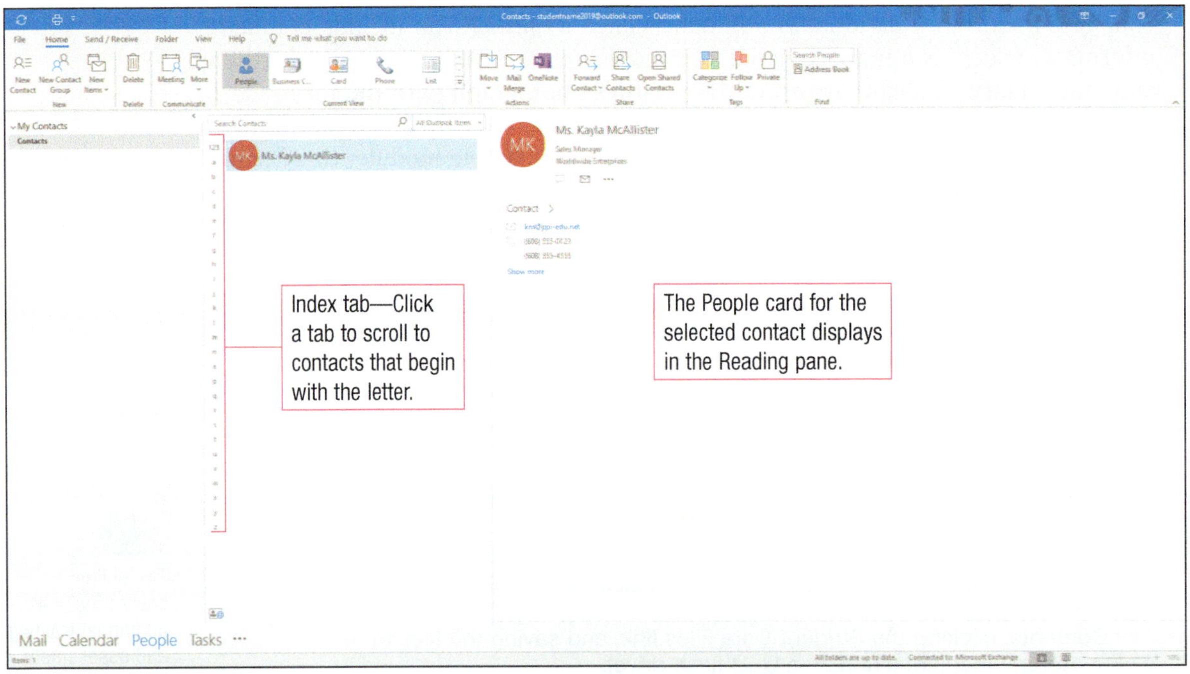

Figure 4.2 New Contact Window with General Page Displayed

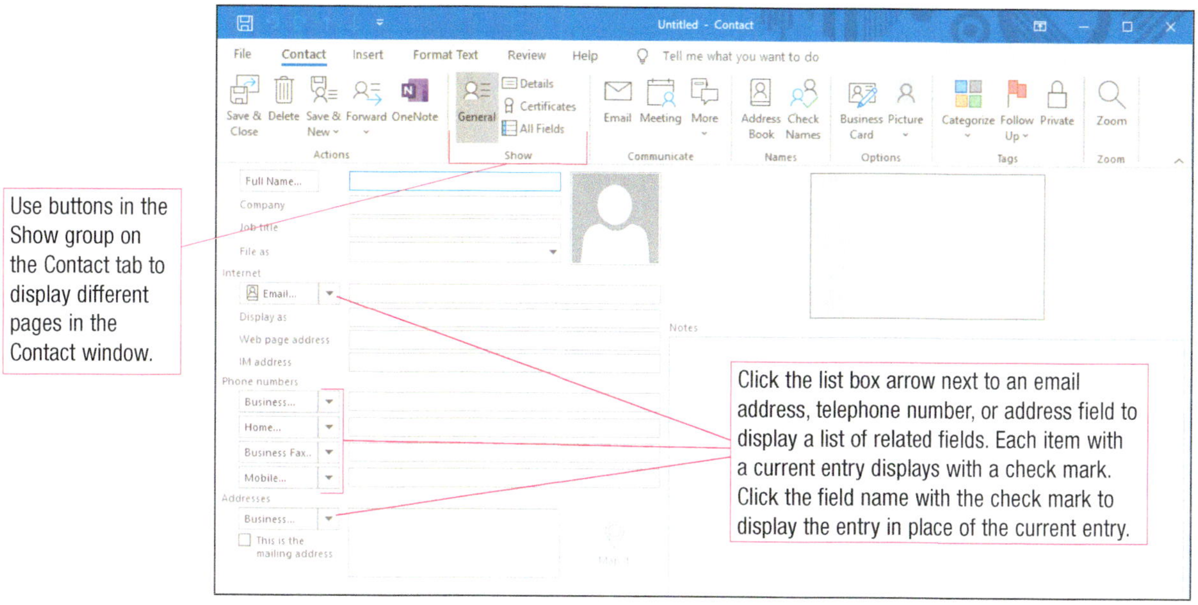

TIP Be mindful of spelling and numeric accuracy while creating a contact record. Contact records are often exported to produce mailing labels.

Buttons in the Show group on the Contact tab display pages with additional fields for the contact. On the Details page, you can enter information about the person in the following fields: *Department*, *Office*, *Profession*, *Manager's name*, and *Assistant's name*. If you would like to keep track of personal information about the individual, type entries in the *Nickname, Title, Suffix, Spouse/Partner, Birthday,* or *Anniversary* fields. If the person will be sharing calendar information, enter his or her web address in the *Internet Free-Busy Address* field.

On the Certificates page, import or export digital IDs that can be used to encrypt mail sent to the individual. Additional fields not shown on the previous pages can be viewed using the All Fields page by selecting a category of fields in the *Select from* drop-down list. The *All Contact fields* option in the *Select from* drop-down list shows all the fields for the active contact in one window.

Consider using the All Fields page to view a subset of related fields. For example, if you have a contact with several phone numbers, you can view all the telephone numbers on one page by selecting *Phone number fields* in the *Select from* drop-down list.

Click the Save & Close button in the Actions group on the Contact tab when you are finished typing information for a new contact. If you are going to add another new contact immediately after saving the current contact, click the Save & New button in the Actions group.

Activity 1 Adding New Contacts

1. With Outlook open, click the People text label or icon on the Navigation bar.
2. Add a new contact record in the People module by completing the following steps:
   a. Click the New Contact button in the New group on the Home tab.

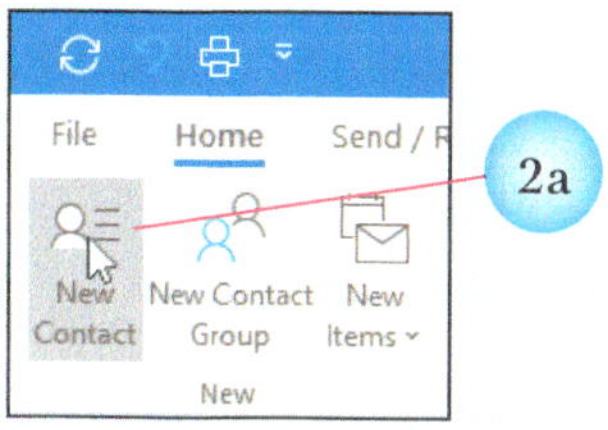

b. With the insertion point positioned in the *Full Name* text box, type Ms. Kayla McAllister and then press the Tab key. The *File as* text box automatically displays the name (with the last name first for sorting purposes) when you move to the next field.
c. With the insertion point positioned in the *Company* text box, type Worldwide Enterprises and then press the Tab key.
d. With the insertion point positioned in the *Job title* text box, type Sales Manager.
e. Click in the *Email* text box in the *Internet* section, type km@ppi-edu.net, and then press the Tab key. The *Display as* text box automatically converts the email entry to *Kayla McAllister (km@ppi-edu.net)*.
f. Click in the *Business* text box in the *Phone numbers* section, type 6085554555, and then press the Tab key. Outlook converts the telephone number to *(608) 555-4555*. You can type telephone numbers with or without spaces or hyphens between sections. ***Note:*** *A Location Information (or Enter Location) dialog box may appear if Windows does not currently have a country and area code set up for the computer you are using. This dialog box stores information related to where you reside and is required for Outlook's telephone features to function correctly. Enter the required location information and then click OK. Click OK if the Phone and Modem dialog box appears, showing your area code.*
g. If necessary, resize the Contact window to view all the fields.
h. Click in the *Mobile* text box in the *Phone numbers* section and then type 6085550123.
i. Click in the *Business* text box in the *Addresses* section and then type the following street address, city, state, and zip code as shown:

   P. O. Box 99
   Middleton, WI 53562

j. Click the Save & Close button in the Actions group on the Contact tab.

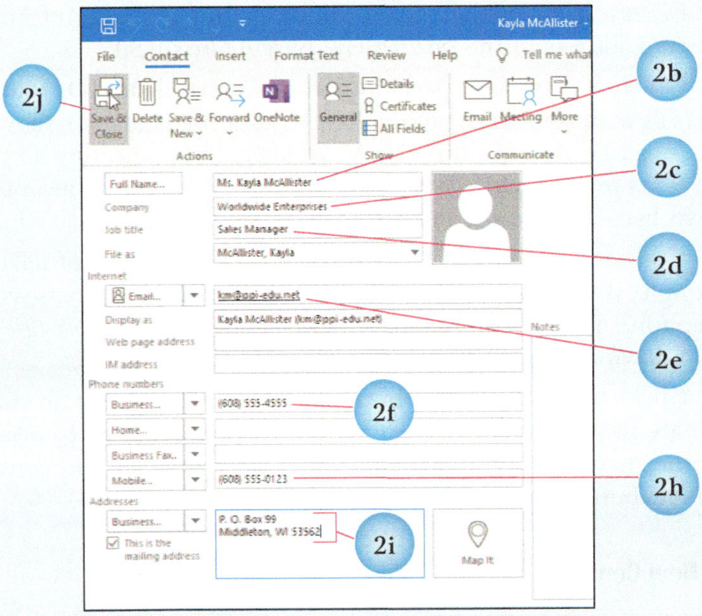

3. Examine the contact record added to the Content pane and the People card displayed in the Reading pane by comparing your screen with the one shown in Figure 4.1.
4. Add a second record to the Contacts module using the Check Full Name and Check Address dialog boxes by completing the following steps:
   a. Double-click in a blank area in the Content pane below the selected contact record for Ms. Kayla McAllister. This action opens a new Contact window.

b. With the insertion point positioned in the *Full Name* text box, click the Full Name button to open the Check Full Name dialog box.

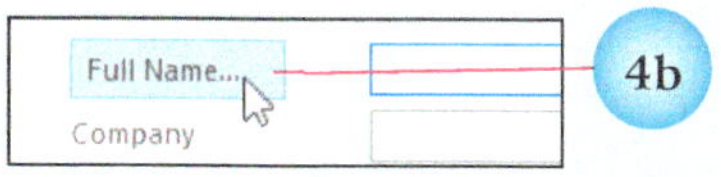

c. With the insertion point positioned in the *Title* text box in the *Name details* section, type Mr. and then press the Tab key or click in the *First* text box.

d. Type Leslie in the *First* text box and then press the Tab key two times or click in the *Last* text box.

e. Type Taylor in the *Last* text box and then press Enter or click OK.

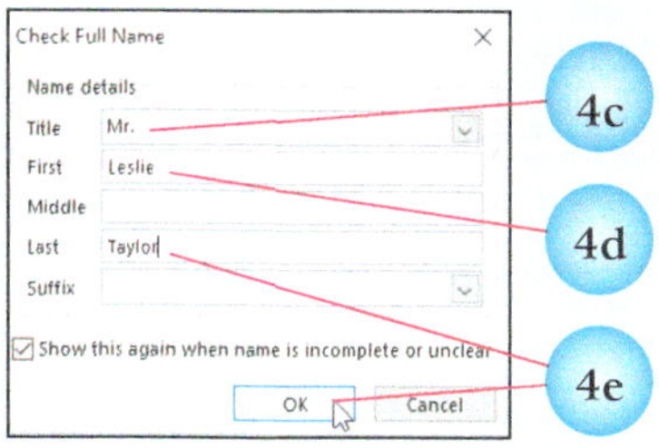

f. Click in the *Company* text box and then type Globalware Distributors.

g. Click in the *Job title* text box and then type Sales Representative.

h. Click in the *Email* text box and then type lt@ppi-edu.net.

i. Type the following telephone numbers in the appropriate fields in the *Phone numbers* section:

Business	6085552199
Mobile	6085554975

j. Click the Business button in the *Addresses* section to open the Check Address dialog box.

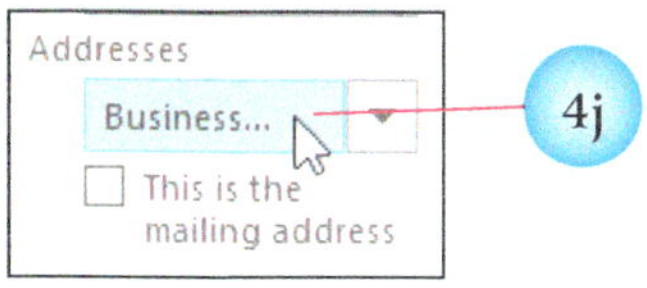

k. With the insertion point positioned in the *Street* text box in the *Address details* section, type 4532 Dundas Street West and then press the Tab key or click in the *City* text box.

l. Type Madison and then press the Tab key or click in the *State/Province* text box.

m. Type WI and then press the Tab key or click in the *ZIP/Postal code* text box.

n. Type 53710 and then press Enter or click OK.

o. Click the Save & Close button in the Actions group on the Contact tab.

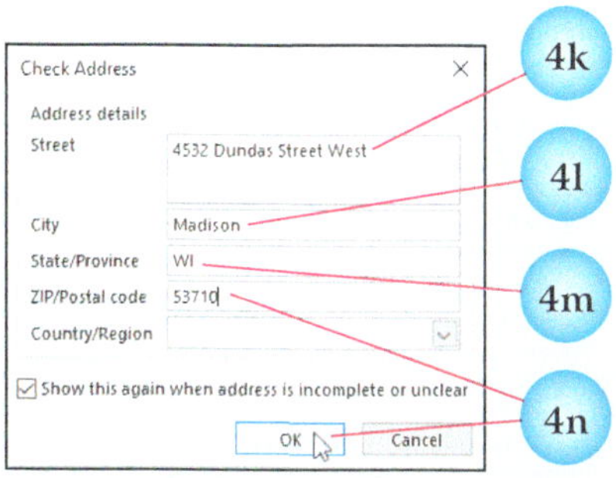

5. Click the Card button in the Current View group on the Home tab.

6. Increase the width of the first column of contacts in the Content pane by pointing to the gray vertical line at the right of the contact names until the pointer displays with a double vertical bar and left-and-right-pointing arrows and then dragging to the right until all data is visible.

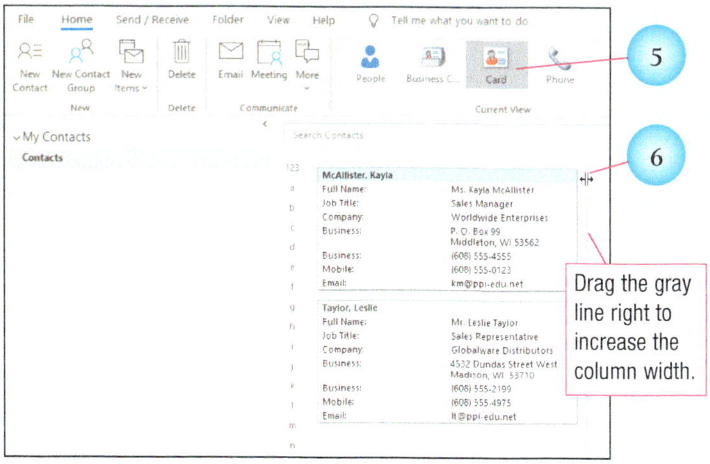

7. Click the File tab and then click *Print*. In the Print backstage area with *Card Style* selected in the *Settings* section, click the Print button or change the printer to the option that prints to PDF and then click the Print button. You determine an appropriate file name if saving as a PDF.

Check Your Work

TIP The Check Address dialog box often appears for international addresses due to differences in zip/postal codes. To save time, type these addresses directly into the Check Address dialog box.

In Activity 1, Step 2, you typed text directly into the *Full Name* and *Business* text boxes, but in Step 4, you typed text into the individual fields for the name and address using the Check Full Name and Check Address dialog boxes. Outlook separates input into the individual fields based on the text that you type unless the entry is not recognized. If the entry is not recognized, the Check Full Name or Check Address dialog box opens automatically. In that case, insert and delete text as required to correct the text in the fields, or click OK to accept the unrecognized entries as you typed them in the text box.

Outlook recognizes the titles *Dr., Miss, Mr., Mrs., Ms.,* and *Prof.* The Check Full Name dialog box opens if you type a title not in this list. The Check Address dialog box opens when an address has been typed that Outlook does not recognize as containing a valid street, city, state or province, and zip or postal code.

Adding a New Contact to People in Outlook.com

Click the App launcher button (waffle icon), click *All apps*, and then click *People* in the Apps pane, or click the People icon on the Navigation bar at the bottom of the Folder pane to display the People module.

Click the New contact button (displays with a plus symbol) on the Menu bar to add a new contact record. Type information in the appropriate fields in the New contact window and then click the Create button when finished.

To add more contact fields to the window, click the *Add more* option near the bottom right of the window to display a pop-up list with additional fields and field categories. For example, to add a business address, click *Add more*, point to *Address*, and then click *Business*. The contact window expands to add a *Business address* section above the *Notes* section.

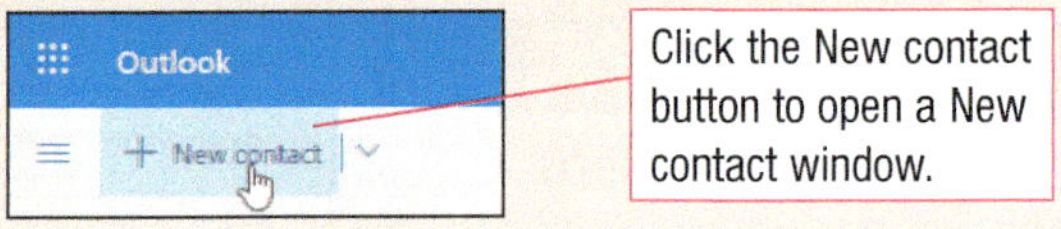

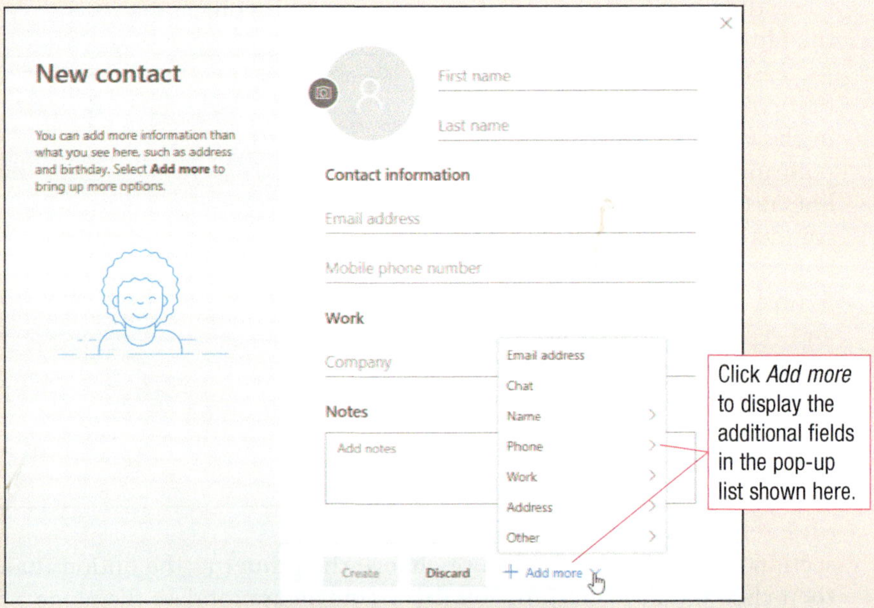

Editing and Deleting Contacts

Maintaining contact records involves activities such as changing addresses, telephone numbers, and email addresses as individuals move or change companies. It also involves adding information to fields not previously completed and deleting contacts for which you no longer require records in the Contacts folder.

To edit a contact, double-click the contact name in the Content pane in People view, Card view, Phone view, or List view to open the Contact window. Edit the data in the fields as required and then click the Save & Close button in the Actions group on the Contact tab when finished.

You can also edit a contact by displaying contacts in People view, right-clicking the contact name in the Content pane, and then clicking *Edit Contact* on the shortcut menu. This action opens the Contact window in which you can make the desired changes and then click the Save & Close button.

Delete

To delete a contact, click to select the name in the Content pane for the contact that you want to remove and then press the Delete key, or click the Delete button in the Delete group on the Home tab. Be cautious when deleting a contact record because Outlook does not prompt you to confirm the deletion. If you delete a contact by mistake and notice the error immediately, click the Undo button on the Quick Access Toolbar to restore the contact record to the list.

Activity 2 Adding and Editing Contacts

1. With Outlook open and the contacts list active in Card view, add a new contact by completing the following steps:
   a. Right-click in a blank area in the Content pane and then click *New Contact* on the shortcut menu.
   b. With the insertion point positioned in the *Full Name* text box, type Celia D'Allario.
   c. Click in the *Email* text box and then type cd@ppi-edu.net.
   d. Type the following telephone numbers in the appropriate text boxes:

      Home 6085554968
      Mobile 6085553795

   e. Click the Business button arrow in the *Addresses* section and then click *Home* in the drop-down list.
   f. With the insertion point positioned in the *Home* text box in the *Addresses* section, type the following text:

      44 Queen Street
      Madison, WI 53562

   g. Click the Private button in the Tags group on the Contact tab.
   h. Click the Save & Close button in the Actions group on the Contact tab.

1b–1f

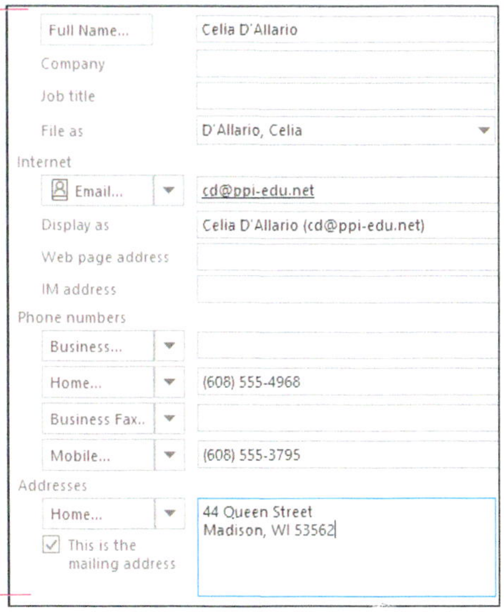

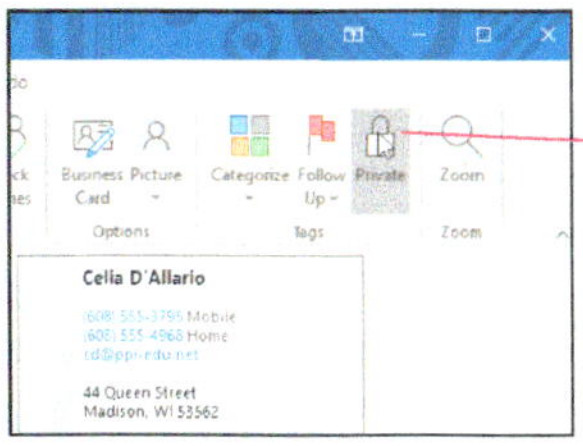

1g

2. Edit the telephone numbers for Leslie Taylor by completing the following steps:
   a. Click the People button in the Current View group on the Home tab.

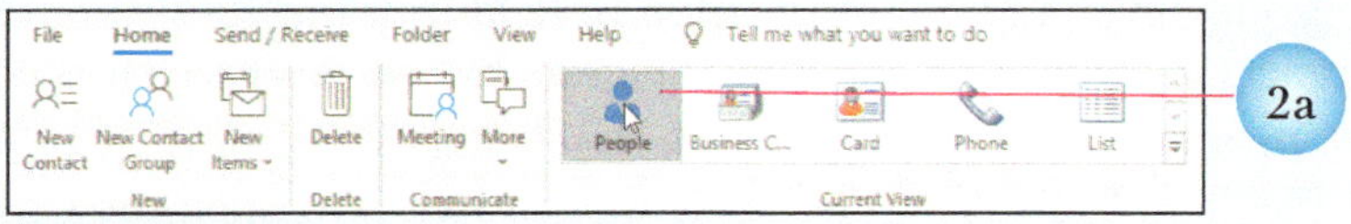

   b. Right-click *Mr. Leslie Taylor* in the Content pane.
   c. Click *Edit Contact* on the shortcut menu.
   d. Click to place the insertion point within the *Business* text box in the *Phone numbers* section and then insert and delete text as required to change the telephone number from *(608) 555-2199* to *(608) 555-2267*.
   e. Change the mobile telephone number from *(608) 555-4975* to *(608) 555-3311* by completing a step similar to Step 2d.
   f. Click the Save & Close button in the Actions group on the Contact tab.

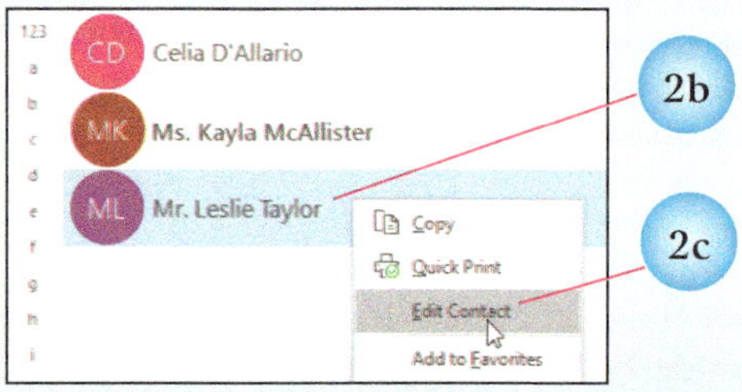

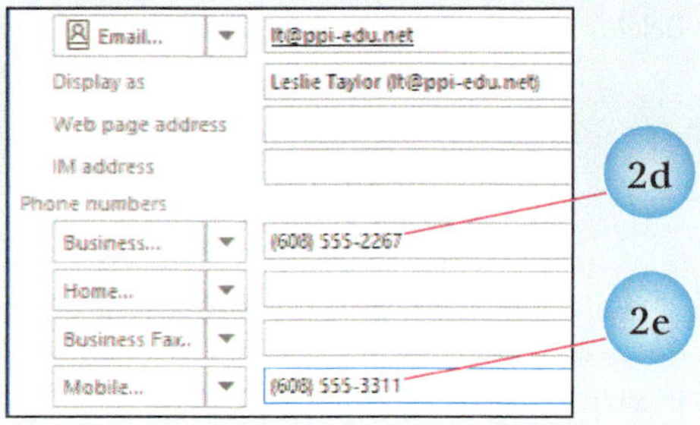

3. Double-click *Ms. Kayla McAllister* in the Content pane to open the Contact window.
4. Change the street address for Kayla McAllister from *P. O. Box 99* to *18 Forsythia Avenue* by completing a step similar to Step 2d.

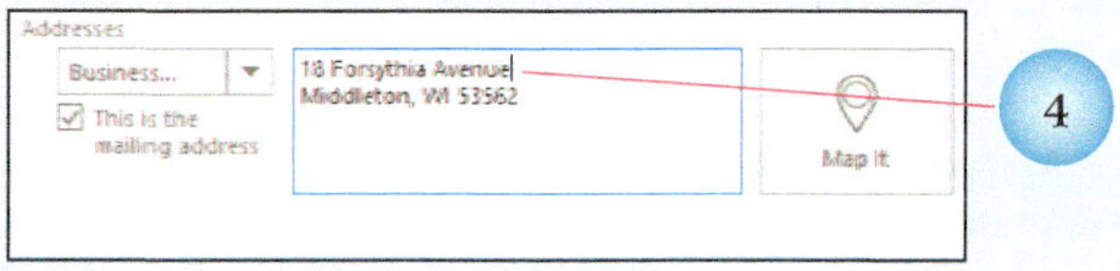

5. Click the Save & Close button.
6. Click the File tab and then click *Print*. With *Card Style* selected in the *Settings* section in the Print backstage area, click the Print button. Enter an appropriate file name if saving as a PDF.

Check Your Work

Editing Contacts in Outlook.com

Edit a contact by clicking to select the contact in the Content pane and then clicking the Edit button on the Menu bar. Make the desired changes in the fields in the Edit contact window and then click the Save button.

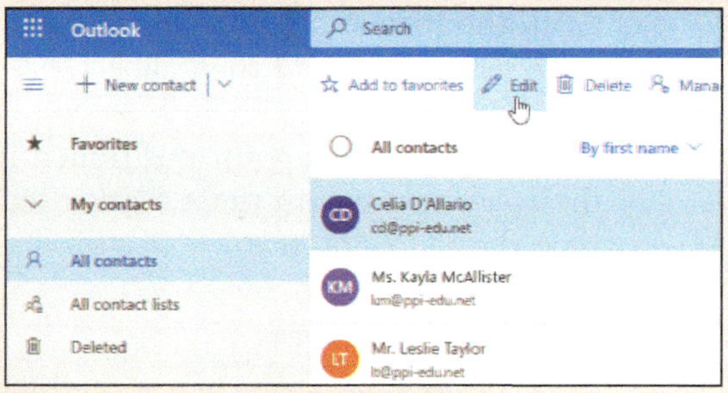

Delete a selected contact by clicking the Delete button on the Menu bar. In the Delete contact? message box that appears, click the Delete button.

Adding a New Contact from an Existing Contact

When you communicate with more than one person from the same company, you can add the second and subsequent records by basing them on the first record. Outlook inserts the company name, company address, and business telephone number in the new record so that you do not have to retype the information. Basing a new record on an existing one not only prevents duplication of effort but also ensures that data in the records is consistent and that typing errors are minimized.

New Items

Once one of the contacts has been created for the company, the remaining contacts for the same company can be added by selecting the contact name in the Contact pane, clicking the New Items button in the New group on the Home tab, and then clicking *Contact from the Same Company* in the drop-down list. Type the name, job title, email address, and other unique information for the new contact and then click the Save & Close button.

Activity 3 Adding a New Contact from an Existing Contact

1. With Outlook open and the contacts list active in People view, add a new contact based on the record of an existing contact by completing the following steps:
   a. If necessary, click to select *Ms. Kayla McAllister* in the Content pane.
   b. Click the New Items button in the New group on the Home tab and then click *Contact from the Same Company* in the drop-down list.
   c. With the insertion point positioned in the *Full Name* text box, type Mr. Henry Miele.
   d. Click in the *Job title* text box and then type Sales Manager, European Division.
   e. Click in the *Email* text box and then type hm@ppi-edu.net.
   f. Click in the *Mobile* text box and then type 6085551884.
   g. Click the Save & Close button.
2. Print or save as a PDF the contacts in Card style, choosing an appropriate file name if saving as a PDF.

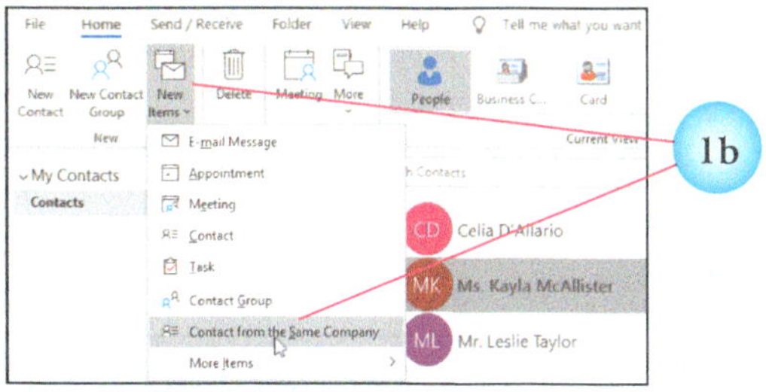

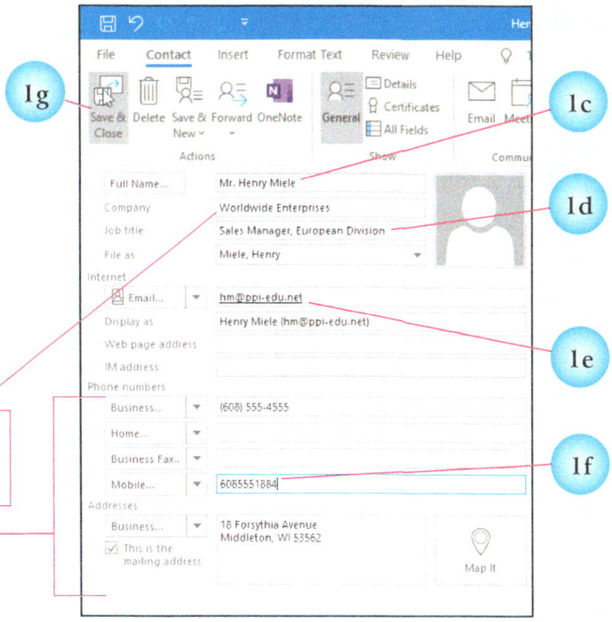

These fields are already completed based on information in Kayla McAllister's record.

Check Your Work

Using the Details and All Fields Pages

Details

All Fields

Approximately 140 fields are available for storing information about a person, including four user-defined fields. The Details page in the Contact window, which is shown in Figure 4.3, groups fields related to the person's business and personal relationships. The All Fields page provides the ability to view subsets of related fields or all the contact fields in a table format. Click the Details or All Fields button in the Show group on the Contact tab to change the page displayed in the Contact window.

Figure 4.3 Contact Window with Details Page Displayed

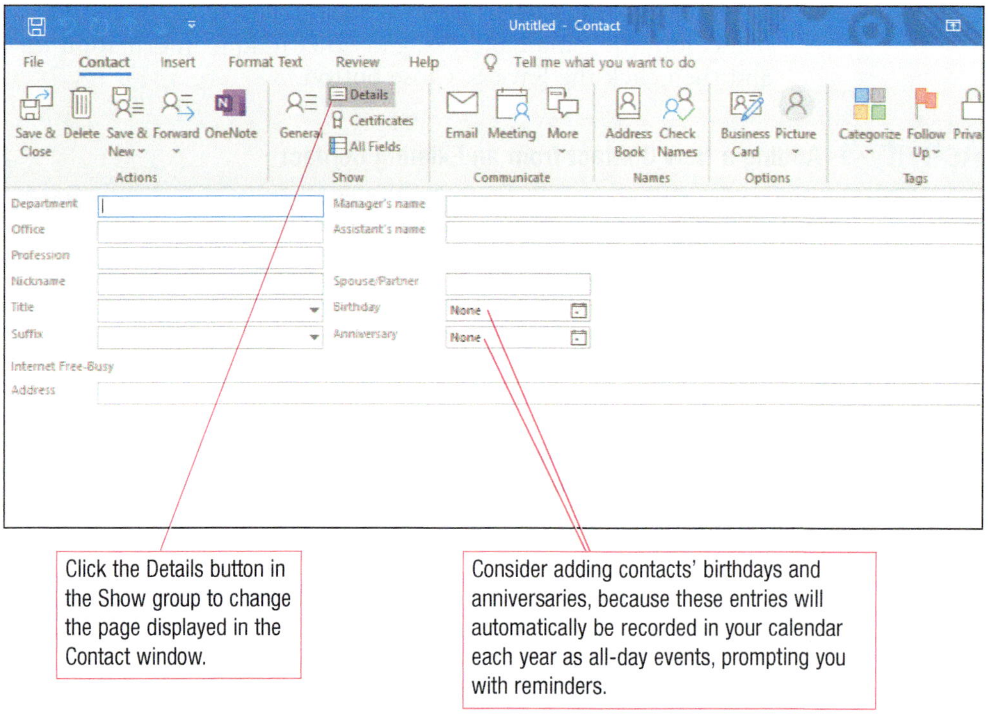

Activity 4 Adding Information in the Details and All Fields Pages

1. With Outlook open and the contacts list active in People view, add a new contact with information on the Details page by completing the following steps:
   a. Click the New Contact button.
   b. Type the following information in the appropriate text boxes on the General page:

Full Name	Dr. Tory Nguyen
Company	Globe Products
Job title	Director, Marketing and Sales
Email	tn@ppi-edu.net
Business	6085552689
Mobile	6085551598
Business	393 Brentwood Road Madison, WI 53562

   c. Click the Details button in the Show group on the Contact tab.

d. With the insertion point positioned in the *Department* text box, type Marketing.
e. Click in the *Manager's name* text box and then type Kyle Winston.
f. Click in the *Assistant's name* text box and then type Dana Gorski.
g. Click in the *Spouse/Partner* text box and then type Chris Greenbaum.

2. View all the contact fields and add the names of the children for the contact by completing the following steps:
   a. Click the All Fields button in the Show group on the Contact tab.

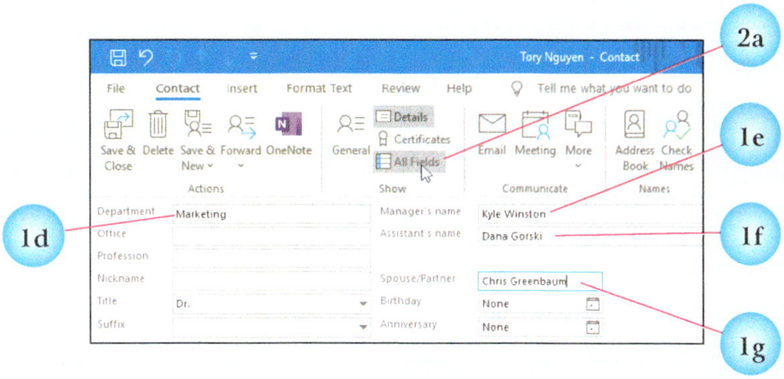

   b. Click the *Select from* list box arrow, scroll down the list box, and then click *All Contact fields*.
   c. Scroll down to the bottom of the list box and examine all the fields that are available for storing information about contacts.
   d. Scroll up the list box until you see the field *Children*. ***Note:*** *The field names are in alphabetical order*.
   e. Click in the column labeled *Value* beside the field *Children* to select the field and position the insertion point inside the dotted text box.
   f. Type Brooke, Justin, Jamie.
   g. Click the File tab inside the Contact window and then click *Print*. With *Memo Style* selected in the *Settings* section in the Print backstage area, click the Print button. Enter an appropriate file name if saving as a PDF.
   h. Click the Save & Close button.

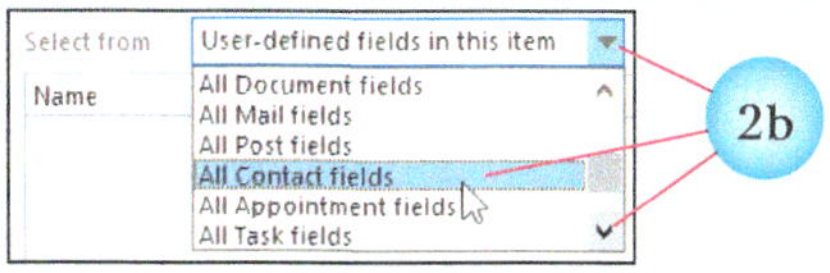

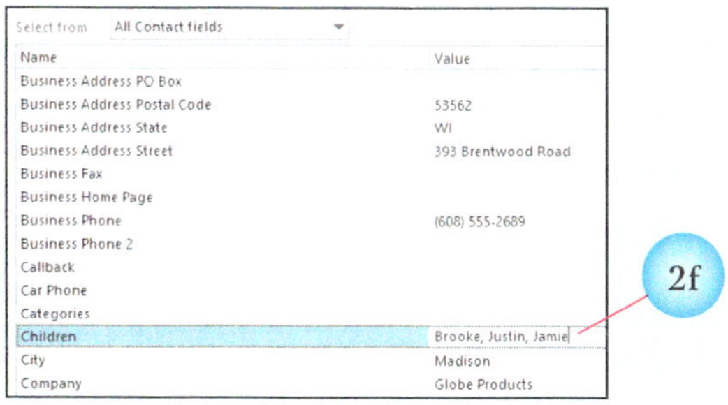

3. Add the birthday information for an existing contact by completing the following steps:
   a. Right-click *Ms. Kayla McAllister* in the Content pane and then click *Edit Contact* on the shortcut menu.
   b. Click the Details button in the Show group.
   c. Select *None* in the *Birthday* text box and then type 10/15/1960.
   d. Click the Save & Close button. A reminder will now automatically occur in the calendar each year on Kayla's birthday.

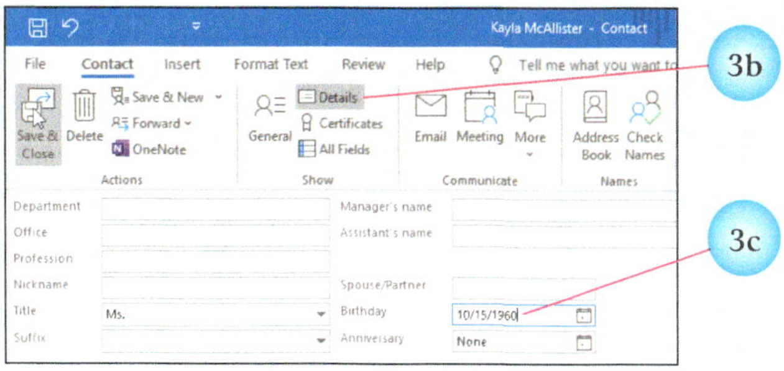

Check Your Work

Adding a Photo for a Contact

Click the *Add Contact Picture* box located within the Contact window to add a photograph of the individual to the contact record. You can also click the Picture button in the Options group on the Contact tab and then click *Add Picture* in the drop-down list. In the Add Contact Picture dialog box, navigate to the drive and folder where the image file is stored and then double-click the file name. Outlook recognizes standard graphics file formats, such as GIF, JPEG, and PNG and their corresponding file extensions *.gif*, *.jpg*, and *.png*. Outlook resizes the image to fit within the picture box, maintaining the aspect ratio so the image does not become distorted.

Add Contact Picture

Figure 4.4 shows Kayla McAllister's Contact window with a photo of her in the *Add Contact Picture* box. (You will add this photo in Activity 5.) If you need to change or remove a picture, open the Contact window for the individual, click the Picture button in the Options group on the Contact tab, and then click *Change Picture* or *Remove Picture* in the Picture button drop-down list.

TIP Photos show next to contact names in the Content pane in People view, in Business Card view, and within a Contact window. Other views do not display the photos.

Figure 4.4 Photograph of Contact Added in Contact Window

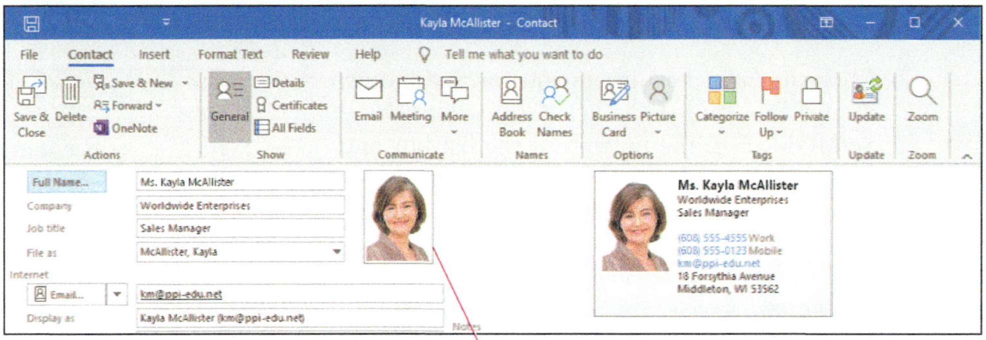

The photo appears in the *Add Contact Picture* box.
You will add Kayla McAllister's photo here in Activity 5.

Activity 5 Adding a Photo in a Contact Record

Note: Make sure you have copied the student data files for this chapter to your storage medium before completing this activity.

1. With Outlook open and the contacts list active in People view, add a photo in Kayla McAllister's contact record by completing the following steps:
   a. If necessary, click to select *Ms. Kayla McAllister* in the Content pane.
   b. Click the More options button (three dots) in the Reading pane next to the message icon and then click *Edit Outlook Contact* to open the Contact window.
   c. Click the *Add Contact Picture* box.
   d. In the Add Contact Picture dialog box, navigate to the drive and folder containing the student data files.
   e. Double-click *K_McAllister.jpg*.
   f. Click the Save & Close button.

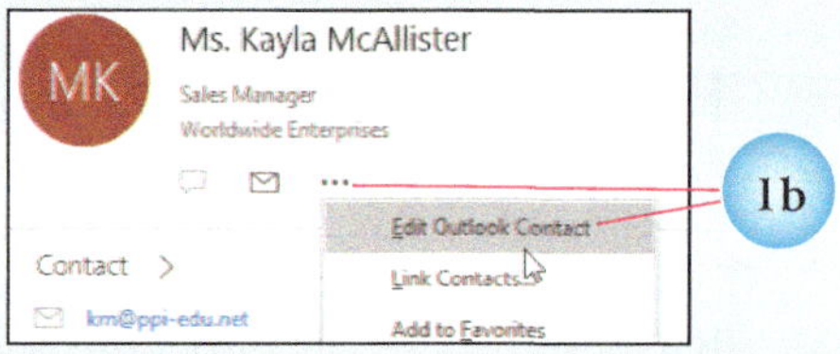

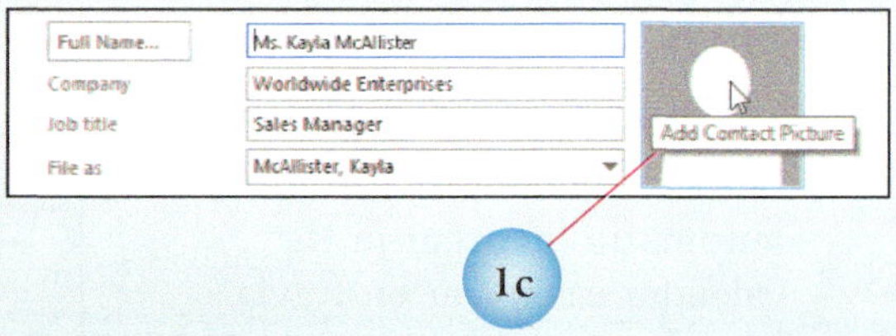

2. Add the following photos to the contact records noted by completing steps similar to Steps 1a through 1f:

Celia D'Allario	***C_DAllario.jpg***
Mr. Henry Miele	***H_Miele.jpg***
Dr. Tory Nguyen	***T_Nguyen.jpg***
Mr. Leslie Taylor	***L_Taylor.jpg***

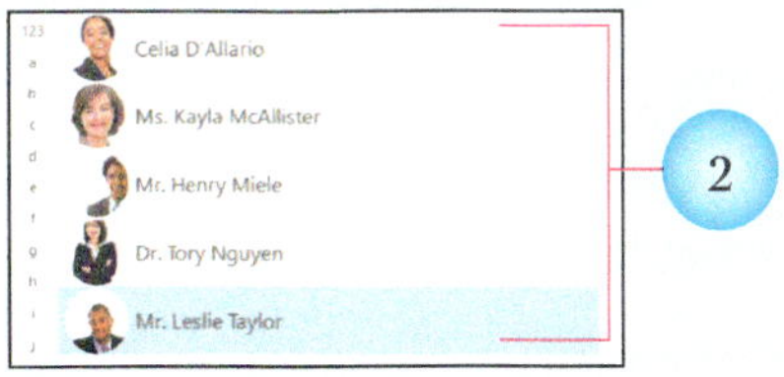

3. Click the Business Card button in the Current View group on the Home tab. In Business Card view, photos are displayed in miniature business cards for those contacts who have an image attached to the record.

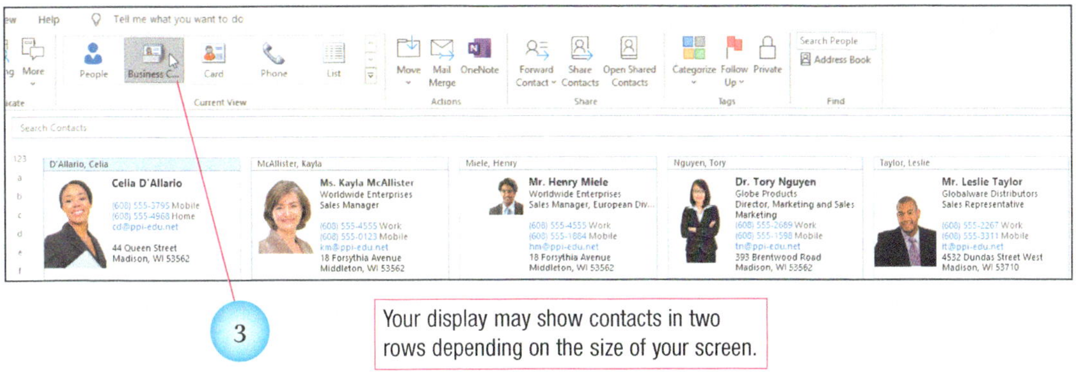

Flagging a Contact for Follow-Up

Follow Up

You can set a reminder to follow up on an outstanding issue with a person by flagging the contact record. To do this, select the record that you want to mark with a flag, click the Follow Up button in the Tags group on the Home tab, and then click the desired follow-up option in the drop-down list. Figure 4.5 displays the predefined follow-up flags.

If none of the predefined flags suit your needs, click *Custom* to open the Custom dialog box. Click the *Flag to* option box arrow in the dialog box and then click the type of flag that you want to set. To enter a Start date or a Due date, type the date in the required text box, or click the option box arrow to select a date in a drop-down calendar. Reminders for flags can also be set in the Custom dialog box by clicking the *Reminder* check box to insert a check mark and then setting the reminder date and time as needed. Click OK when you have finished defining the criteria for the custom flag.

Figure 4.5 Follow-up Flags

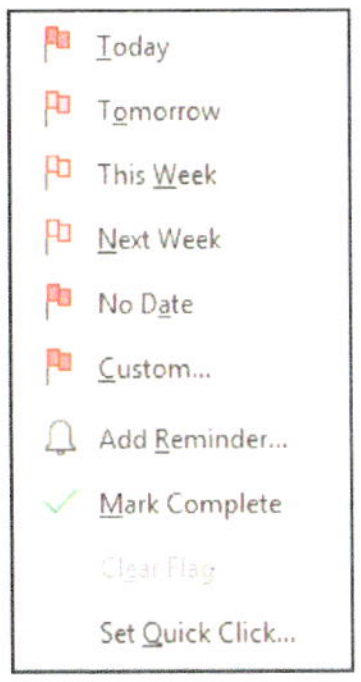

Activity 6 Flagging Contacts for Follow-Up

1. With Outlook open and the contacts list active in Business Card view, complete the following steps to attach a follow-up flag to a contact record that will remind you to schedule a meeting.
   a. Click to select the business card for Ms. Kayla McAllister.
   b. Click the Follow Up button in the Tags group on the Home tab and then click *Custom* in the drop-down list.
   c. In the Custom dialog box, click the *Flag to* option box arrow and then click *Arrange Meeting*.
   d. Select the current date in the *Due date* text box, type one week from today, and then press Enter or click OK. Outlook allows all dates to be entered using natural language phrases. The *Due date* will be set to one week from the current date.

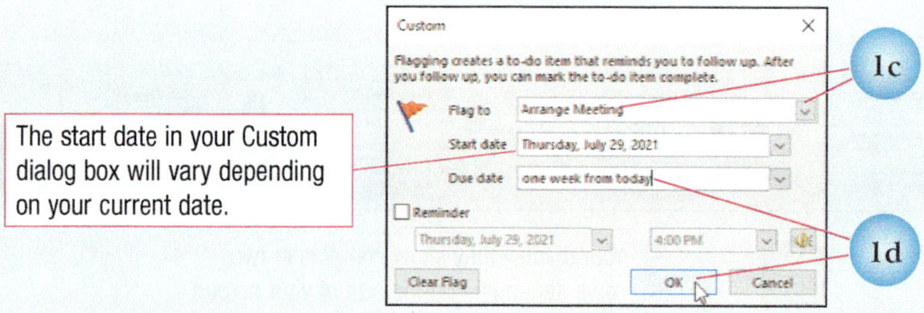

2. Click the Card button in the Current View group on the Home tab. Look at the Follow Up Flag information that appears in the card below the name banner for Kayla McAllister. Outlook also adds an item to the task list in the Tasks module.
3. Click the People button in the Current View group and then double-click *Ms. Kayla McAllister* to open the Contact window and view the Follow Up message above the Full Name button.

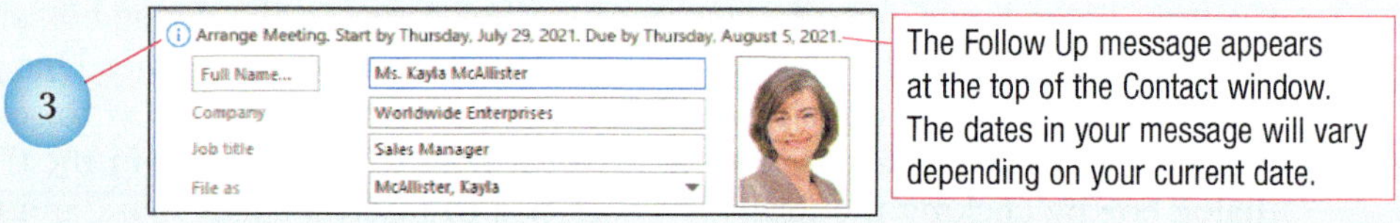

4. Close the Contact window.
5. Add a follow-up flag to the contact record for Dr. Tory Nguyen by completing the following steps:
   a. Right-click *Dr. Tory Nguyen* in the Content pane.
   b. Point to *Follow Up* and then click *No Date* on the shortcut menu.
6. Change the current view to Card view and then print or save as a PDF the contacts in Card style. Enter an appropriate file name if saving as a PDF.

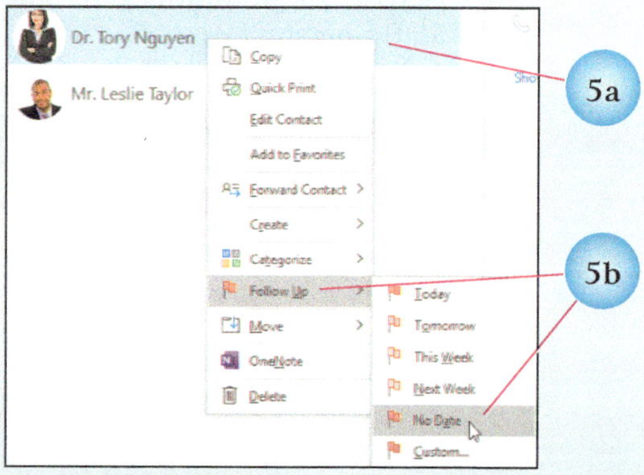

Check Your Work

TIP In Card view, the data for a contact in which a follow-up flag due date has passed without the flag being cleared or marked complete displays in red.

Once the follow-up activity has been completed, remove the flag by selecting the contact in the Content pane, clicking the Follow Up button, and then clicking *Clear Flag* in the drop-down list. Alternatively, you can choose the *Mark Complete* option in the Follow Up drop-down list to note the activity has been finished. By choosing *Mark Complete*, you leave the follow-up flag in place in the contact record along with the date the follow-up activity was marked complete. Use this method if retaining the activity details is important to you.

Tutorial

Sorting Contacts

Sorting Contacts

Contacts are displayed in the Content pane alphabetically in ascending order by the *File As* field, which defaults to the contact's last name followed by his or her first name. In the Sort dialog box, shown in Figure 4.6, you can specify up to four fields by which to sort the contacts list.

The drop-down list of fields for *Sort items by* and *Then by* defaults to *Frequently-used fields*. Click the *Select available fields from* list box arrow to change to any of the subsets of related fields or all the contact fields.

View Settings

To begin a sort, click the View tab, click the View Settings button in the Current View group, and then click the Sort button in the Advanced View Settings dialog box. The Sort dialog box opens, which is where you define the sort criteria. Click OK two times after defining the sort field(s), and the contact list reorders to the new sort settings.

Figure 4.6 Sort Dialog Box

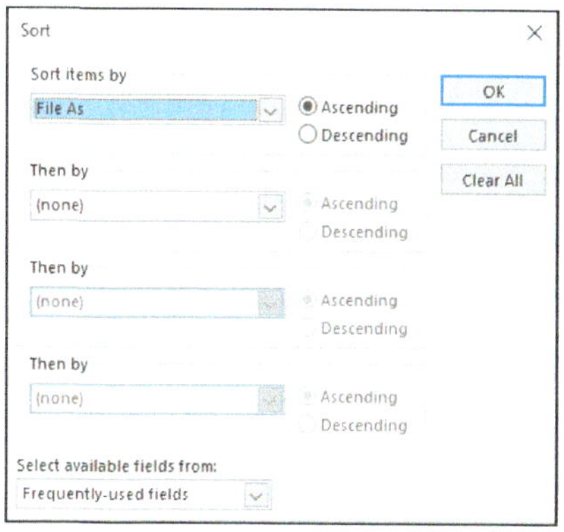

Activity 7 Sorting Contacts

1. With Outlook open and the contacts list active in Card view, sort the contacts list by company name and then by last name within each company by completing the following steps:
   a. Click the View tab and then click the View Settings button in the Current View group.
   b. Click the Sort button in the Advanced View Settings dialog box.

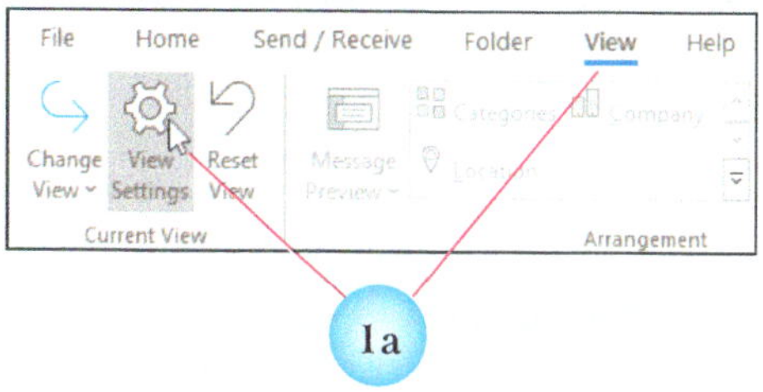

c. Click the *Sort items by* list box arrow, scroll up the list box, and then click *Company*. The default sort order is *Ascending*.

d. Click the first *Then by* list box arrow, scroll down the list box, and then click *Last Name*. The default sort order is *Ascending*.

e. Click OK to close the Sort dialog box.

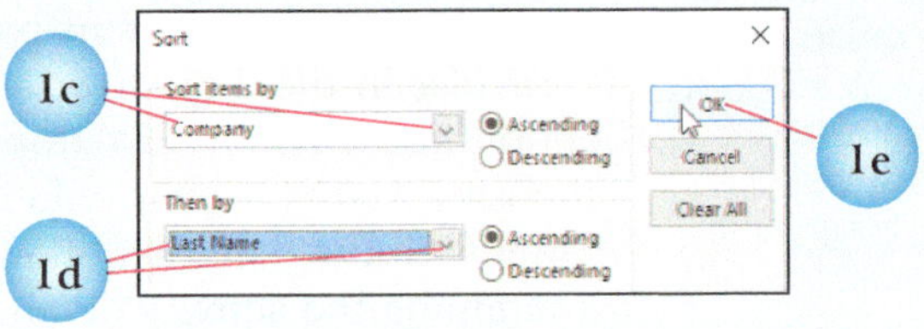

f. In the Microsoft Outlook message box informing you that the field *Last Name* is not shown in the view and asking if you want to show it, click the No button. You do not need to display the *Last Name* field because the banner for each card displays the *File As* field, which includes the last name.

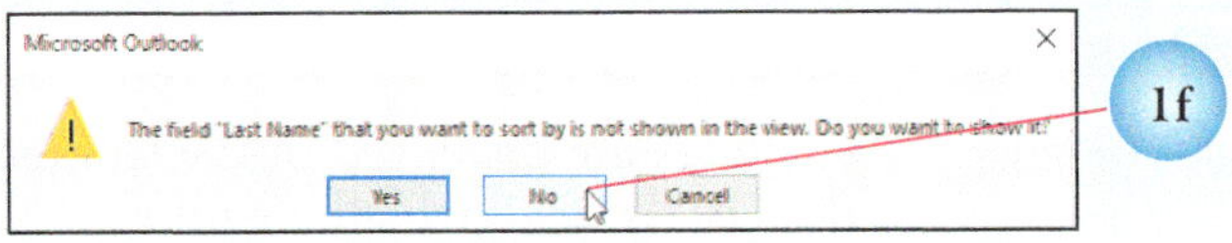

g. With the current sort settings displayed next to the Sort button in the Advanced View Settings dialog box, click OK.

h. Examine the order of the records in the Content pane. If necessary, scroll in the Content pane to view all the contact records.

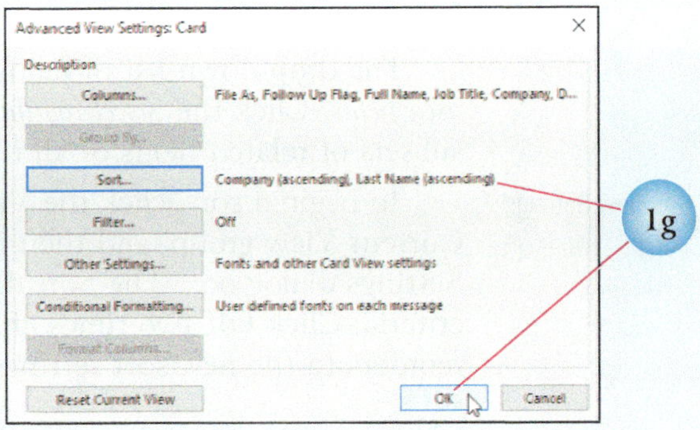

2. Add a new contact that is based on an existing contact by completing the following steps:

a. Click to select the card for Dr. Tory Nguyen.

b. Click the Home tab, click the New Items button in the New group, and then click *Contact from the Same Company*.

c. Type the following information in the appropriate text boxes:

Full Name	Mr. Luis Phillips
Job title	Sales Manager
E-mail	lp@ppi-edu.net
Mobile	6085553884

d. Replace the picture of Tory Nguyen with the correct image by completing the following steps:

1) Click the Picture button in the Options group on the Contact tab.

2) Click *Change Picture* in the drop-down list.

3) If necessary, navigate to the student data files.

4) Double-click ***L_Phillips.jpg***.

This is the business card for the new contact added in Step 2 from inside the Contact window.

e. Click the Save & Close button. Notice that the new record is arranged in the list in the correct position sorted first by company and then by the last name within each company.

3. Print or save as a PDF the contacts in Card style, entering an appropriate file name if saving as a PDF.
4. Restore the sort order to the default settings by completing the following steps:
   a. Click the View tab.
   b. Click the Reset View button in the Current View group.

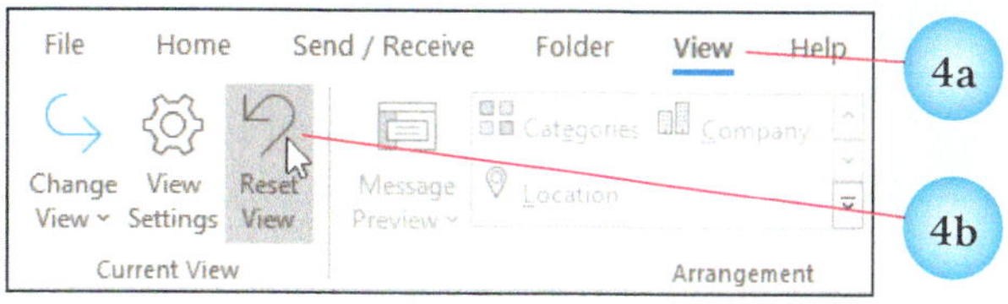

   c. Click the Yes button in the Microsoft Outlook message box asking if you want to reset the Card view to the original settings.

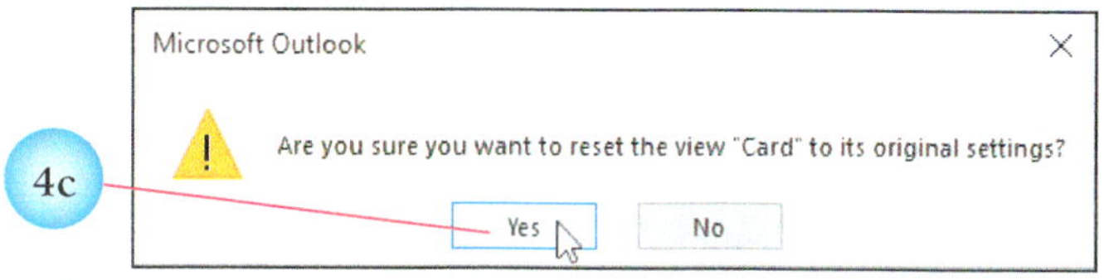

   d. Drag the gray, vertical bar at the right of the first column to widen the columns until all the data within each card is entirely visible.

Check Your Work

Sorting Contacts in Outlook.com

Contacts are sorted by first name and display the contact's first name followed by his or her last name. To change the sort order to last name, click the *By first name* option arrow at the top of the list in the Content pane and then click *Last name* in the drop-down list.

In the image shown below, the *Company* option was selected as the sort option to display contacts in order by company name.

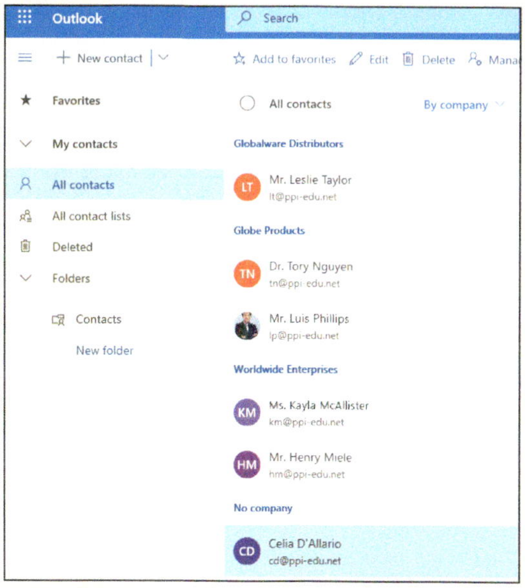

Tutorial

Filtering Contacts

Filtering Contacts

A filtered contacts list is a subset of records selected based on a criterion specified in the Filter dialog box. Records that do not meet the condition are temporarily removed from the list. The message *Filter applied* appears in the Status bar next to the total number of records (labeled *Items*) to indicate that not all records are currently displayed.

To specify the condition upon which to display records, click the View tab and then click the View Settings button in the Current View group. Click the Filter button in the Advanced View Settings dialog box and then specify the criterion by which records will be selected in the Filter dialog box with the Contacts tab selected (as shown in Figure 4.7).

TIP Another way to restore all records is to click the *Filter applied* message in the Status bar, click the Clear All button in the Filter dialog box, and then click OK.

View and print the filtered list as necessary, then restore all records by completing the following steps:

1. Click the View tab.
2. Click the View Settings button.
3. Click the Filter button.
4. Click the Clear All button in the Filter dialog box.
5. Click OK two times.

Figure 4.7 Filter Dialog Box with Contacts Tab Selected

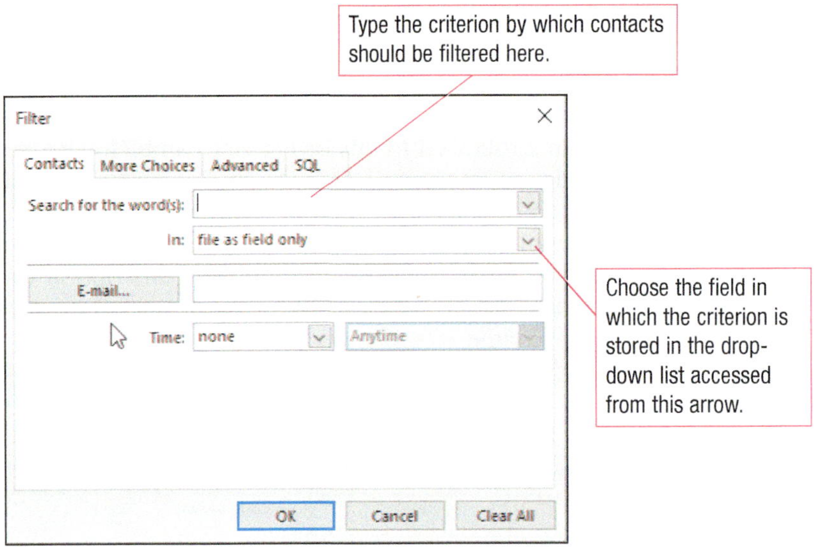

Activity 8 Filtering Contacts

1. With Outlook open and the contacts list active in Card view, filter the contacts list to display only those records for Globe Products by completing the following steps:
   a. Click the View Settings button on the View tab.
   b. Click the Filter button in the Advanced View Settings dialog box.

c. In the Filter dialog box with the Contacts tab selected and the insertion point positioned in the *Search for the word(s)* text box, type Globe Products.
d. Click the *In* list box arrow and then click *company field only* in the drop-down list.
e. Click OK to close the Filter dialog box.

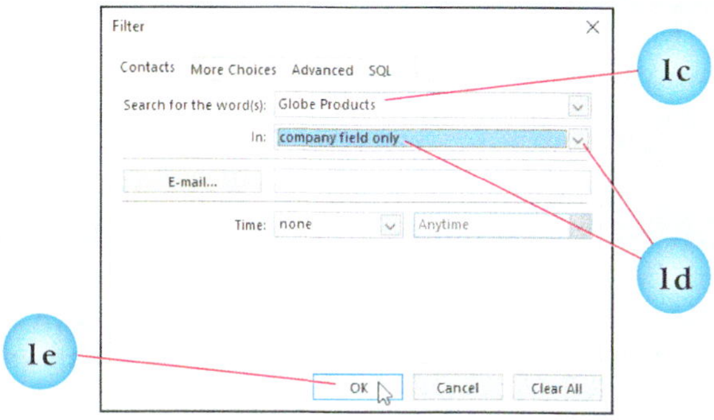

f. With the current filter settings displayed next to the Filter button in the Advanced View Settings dialog box, click OK. Only two records are displayed in the Content pane, as shown in the second image below. The message *Filter applied* displays at the left edge of the Status bar to indicate you are not seeing the entire contacts list.

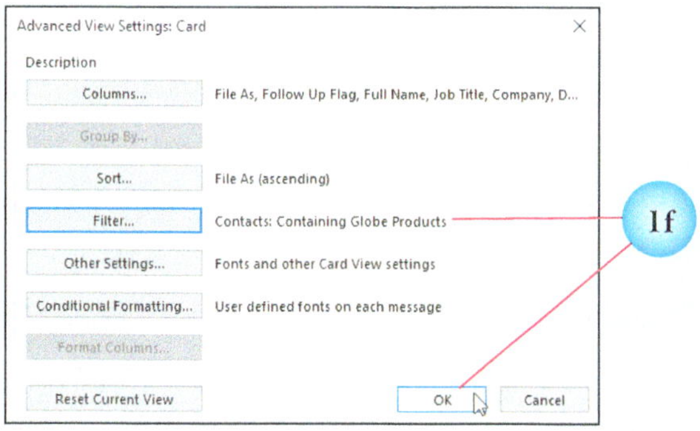

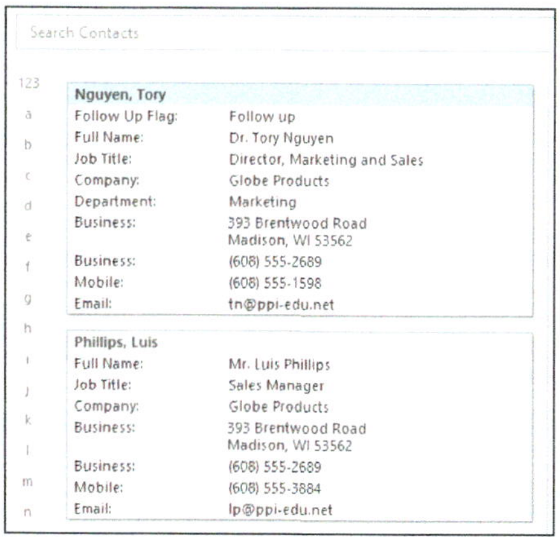

2. Print or save as a PDF the filtered list in Phone Directory style by completing the following steps:
   a. Click the File tab and then click *Print*.
   b. Click *Phone Directory Style* in the *Settings* section in the Print backstage area.
   c. Click the Print button. You determine an appropriate file name if saving as a PDF.
3. Restore the Content pane to display all contacts by completing the following steps:
   a. Click the View Settings button.
   b. Click the Filter button in the Advanced View Settings dialog box.
   c. Click the Clear All button in the Filter dialog box. Notice the search text box and *In* field entry are cleared.
   d. Click OK two times.

Check Your Work

Applying Color Categories to Contacts

The same six color categories that can be applied to messages and appointments can be applied to contacts. The various methods you learned to apply a color category and rename a color category for messages and appointments can be used to categorize contacts.

In Card view, the category applied to a contact displays at the bottom of the address card. You can also display the contacts list in table format using the *List* option and then group the contacts by color category. To do this, click the List button in the Current View group on the Home tab. You can also change to List view using the *List* option in the Change View button drop-down list in the Current View group on the View tab. List view displays the contacts in table format with the column headings *Full Name*, *Job Title*, *Company*, and so on. Next, click the Categories button in the Arrangement group on the View tab to group the contacts by color categories.

Categories

Activity 9 Renaming a Color Category, Applying Color Categories to Contacts, and Viewing Contacts by Category

1. With Outlook open and the contacts list active in Card view, rename a color category and apply a color category to a contact by completing the following steps:
   a. Click to select the card for Mr. Henry Miele.
   b. Click the Home tab.
   c. Click the Categorize button in the Tags group and then click *All Categories* in the drop-down list.
   d. In the Color Categories dialog box, click to insert a check mark in the *Yellow category* check box.
   e. Click the Rename button.
   f. Type Association Member and then press Enter.
   g. Click OK.

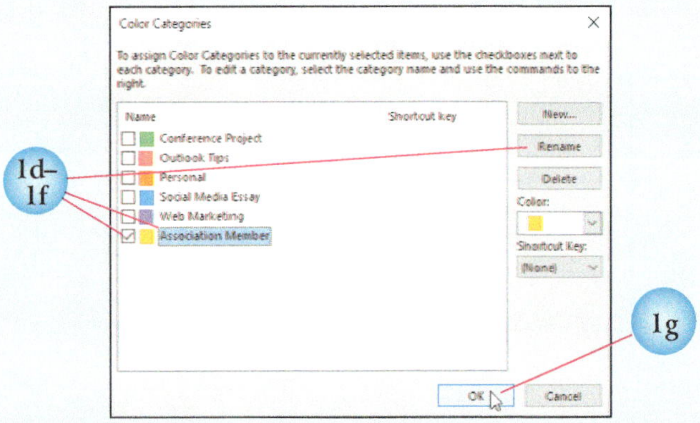

2. Look at the bottom of the card for Henry Miele. Notice that Outlook added a new line to the bottom of the card with the category name you created in Step 1.

3. Right-click the card for Mr. Luis Phillips, point to *Categorize*, and then click *Association Member* on the shortcut menu.
4. Assign the Association Member color category to the card for Dr. Tory Nguyen.
5. Display the contacts grouped by color category in table format by completing the following steps:
   a. Click the View tab, click the Change View button in the Current View group, and then click *List* in the drop-down list. This view displays the contacts in table format grouped by company name.

b. Click the Categories button in the Arrangement group option box on the View tab. The contacts are grouped according to the categories to which they were assigned in an expanded list.

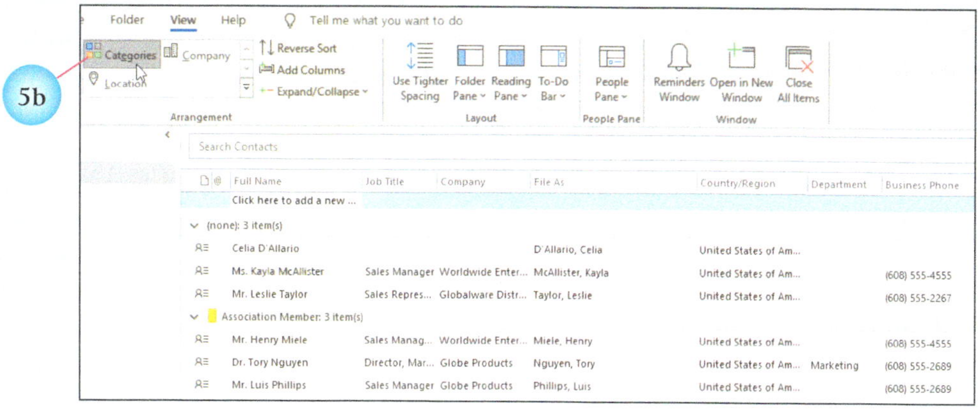

6. Print or save as a PDF the contacts in Table style. You determine an appropriate file name if saving as a PDF.

Check Your Work

Activity 10 Applying a Color Category While Creating a Contact

1. With Outlook open and the contacts list active in List view, apply a color category while adding a new contact by completing the following steps:
   a. Click the miniaturized people card icon in the first column of the table next to *Mr. Leslie Taylor* to select the record.

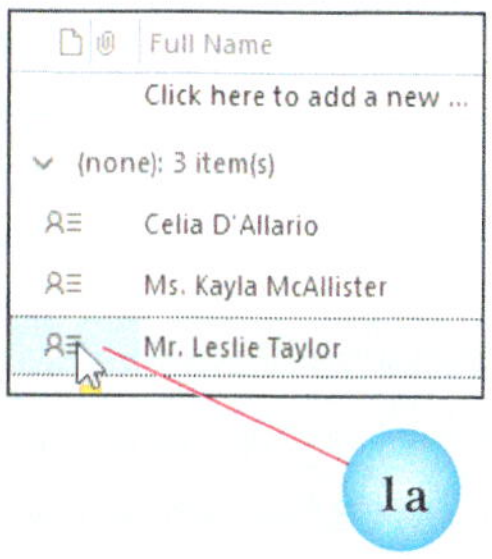

   b. Click the Home tab, click the New Items button in the New group, and then click *Contact from the Same Company*.
   c. Type the following information in the appropriate text boxes:

Full Name	Ms. Leigh Avaire
Job title	District Sales Manager
E-mail	la@ppi-edu.net
Mobile	6085551158

   d. Click the Picture button in the Options group on the Contact tab and then click *Remove Picture* in the drop-down list.
   e. Click the Categorize button in the Tags group on the Contact tab and then click *Association Member* in the drop-down list. Notice that Outlook displays the color category assigned to the contact in the information bar along the top of the Contact window below the ribbon.
   f. Click the Save & Close button. Outlook automatically adds the new contact to the bottom of the *Association Member* color category in the table.

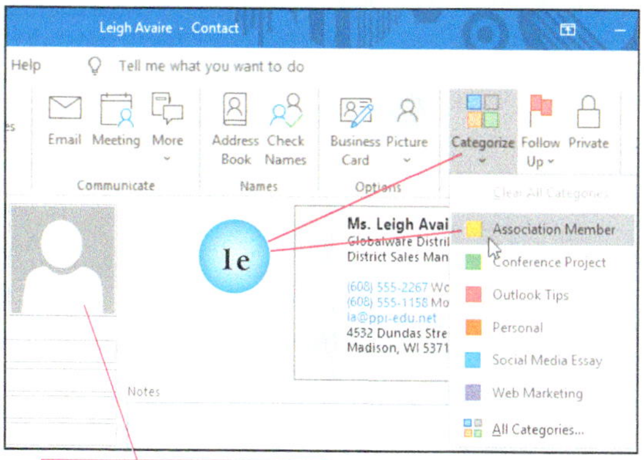

Leslie Taylor's photo was removed in Step 1d.

2. Print or save as a PDF the contacts in Table style.

Check Your Work

Activity 11 Filtering a Contact List by Category

1. With Outlook open and the contacts list active in List view, filter the contacts list to produce a list of only those contacts in the *Association Member* category by completing the following steps:
   a. Click the View tab and then click the View Settings button.
   b. Click the Filter button in the Advanced View Settings dialog box.
   c. Click the More Choices tab in the Filter dialog box.
   d. Click the Categories button.
   e. In the Color Categories dialog box, click to insert a check mark in the *Association Member* check box and then click OK.
   f. Click OK to close the Filter dialog box and then click OK to close the Advanced View Settings dialog box. Only four records are displayed in the Content pane. The message *Filter applied* appears at the left end of the Status bar.

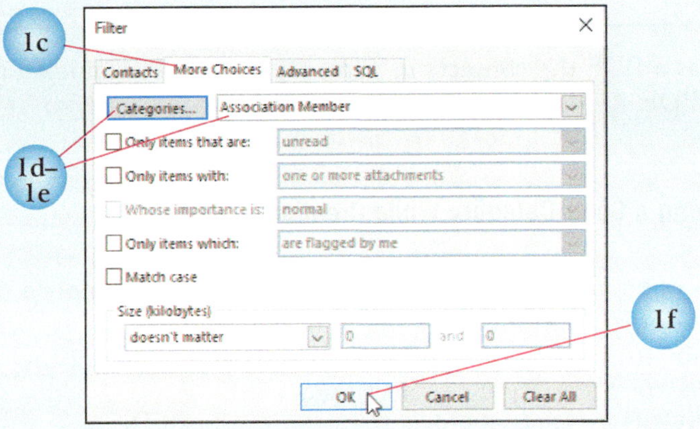

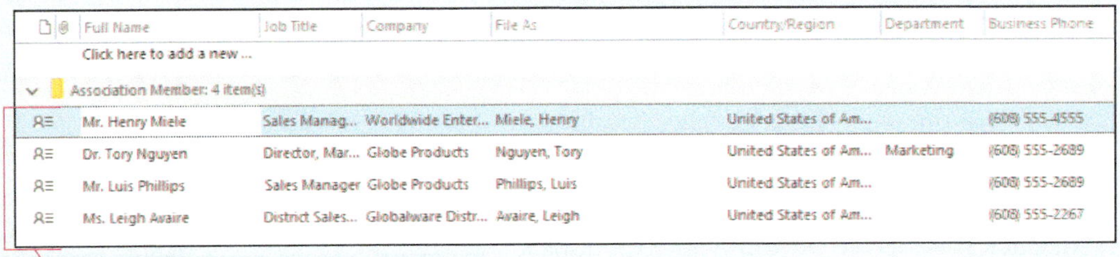

Contacts are filtered by *Association Member* color category in Step 1.

2. Print or save as a PDF the filtered list in Table style, entering an appropriate file name if saving as a PDF.
3. Restore the Content pane to display all contacts by completing the following steps:
   a. Click the Reset View button in the Current View group on the View tab.
   b. In the Microsoft Outlook message box asking if you are sure you want to reset the List view to its original settings, click the Yes button.
4. Click the Change View button and then click *Card* in the drop-down list.

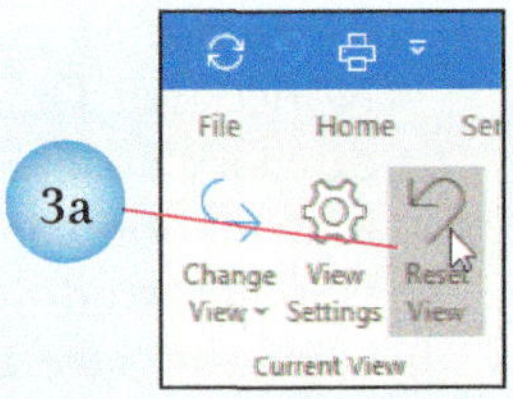

Check Your Work

Tutorial

Search for People and Appointments

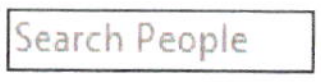

Search People

Finding a Contact

When a contacts folder contains a lot of records, browsing through the folder to find a contact record can be time consuming. Outlook provides three tools to assist with locating a record quickly:

- the *Search People* box in the Find group on the Home tab
- the *Search Contacts* box above the People list in the Content pane
- the Advanced Find dialog box

In addition to the three tools listed above, the letter tabs (called the *alphabet index*) along the left side of the Content pane in the Card, Business Card, and People views can be used to move to the first record that begins with the letter. For example, to move the selected record to the first contact whose last name begins with *w*, click the *w* letter tab in the alphabet index.

Using the *Search People* Box

To find a record quickly, click in the *Search People* box in the Find group on the Home tab (currently displays *Search People*), type the name of the individual whose record you want to see, and then press Enter. Outlook can locate records based on a partial entry (e.g., *Joe Sm*), a first name only, a last name only, an email alias, or a company name. The *Search People* box cannot be used to find people based on a telephone number or address. For these types of searches, use the *Search Contacts* box, which is described in the next section.

Activity 12 Locating Contacts Using Letter Tabs and the *Search People* Box

1. With Outlook open and the contacts list active in Card view, locate and select records using the alphabet index tabs by completing the following steps:
   a. Click the *t* letter tab along the left edge of the Content pane. ***Note:*** *Depending on your screen size and resolution setting, your letter tabs may display with two letters per tab.* The screen scrolls if necessary, and the card for Mr. Leslie Taylor is selected.

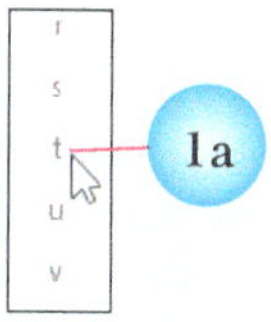

   b. Click the *a* letter tab. The screen scrolls if necessary, and the card for Ms. Leigh Avaire is selected.

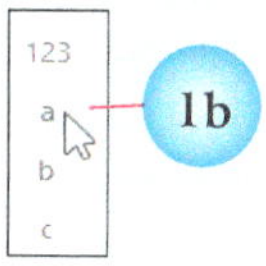

   c. Click the *m* letter tab. The card for Ms. Kayla McAllister is selected.
2. Locate and view records using the *Search People* box by completing the following steps:
   a. Click the Home tab.
   b. Click inside the *Search People* box in the Find group and then type leslie. Outlook displays the search results immediately as it begins locating records that match your search text.
   c. Click *Mr. Leslie Taylor* in the search results drop-down list. Review the information in the Contact window that opens and then click the Close button (displays as ×) in the top right corner of the Contact window.

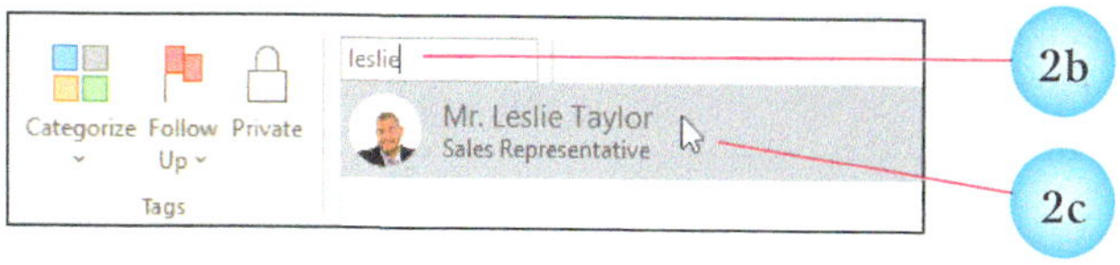

d. Click inside the *Search People* box and then type worldwide. You can locate contacts by a person's name or by a company name.
e. Click *Ms. Kayla McAllister* in the search results list to open her Contact window.

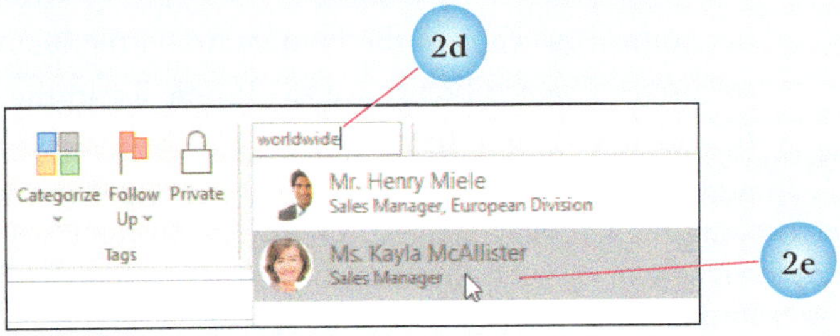

f. Review the information in the Contact window for Ms. Kayla McAllister and then close the Contact window.

Using the *Search Contacts* Box

The *Search Contacts* box, with the text *Search Contacts*, is at the top of the Content pane. To find a contact in the current Contacts folder, click in the box and start typing the name by which you want to search the folder. As soon as you begin typing, Outlook begins filtering the Content pane to include only those records that match your search text. Continue typing the name until the list is filtered to the contact(s) for whom you are looking.

The Search tab, shown in Figure 4.8, displays when you type an entry in the *Search Contacts* box. Use buttons in the Scope group to change the target folders for the search. Notice that the current folder is automatically the target for the current search word. Use buttons in the Refine group to narrow the search results to a specific color category, telephone number, address, or other contact field property.

Recent Searches

The Recent Searches button in the Options group displays a history of your recent search requests. To repeat a search, click the search word or phrase in the Recent Searches button drop-down list. Click the Search Tools button in the Options group to display the indexing status of your Outlook items, to change the location in which to search (that is, to search in a different email account), to open the Advanced Find dialog box, or to modify search options in the Outlook Options dialog box.

Figure 4.8 Search Tab for Contacts

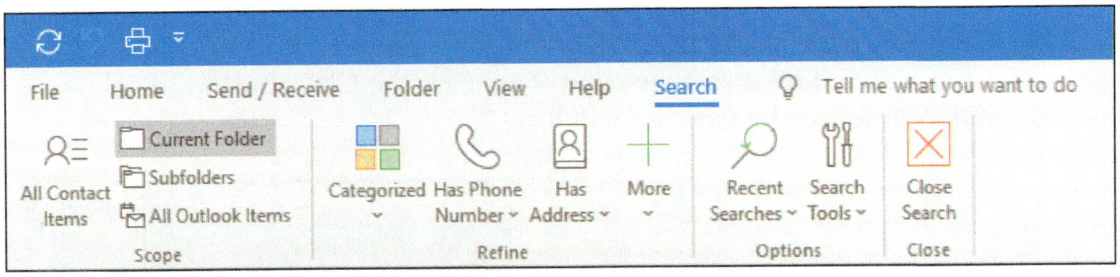

Activity 13 Locating Contacts Using the *Search Contacts* Box

1. With Outlook open and the contacts list active in Card view, locate records for contacts from Globe Products using the *Search Contacts* box by completing the following steps:
   a. Click in the *Search Contacts* box that displays the text *Search Contacts* at the top of the Content pane and then type globe.
   b. Examine the records for the two contacts that met the search criterion—Dr. Tory Nguyen and Mr. Luis Phillips—in the Content pane.

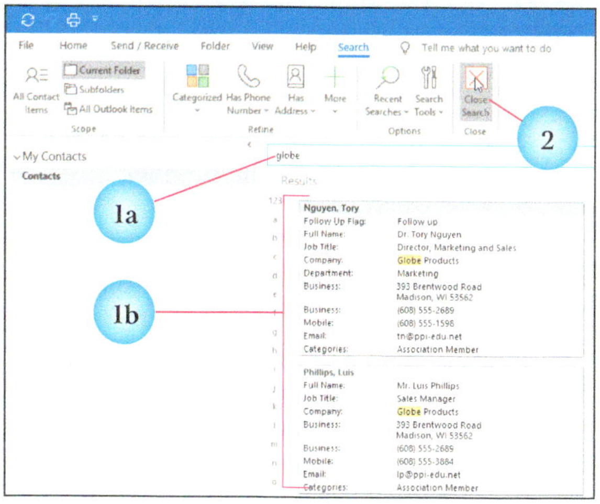

2. Click the Close Search button in the Close group on the Search tab or at the right end of the *Search Contacts* box. All contact records are restored to the Content pane.
3. Conduct another search to locate the records of sales manager contacts that are association members by completing the following steps:
   a. Click in the *Search Contacts* box and then type sales manager. Outlook filters the Content pane to show four contacts that have *Sales Manager* in the *Job Title* field.
   b. Click the Categorized button in the Refine group on the Search tab and then click *Association Member* in the drop-down list.

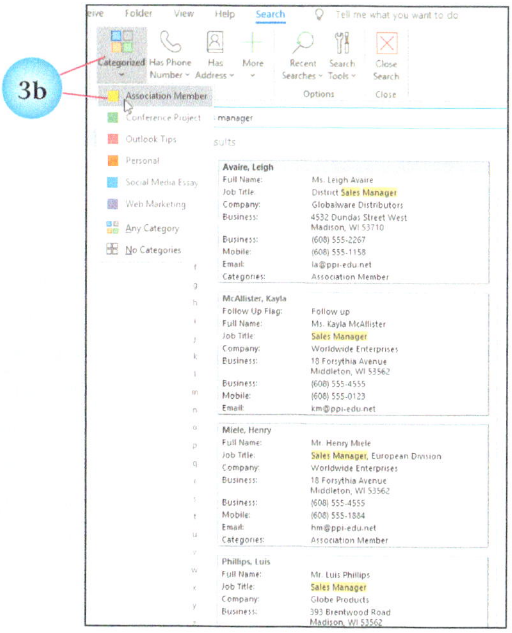

4. Look in the *Search Contacts* box at the entry added after *sales manager* in Step 3b—*category:="Association Member"*. Notice also that three contacts remain in the filtered list.
5. Click the Close Search button.

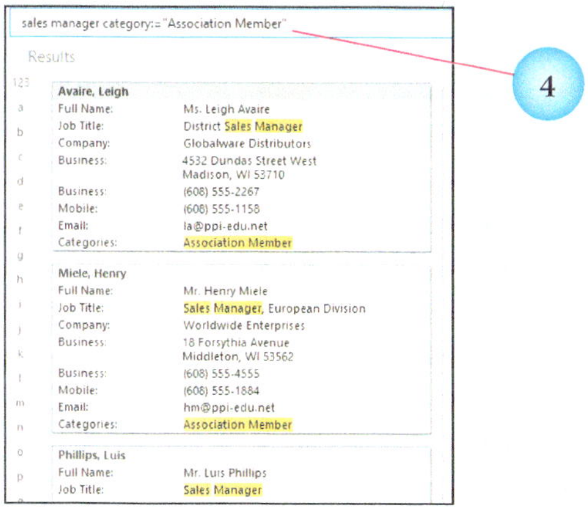

Using the Advanced Find Dialog Box

Search Tools

If you cannot locate a record using the *Search People* or *Search Contacts* box, consider opening the Advanced Find dialog box. Click in or type a search word in the *Search Contacts* box to begin a search using the Advanced Find feature, or, if the contacts are already filtered in the Content pane, click the Search Tools button in the Options group on the Search tab and then click *Advanced Find* in the drop-down list. The Contacts tab that is active when the dialog box opens contains options to locate records by typing a word that exists within the record, such as a name, telephone number, or email address; to search within a set of related fields, such as address fields; and to restrict the search to records created or modified within a specific time frame.

Click the Advanced tab to enter a conditional statement for a field to use as the criterion on which to locate contact records. For example, on the Advanced tab, you could create a conditional statement to locate a record based on a manager's name you know exists in the contact record. Following this example, to enter the conditional statement, complete the following steps:

1. Open the Advanced Find Dialog box and click the Advanced tab.
2. Click the Field button arrow.
3. Point to *Name fields* in the drop-down list.
4. Click *Manager's Name* in the Name fields pop up list.
5. Click in the *Value* column text box that appears in the Manager's Name row.
6. Type the name of the person's manager.
7. Click the Add to List button to add the search criteria to the *Find items that match these criteria* list box.
8. Click the Find Now button to begin the search.

Figure 4.9 displays the search results list for the example described in Step 1 to Step 8. Contacts that meet the search specifications display in the bottom of the dialog box (below the search criteria). Double-click a contact name in the search results list to open the contact record. Click the Close button in the Advanced Find dialog box title bar when you are finished searching and viewing contacts. If necessary, click the Close Search button on the Search tab to restore the full list of contacts.

Figure 4.9 Advanced Find Dialog Box with Search Criteria to Find a Contact by a Manager's Name

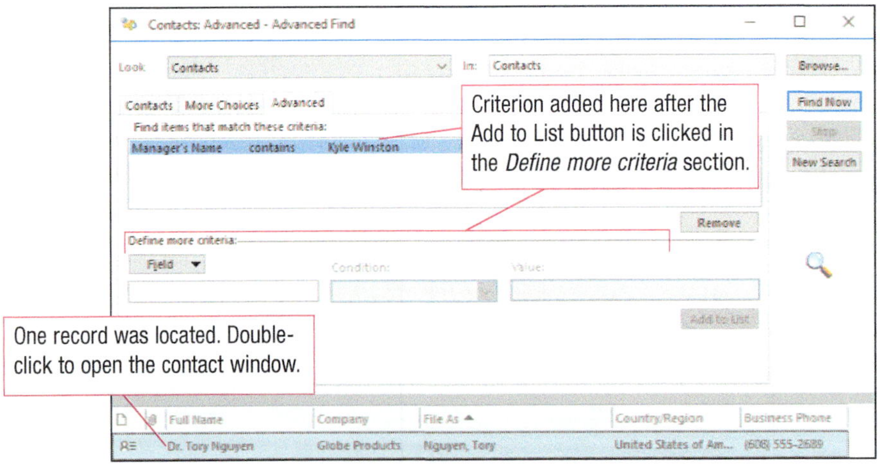

Finding a Contact in Outlook.com

A search box (displays with the text *Search*) is next to Outlook in the blue banner along the top of the browser window. Click in the box, type the name of the person whose record you want to view, and then press Enter or click the search button (magnif… name in the search results list to view the record in the Reading pane. Click the back button (left arrow) in the search box to restore the full list of contacts.

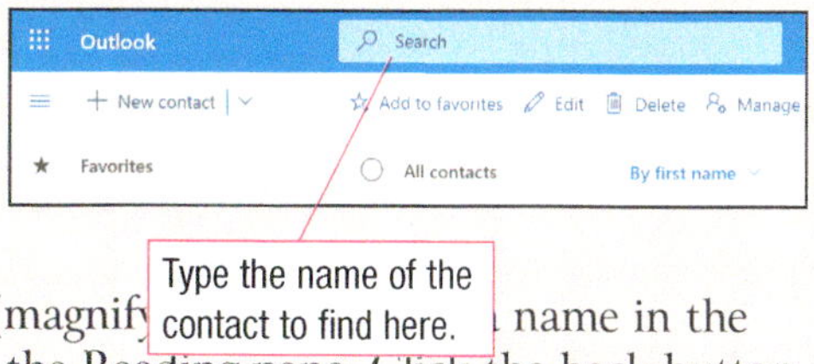

Sending an Email Message to a Contact

You can create an email message to a contact without leaving the People module and displaying the Inbox. To do this, first click to select the name of the person to whom you want to send an email and then perform one of the following actions:

- Click the Email icon below the person's name in the Reading pane (People view) or click the Email button in the Communicate group on the Home tab (Card or Business Card view).
- In Card or Business Card view, right-click the card for the desired contact, point to *Create*, and then click *Email*.
- Open the Contact window for the individual and then click the Email button in the Communicate group on the Contact tab.

Email

Activity 14 Sending an Email Message to a Contact

1. With Outlook open and the contacts list active in Card view, send an email message to a contact by completing the following steps:
   a. Select the card for Mr. Leslie Taylor.
   b. Click the Email button in the Communicate group on the Home tab. A message window opens with the email address for Leslie Taylor already entered in the *To* text box.
   c. With the insertion point positioned in the *Subject* text box, type New products (see figure on the next page).
   d. Click in the message editing window and then type the following text, adding your name a double space below the closing.

      Leslie,

      I would like to arrange a meeting with you sometime next week to review the new products. Please let me know a day and time that work best for you.

      Regards,

   e. Click the Send button.

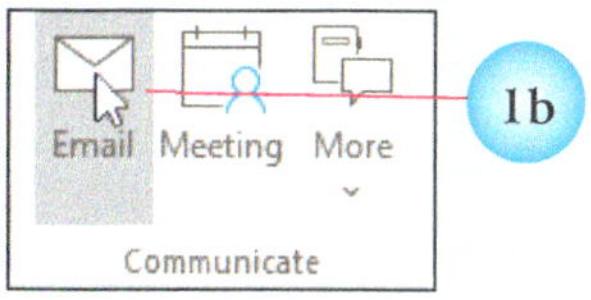

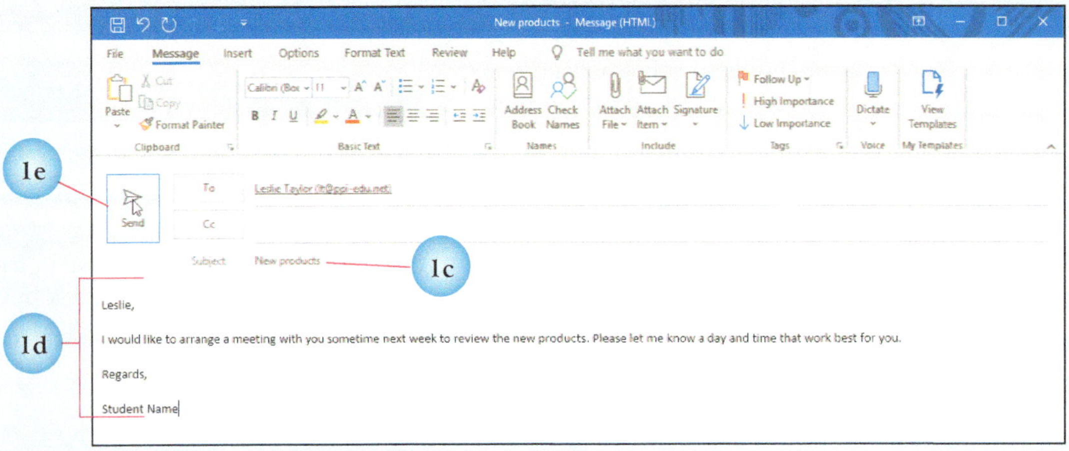

2. View and print the message by completing the following steps:
   a. Switch to the Mail module and display the Sent Items folder in the Content pane.
   b. Double-click the message header for the message created in Step 1.
   c. Print or save as a PDF the message from the message window, entering an appropriate file name if saving as a PDF. Close the message window.
3. Switch back to the People module and the contacts list in Card view. ***Note:*** *You will eventually receive a message in your Inbox stating that the message was not delivered because the email address for Leslie Taylor is fictitious.*

Check Your Work

Sending an Email Message to a Contact in Outlook.com

Click to select a name in the Content pane and then click the Send email button in the Reading pane. Outlook.com opens a message window addressed to the contact. Type the subject and message text and then click the Send button.

Scheduling a Meeting with a Contact

You can schedule a meeting with a contact without leaving the People module. If you already know that you are available on the required day and time, you do not need to display your calendar to complete the scheduling. Click to select the person's name and then complete one of the following actions:

Meeting

- Click the Meeting button in the Communicate group on the Home tab.
- Right-click the person's name or card, point to *Create*, and then click *Meeting*.
- Open the Contact window for the individual and then click the Meeting button in the Communicate group on the Contact tab.

Enter the title, start day and time, end day and time, and location details and then click the Send button.

Activity 15 Scheduling a Meeting with a Contact

1. With Outlook open and the contacts list active in Card view, schedule a meeting with a contact by completing the following steps:
   a. If necessary, click to select the card for Mr. Leslie Taylor.
   b. Click the Meeting button in the Communicate group on the Home tab. A meeting window opens with Leslie Taylor's information entered in the *Required* text box.

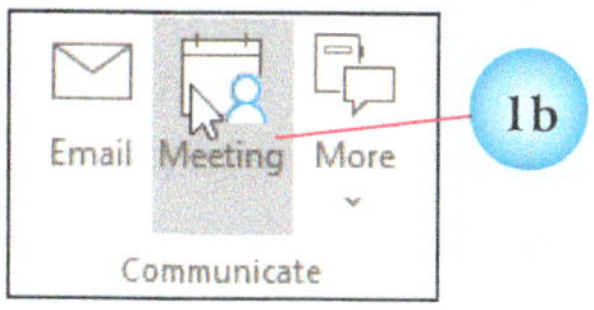

   c. With the insertion point positioned in the *Title* text box, type New products review meeting.
   d. Select the current date in the *Start time* day text box and then type one week from today. (The date one week from today is displayed when you move to the next field.)
   e. Select the current time in the *Start time* time text box and then type noon. (*12:00 PM* is displayed in the field when you move to another field.)
   f. Change the *End time* time to *1:30 PM*.
   g. Click next to the Location button and then type Globalware Distributor's office in the *Location* text box.
   h. Click the Send button.

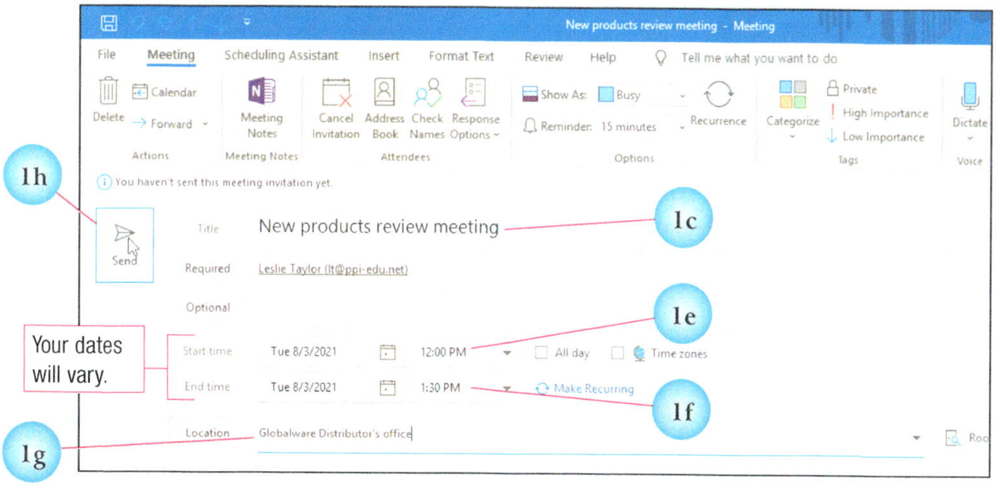

2. Switch to the Mail module and display the Sent Items folder in the Content pane if necessary. Double-click the message header for the meeting invitation message sent to Leslie Taylor in Step 1, print or save as a PDF the message from the message window, entering an appropriate file name if saving as a PDF. Close the message window.
3. Switch back to the People module and the contacts list in Card view. ***Note:*** *You will eventually receive a message stating that the message was not delivered.*

Check Your Work

Tutorial

Creating a Contact Group

Creating a Contact Group

If you frequently send email messages to the same group of people, consider creating a contact group to enable you to create and send the messages more quickly. This feature is sometimes referred to as a ***distribution list***. A ***contact group*** is a name associated with a group of contact records. For example, if you send a weekly status message to members of a project team, you could create a contact group named *Project Team* that contains the names of all the people working on the project. Whenever you need to send a status message, type *Project Team* in the Message window *To* text box and Outlook sends the message to the email addresses of all the members stored in the contact group. Contact groups can also be used in meeting requests. A contact group displays with the group name in the Content pane.

New Contact Group

Click the New Contact Group button in the New group on the Home tab to open the Contact Group window, as shown in Figure 4.10. Type a name for the group in the *Name* text box. Click the Add Members button in the Members group on the Contact Group tab and then click *From Outlook Contacts*, *From Address Book*, or *New Email Contact* in the drop-down list to add names to the group list. When you are finished adding members to the group, click OK and then click the Save & Close button in the Actions group on the Contact Group tab.

Figure 4.10 Contact Group Window

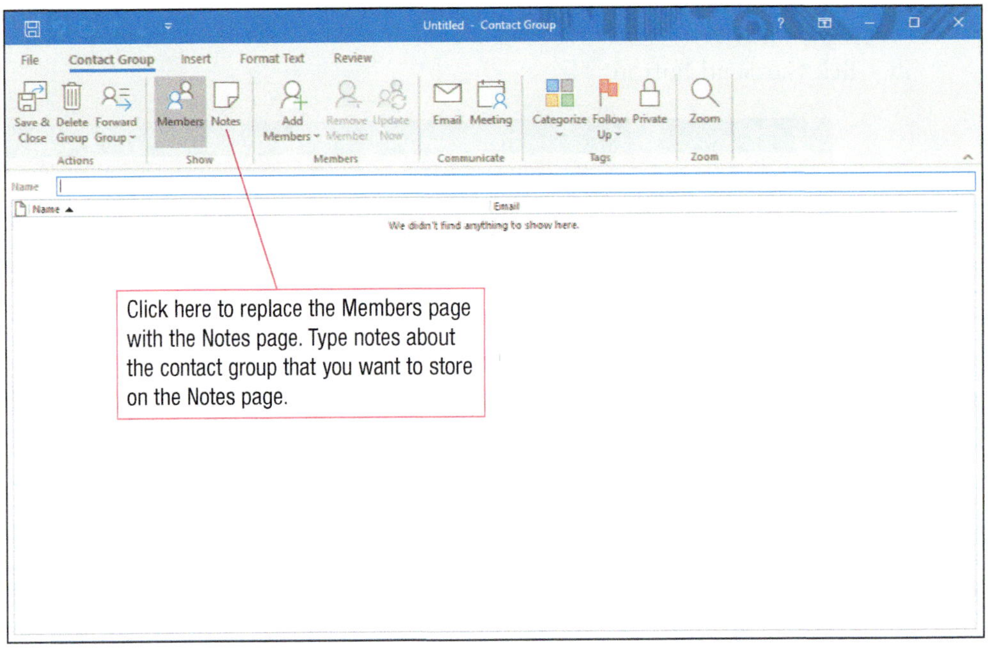

Creating a Contact List in Outlook.com

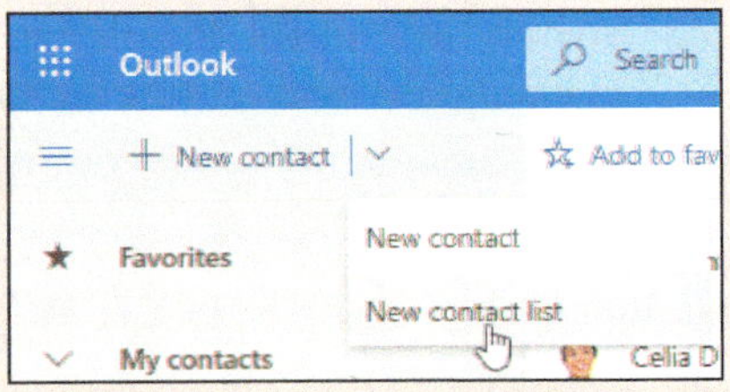

In Outlook.com a contact group is called a *contact list*. To create a new contact list, begin by clicking the New contact button arrow and then clicking *New contact list*. In the New contact list window that appears, type a name for the list in the *Contact list name* text box. Next, click in the *Add email addresses* text box and type a name or click to select a name in the drop-down list. Continue adding member names until finished. Click the Create button to save the new list.

Activity 16 Creating and Using a Contact Group

1. With Outlook open and the contacts list active in Card view, create a new contact group for the sales managers by completing the following steps:
   a. Click the New Contact Group button in the New group on the Home tab.
   b. In the Untitled - Contact Group window with the insertion point positioned in the *Name* text box, type Sales Managers.
   c. Click the Add Members button in the Members group on the Contact Group tab and then click *From Outlook Contacts* in the drop-down list.

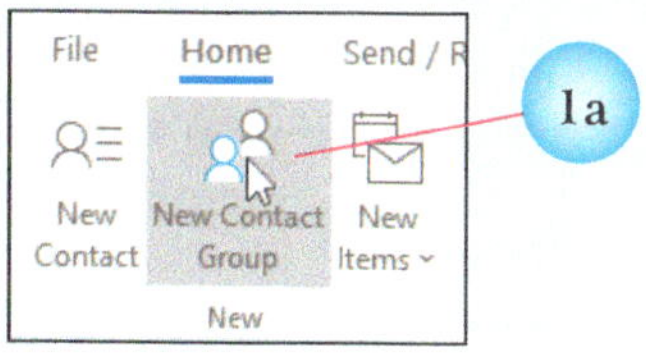

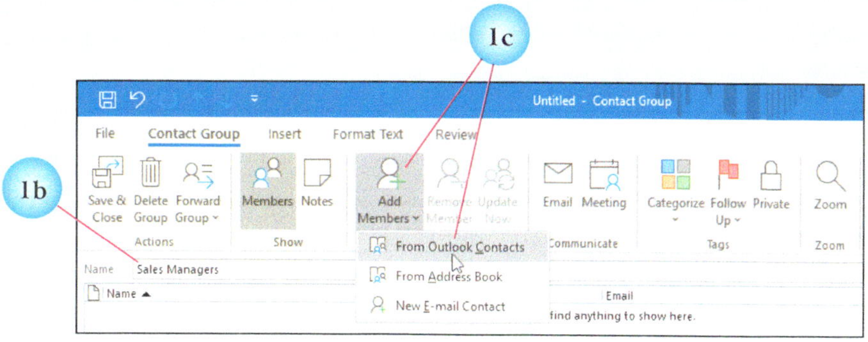

   d. In the Select Members: Contacts dialog box, double-click *Celia D'Allario (cd@ppi-edu.net)* to add the email address for Celia D'Allario to the *Members* text box at the bottom of the dialog box.
   e. Double-click the following sales managers' names to add them to the *Members* list:

      Henry Miele
      Kayla McAllister
      Luis Phillips

   f. Click OK to close the Select Members: Contacts dialog box.

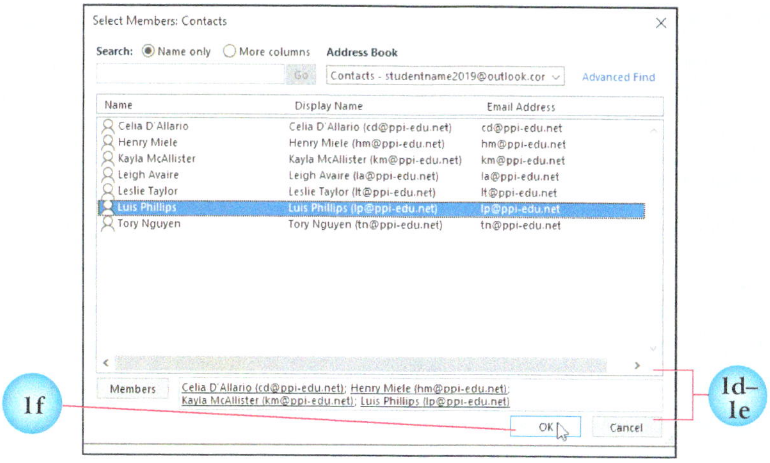

g. Click the Notes button in the Show group on the Contact Group tab.
h. Type All the members in this group have accounts on the supplier web portal.
i. Click the Save & Close button in the Actions group on the Contact Group tab. A contact group entry appears in the Content

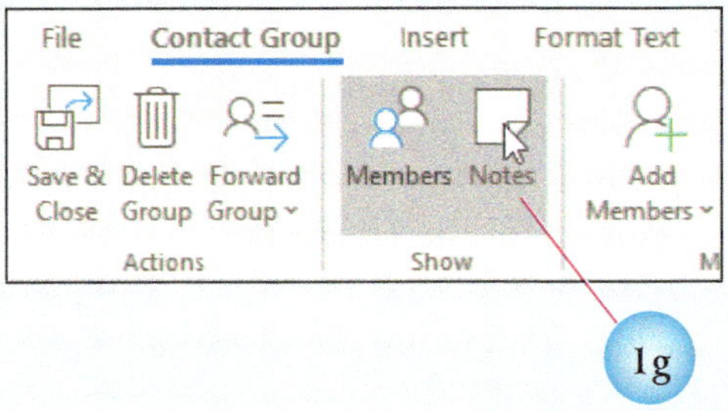

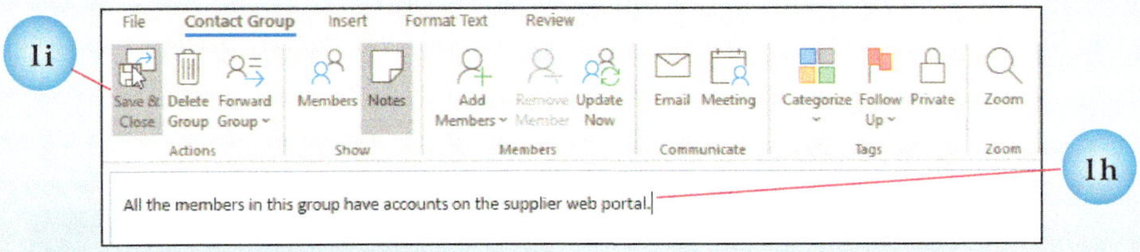

pane with the name of the group.

2. Send an email message to the members in the Sales Managers contact group by completing the following steps:
   a. Click the *Sales Managers* card in the Content pane and then click the Email button, or right-click the Sales Managers card, point to *Create*, and then click *Email*. An email message window opens with the contact group name added in the *To* text box.

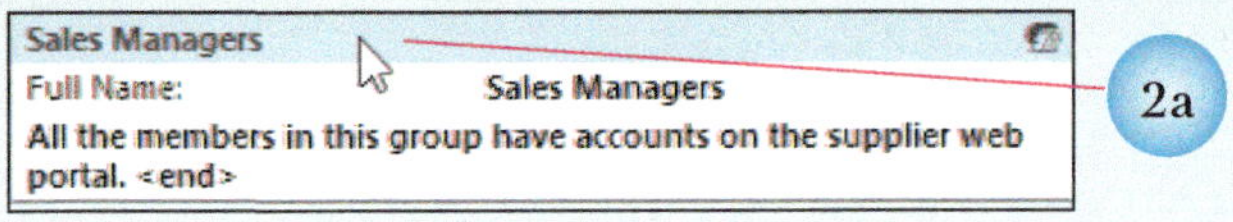

   b. With the insertion point positioned in the *Subject* text box, type Supplier Web Portal and then press Enter.
   c. Type the following message text, adding your name a double space below the closing:

      Dear Valued Supplier,

      A new supplier web portal will be activated the first of next month. Existing accounts are already converted for the new website. We have incorporated many improvements to streamline order entry and provide real-time stock updates. Call or email me if you have any questions.

      Regards,

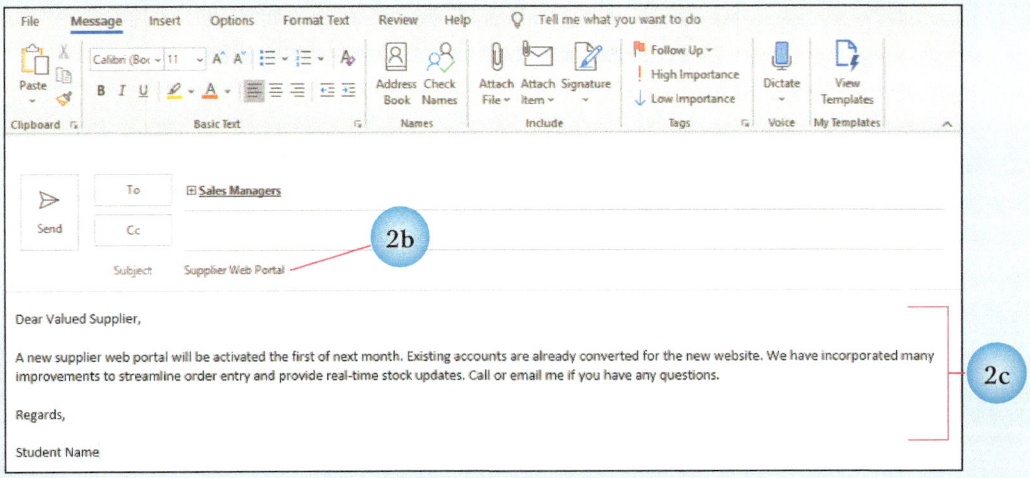

d. Print or save as a PDF the message from the message window, entering an appropriate file name if saving as a PDF.

e. Send the message. ***Note:*** *Check with your instructor before sending the message. Since the email addresses are fictitious, you will receive a message saying that your message was undeliverable for each member in the group. Your instructor may prefer that you close the message after completing Step 2d.*

3. Change the view to People view.

Check Your Work

Maintaining Contact Groups

TIP You can nest contact groups. For example, in a group that is divided into two teams, you can create a group for each team and then add the two team group names as members in the main contact group. By nesting the groups, you can send messages to an individual team or use the main contact group to send a message to all team members.

Double-click the group name in the Content pane to open the Contact Group window with the names of the members shown in the Members page, as shown in Figure 4.11. Use the Add Members button in the Members group on the Contact Group tab to add new members to the group following the process you learned in Activity 16. To delete a member from the group, click to select the member's name in the list box and then click the Remove Member button in the Members group.

If you change an email address in a contact record, the corresponding entry in the contact group does not automatically update to reflect the same change. Open a contact group window and click the Update Now button in the Members group to update changes to members' email addresses. Click the Save & Close button when you have finished adding, deleting, or updating group members.

Deleting a Contact Group

Some contact groups are created to facilitate messaging and scheduling for a limited time period, such as the duration of a project. When the project is finished, the contact group is no longer needed. To remove the contact group from the contacts list, select the group name in the Content pane and then click the Delete button in the Delete group on the Home tab.

Figure 4.11 Contact Group Window with Members Page Shown

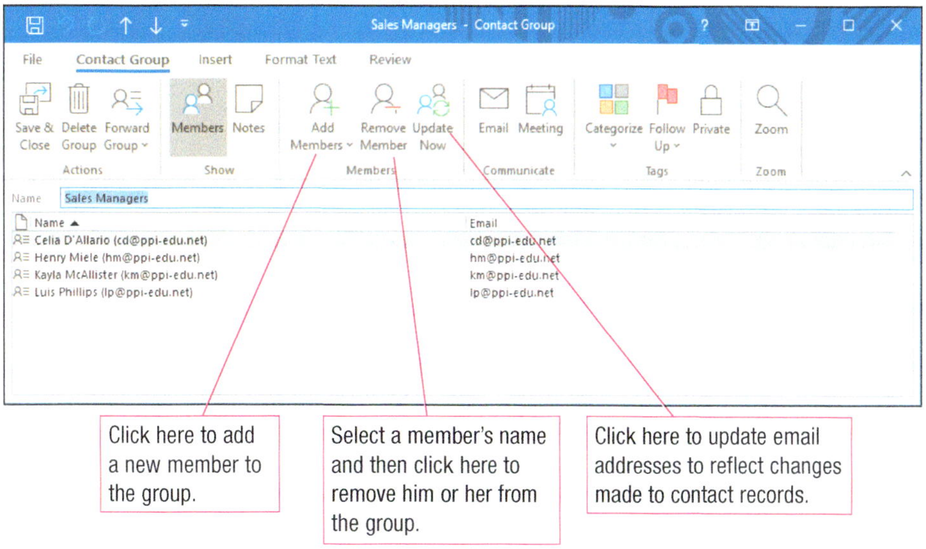

Tutorial

Adding Tasks

Creating and Managing Tasks

Adding activities in Tasks is similar to jotting down jobs in a to-do list on your desk. Tasks are added using the *Type a new task* text box or in the Task window. *Type a new task* may display as *Click here to add a new Task* if Outlook has been customized.

Creating Tasks in the *Type a new task* Text Box and Deleting Tasks

The Tasks module in To-Do List view is shown in Figure 4.12. Add new tasks by clicking in the *Type a new task* text box located at the top of the To-Do list, typing a short description of the job or activity, and then pressing the Enter key.

Delete a task by selecting the task in the task list and then pressing the Delete key or by clicking the Delete button in the Delete group on the Home tab.

Figure 4.12 Tasks Module in To-Do List View

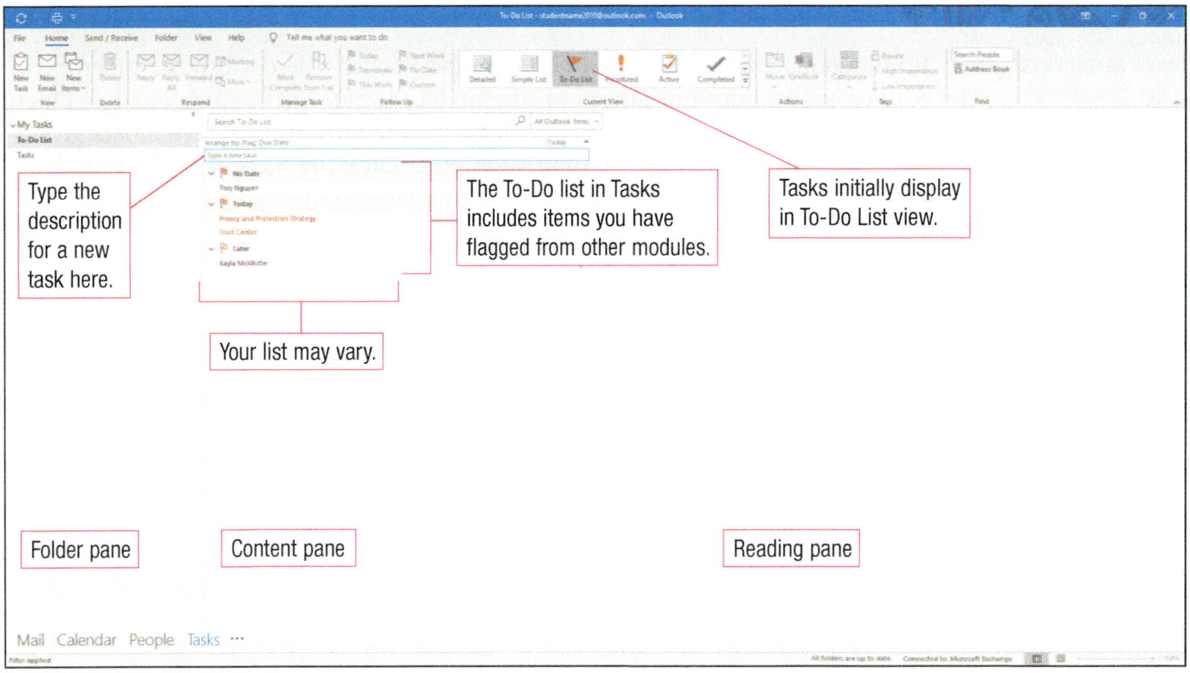

Activity 17 Deleting Tasks and Creating Tasks Using the *Type a new task* Text Box

1. With Outlook open, access the Peek feature by pointing to the Tasks text label or icon on the Navigation bar. If you are using a touch device, press and hold the Tasks icon or text label on the Navigation bar and then tap *Show the peek*. The Peek feature in Outlook shows a preview of the tasks in the To-Do list. The items that appear in the illustrations for this activity have been added to the To-Do list as a result of flagging email messages and contacts in activities and assessments in Chapter 1 and earlier in this chapter.

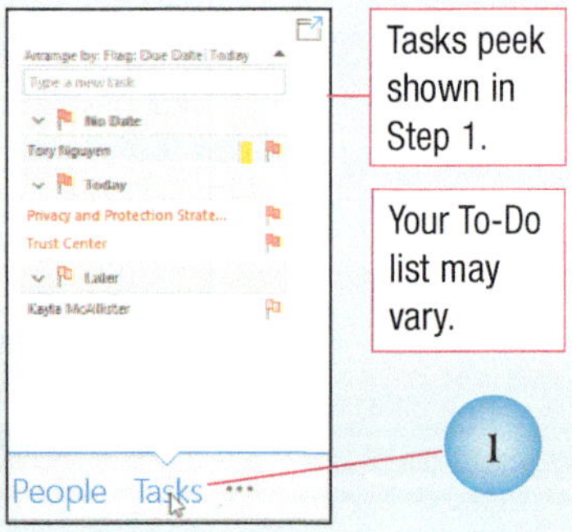

2. Click the Tasks text label or icon on the Navigation bar to display the Tasks module in the Content pane.
3. Delete the tasks added in Chapter 1 and earlier in this chapter that appear in the To-Do list by completing the following steps:
   a. Press Ctrl + A to select all the items in the To-Do list. ***Note:*** *If you have items in your To-Do list in addition to the tasks created by completing activities in this textbook, do not use the Select All feature. Instead, select only those items shown in the image at the right by holding down the Ctrl key while clicking each item.*

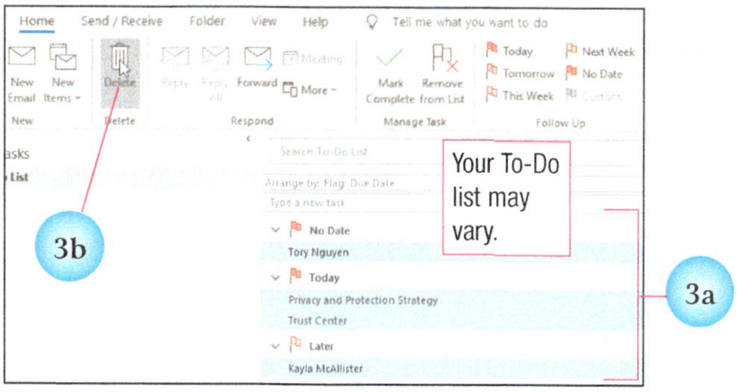

   b. Click the Delete button in the Delete group on the Home tab.
   c. In the Microsoft Outlook message box that indicates deleting these items will also delete associated email messages and/or contacts, click OK.

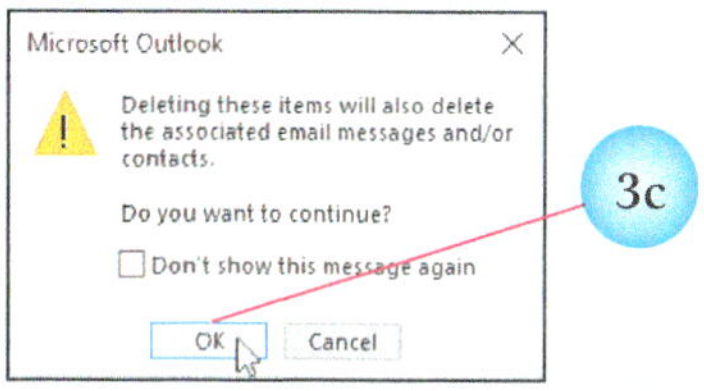

4. Add new tasks to the Tasks folder by completing the following steps:
   a. Click in the text box located at the top of the To-Do list that contains the text *Type a new task*.
   b. Type Assemble research on social media and then press Enter. Outlook adds the item to the To-Do list under a flag with the heading *Today* and at the same time clears the task entry text box so that it displays the insertion point, indicating another new task can be typed.

   c. Type Upload photos to Flickr.com in the task entry text box and then press Enter.
   d. Click in a blank area in the Content pane to deactivate the new task entry box.

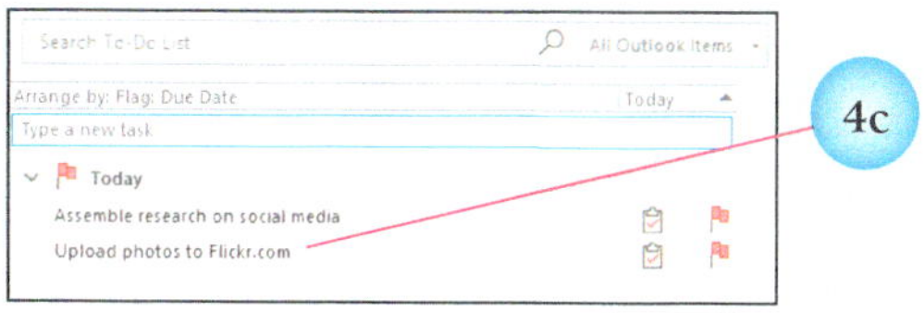

5. Click the File tab and then click *Print*. With *Table Style* selected in the *Settings* section in the Print backstage area, click the Print button. You determine an appropriate file name if saving as a PDF.

Check Your Work

Creating Tasks in the Task Window

New Task

You can also create tasks in the Task window, as shown in Figure 4.13. Open the Task window by clicking the New Task button in the New group on the Home tab. In the Task window, type a description of the task in the *Subject* text box, change other fields as required, and then click the Save & Close button in the Actions group on the Task tab.

Create a task using the Task window to assign a start date and a due date to the task or to attach other information, such as a status, priority, or instructional notes. The default status for a new task is *Not Started*. Enter a different status by clicking the *Status* list box arrow and choosing from *In Progress, Completed, Waiting on someone else*, and *Deferred* in the drop-down list. The default priority for a task is *Normal*, and it can be changed to *Low* or *High*. Outlook inserts the name of the current user as the task *Owner*. Use the Categorize button in the Tags group on the Home tab to assign a color category to the task, just as you would assign a color category to other Outlook items. Use the white text box below the *Reminder* check box and option boxes to type additional notes, instructions, or other information that you want to store with the task details.

Click the Details button in the Show group on the Task tab to display the Details page. On this page, you can store the date the task was completed, the number of hours estimated to complete the task, and the actual number of hours worked on the task. If the work you are doing is to be billed out, enter information in the *Company*, *Mileage*, and *Billing information* text boxes.

Figure 4.13 Task Window with Task Page Selected

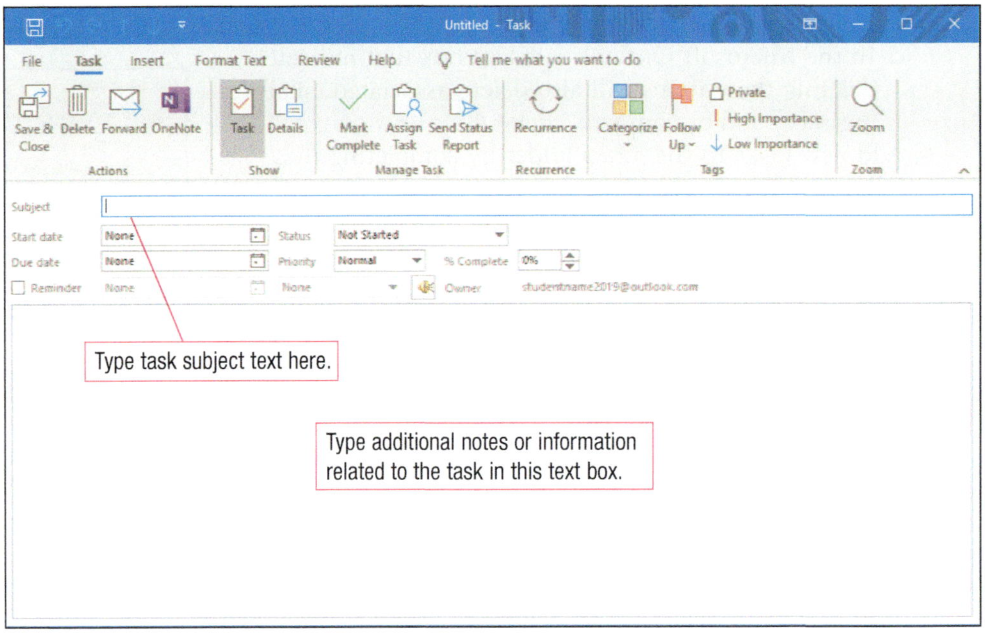

Activity 18 Creating a Task Using the Task Window

1. With Outlook open and the Tasks module active, add a new task using the Task window by completing the following steps:
   a. Click the New Task button in the New group on the Home tab.
   b. With the insertion point positioned in the *Subject* text box, type Start budget estimates for next year (see figure on the next page).
   c. Click the *Status* list box arrow and then click *In Progress* in the drop-down list.

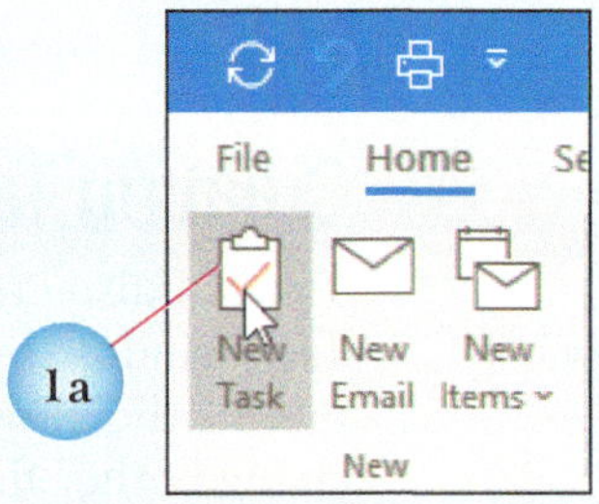

d. Click the Save & Close button in the Actions group on the Task tab. Outlook adds the task below a flag with the heading *No Date*.

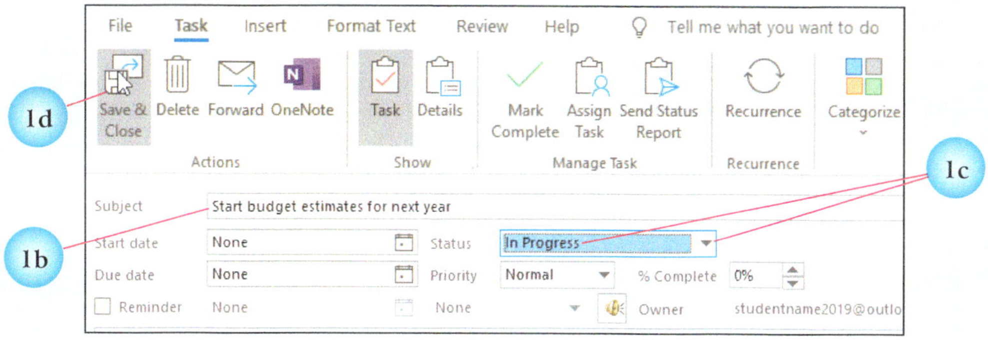

2. Click to select the task *Start budget estimates for next year* in the To-Do list and then read the task information that displays in the Reading pane. ***Note:*** *If the Reading pane is not visible, click the View tab, click the Reading Pane button in the Layout group, and then click* Right *in the drop-down list.*

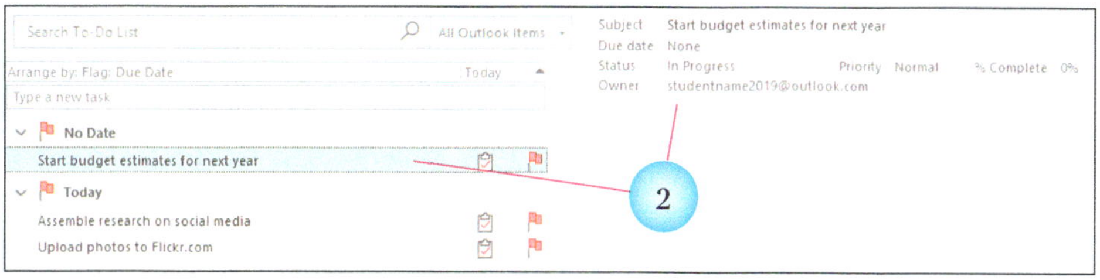

3. Print or save as a PDF only the task added in Step 1 by clicking the File tab and then clicking *Print*. With *Memo Style* selected in the *Settings* section in the Print backstage area, click the Print button. You determine an appropriate file name if saving as a PDF.

Check Your Work

Creating Tasks in Outlook.com

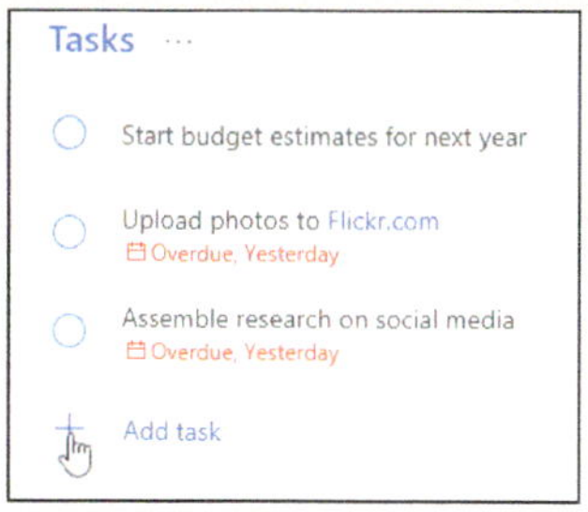

To display the Tasks module, click the App launcher button, click *All apps*, and then click *Tasks* in the Apps pane. You can also navigate to Tasks by clicking the More options button (three dots) on the Navigation bar and then clicking *Tasks* in the pop-up list. Click the Add task button (plus symbol) at the bottom of the To-Do list to open a new task entry in the list. Type a description of the task (type over the dimmed text *Add task*) and then press the Enter key. To add more options, such as a reminder or due date, click to select the task subject in the task list and then change the desired option in the Task pane that opens at the right side of the window.

Tutorial

Editing Tasks

Mark Complete

TIP In Simple List or Detailed view, mark a task as completed by clicking to insert a check mark in the check box at the left of the task subject.

Updating Tasks

Updating tasks can include activities such as changing the due date, start date, status, priority, or percentage (%) complete. When a task is finished, you can either delete the task from the task list or change the task status to *Completed*. To change the task status, open the Task window and change the *Status* field to *Completed*, or click the Mark Complete button in the Manage Task group on the Task tab. Marking a task as completed automatically changes the *% Complete* option to *100%*. A task that is marked as completed is removed from the To-Do List view; however, the task is not deleted from the Tasks folder. In a view other than To-Do List view, a completed task is displayed with a line drawn through dimmed text.

Double-click a task in the task list to open the Task window and make changes to the task details as required. To edit only the subject text, click to select the task entry in the task list. With the task highlighted, click the task text box a second time to open the task text box for editing and display an insertion point. Insert or delete text as required and then click outside the task text box to finish editing.

Activity 19 **Updating Tasks**

1. With Outlook open and the Tasks module active, change the status for the task entry *Assemble research on social media* by completing the following steps:
   a. Double-click the task entry *Assemble research on social media* to open the Task window.
   b. Click the *Status* list box arrow and then click *In Progress* in the drop-down list.
   c. Select *0%* in the *% Complete* measurement box and then type 60. ***Note:*** *The up- and down-pointing arrows on the right of the* % Complete *measurement box incrementally increase or decrease the value by 25%.*
   d. Click the Save & Close button in the Actions group on the Task tab.

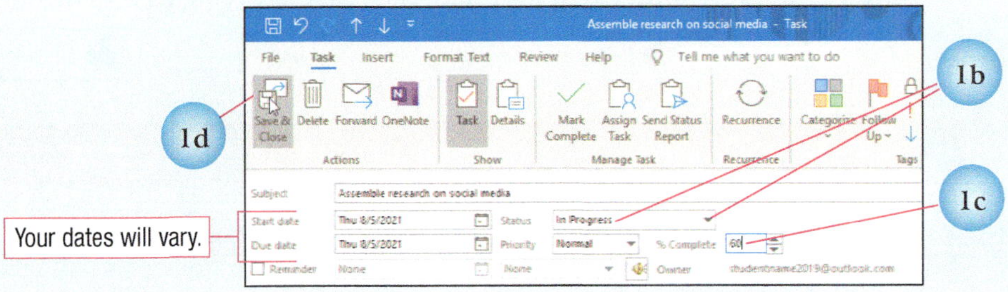

2. Change the status for a task to *Completed* by completing the following steps:
   a. Double-click the task entry *Upload photos to Flickr.com*.
   b. Click the Mark Complete button in the Manage Task group on the Task tab. A task marked as completed is removed from the To-Do List view; however, the task information is retained in the Tasks folder and can be accessed in a view other than To-Do List view.

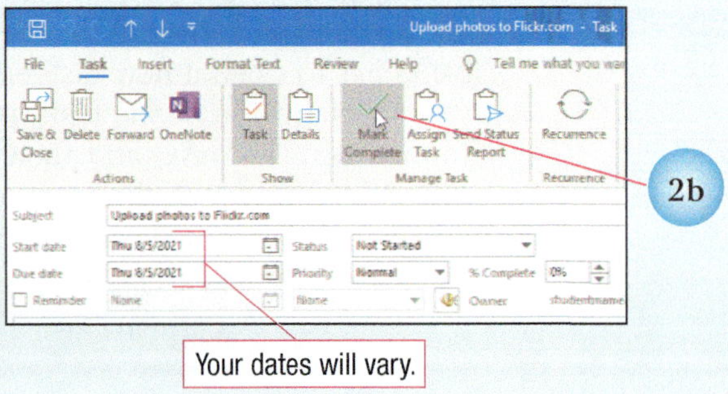

3. Change the current view and expand column widths by completing the following steps:
   a. Click the Detailed button in the Current View group on the Home tab. In Detailed view, the columns *Status*, *Due Date*, *Modified*, *Date Completed*, *In Folder*, and *Categories* are added to the task list. Notice that tasks marked as completed are displayed with a line drawn through dimmed text.
   b. If necessary, double-click the right column boundaries for the *Task Subject* column and the *Status* column to expand the column widths to fit the longest entries.
   c. Double-click the right column boundary for the *Modified* column.

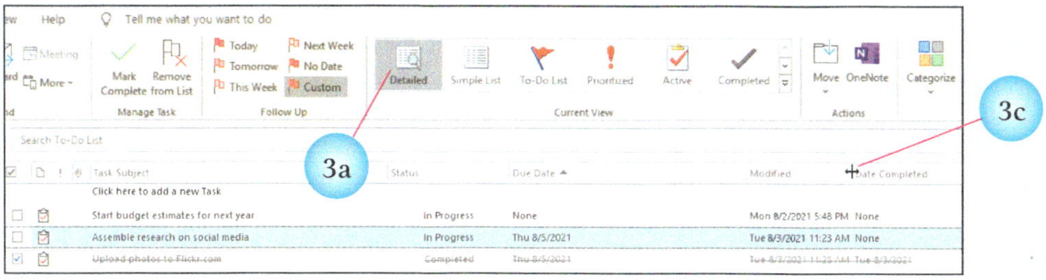

4. Click the File tab and then click *Print*. If necessary, click *Table Style* to select it in the *Settings* section in the Print backstage area. Click the Print button. You determine an appropriate file name if saving as a PDF.

Check Your Work

Updating Tasks in Outlook.com

Click a task subject entry to open the Task pane at the right side of the window and update fields as required. To mark a task complete, click the check circle next to a task in the task list. Tasks marked as completed are removed from the To-Do list.

You can also right-click a task subject to choose options on the shortcut menu such as *Mark as completed*, *Mark as important*, *Due today*, *Due tomorrow*, or *Delete task*.

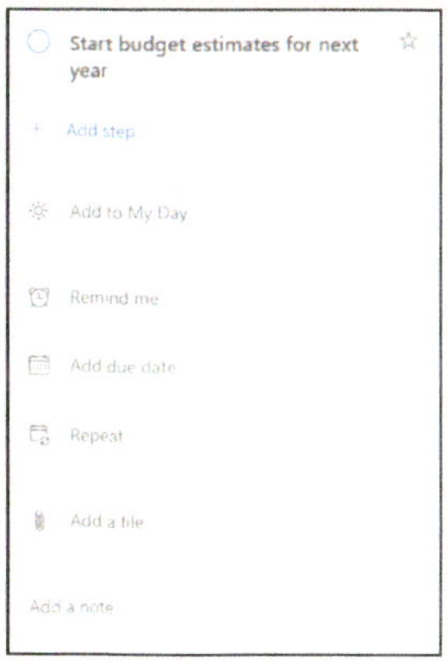

Creating a Recurring Task

A task that you perform on a regular basis can be set up in a manner similar to a recurring appointment. A recurring task appears only once in the task list. When you change the status for that occurrence of the task to *Completed*, Outlook automatically generates the next occurrence in the task list.

Recurrence

To create a recurring task, open the Task window, type a description of the task in the *Subject* text box, and then click the Recurrence button in the Recurrence group on the Task tab. Select the options as required in the *Recurrence pattern* and *Range of recurrence* sections in the Task Recurrence dialog box and then click OK.

Activity 20 Creating a Recurring Task

1. With Outlook open and the Tasks module active in Detailed view, add a recurring task to the task list by completing the following steps:
   a. Click the New Task button in the New group.
   b. With the insertion point positioned in the *Subject* text box, type Compile month end reports.
   c. Click the Recurrence button in the Recurrence group on the Task tab.
   d. In the Task Recurrence dialog box, click *Monthly* in the *Recurrence pattern* section.
   e. Click *The* in the *Recurrence pattern* section. Depending on the current date, the options next to *The* display the occurrence as *first*, *second*, *third*, *fourth*, or *last* and the current day of the week. If necessary, click the occurrence list box arrow and then click *first*. Click the day-of-the-week list box arrow and then click *Thursday* so that the Recurrence pattern becomes *The [first] [Thursday] of every [1] month(s)*.

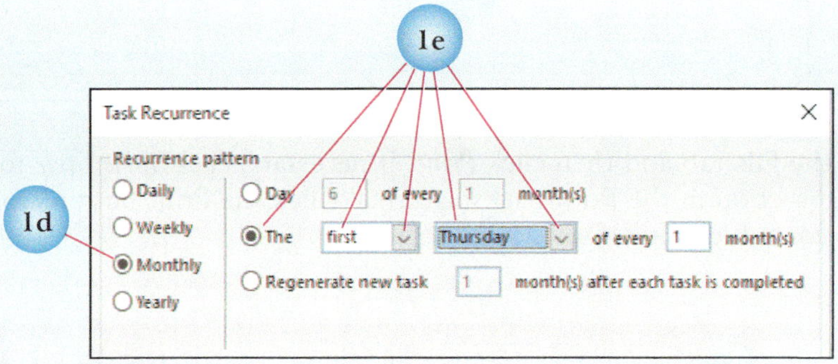

   f. Click OK to close the Task Recurrence dialog box. The information bar in the Task window above the subject text displays the recurrence pattern details.

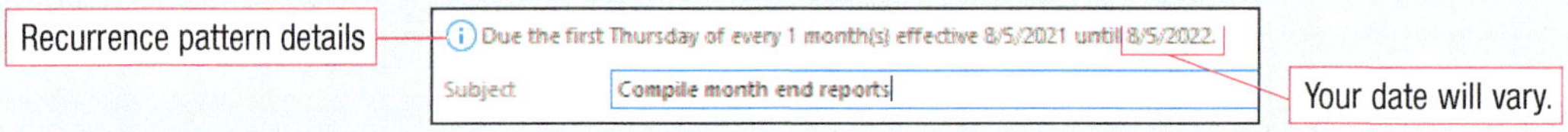

   g. Click the Save & Close button in the Actions group on the Task tab. The first recurring task appears in the list. Notice the recurring icon for the task next to the task subject.
2. Click the Simple List button in the Current View group on the Home tab.
3. Print or save as a PDF the tasks in Table style, entering an appropriate file name if saving as a PDF.

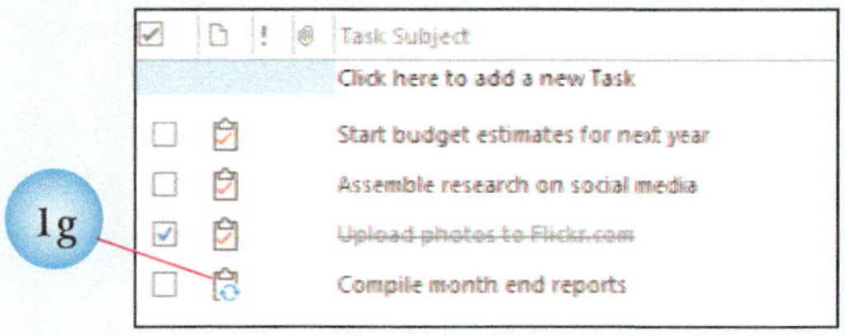

Check Your Work

Assigning a Task to Someone Else

A task can be assigned to someone else by emailing the individual a task request. The recipient of the task request can choose to accept the task, decline the task, or assign the task to someone else. When the recipient accepts the task, the task is automatically added to his or her task list. To create a task request, click the New Items button in the New group on the Home tab and then click *Task Request* in the drop-down list. The process for responding to a task request is similar to responding to a meeting request, which you learned in Chapter 3.

Chapter Summary

- Add a new contact using the New Contact button in the New group on the Home tab. Type information into the General, Details, and All Fields pages.
- Outlook displays the Check Full Name and Check Address dialog boxes when the entry typed into a name or address field is not recognized.
- Double-click a name in the People list to open the Contact window and add, edit, or delete information as required.
- Delete a selected contact by pressing the Delete key or by clicking the Delete button in the Delete group on the Home tab.
- Add a contact from the same company by selecting a contact and choosing *Contact from the Same Company* in the New Items button drop-down list.
- Use the *Add Contact Picture* box in the Contact window to attach a photograph of the person in a contact record.
- Attach a follow-up flag to a contact as a reminder to follow up on an issue.
- Contact records can be sorted by up to four fields in the Sort dialog box.
- Open the Filter dialog box to temporarily remove from the contacts list records that do not meet the specified condition.
- The same six color categories that can be applied to messages and appointments can be applied to contacts.
- Use the letter tabs in the alphabet index along the left side of the Content pane to move to records.
- Find a contact by typing a name or other entry in the *Search People* box in the Find group on the Home tab or in the *Search Contacts* box at the top of the Content pane. Buttons on the Search tab help you narrow the results.
- Use the Advanced Find dialog box to locate contact records by performing more complex searches based on a conditional statement by which to find records.
- Click the Email or Meeting button in the Communicate group on the Home tab to create a message to, or schedule a meeting with, a selected contact.
- A contact group is a distribution list of contacts that is stored using a group name, which can be used to send email messages or meeting invitations.
- Add and delete members and update member data by using the Add Members, Remove Member, and Update Now buttons in the Members group on the Contact Group tab.
- You can delete a contact group when the distribution list is no longer needed.
- Add jobs to your To-Do list as tasks in the Task module. To add a new task, type the task description in the *Type a new task* text box at the top of the task list.
- Create a task in a Task window to add additional options, such as the task status and priority.
- When you have finished a task, you can either delete it from the task list or mark it as completed.
- Update or edit a task by double-clicking the task entry to open the Task window and then making changes to the task details.
- A task that you perform on a regular basis can be set up as a recurring task.
- You can assign a task to someone else by emailing him or her a task request. The task recipient can choose to accept the task, decline the task, or reassign the task to another person.

Commands Review

FEATURE	BUTTON	RIBBON TAB AND GROUP, OR OTHER METHOD	SHORTCUT
Add contact		Home, New	Ctrl + N
Add contact from existing contact		Home, New	
Add contact group		Home, New	Ctrl + Shift + L
Add, change, or view contact details		Contact, Show	
Add, change, or view contact fields		Contact, Show	
Add contact photo		Contact, Options	
Apply color category		Home, Tags OR Contact, Tags	
Create task		Home, New	Ctrl + N
Delete contact or task		Home, Delete OR Contact, Actions OR Task, Actions	Ctrl + D
Filter contacts		View, Current View	
Find contact using *Search Contacts* box		Click in *Search Contacts* box	Ctrl + E
Find contact using *Search People* box	Search People	Home, Find	
Flag contact for follow-up		Home, Tags OR Contact, Tags	Ctrl + Shift + G
Mark task as completed		Task, Manage Task	
Schedule meeting with contact		Home, Communicate OR Contact, Communicate	Ctrl + Shift + Q
Send email to contact		Home, Communicate OR Contact, Communicate OR Email button in Reading pane (People view)	
Sort contacts		View, Current View	
View history of recent search requests		Search Tools Search, Options	

Quick Steps

Add a Contact
1. Click New Contact button in New group on Home tab.
2. Type data in required fields.
3. Click Save & Close button.

Edit a Contact
1. Double-click contact name in Content pane.
2. Edit fields as required in Contact window.
3. Click Save & Close button.

Delete a Contact
1. Click to select name in Content pane.
2. Click Delete button in Delete group on Home tab.

Add a Contact From Same Company
1. Select existing contact in Content pane.
2. Click New Items button in New group on Home tab.
3. Click *Contact from the Same Company*.
4. Type data as required.
5. Click Save & Close button.

Add a Photo to a Contact Record
1. Open Contact window.
2. Click *Add Contact Picture* box.
3. Navigate to drive and folder.
4. Double-click image file name.
5. Click Save & Close button.

Flag a Contact for Follow-Up
1. Select record in Content pane.
2. Click Follow Up button in Tags group on Home tab.
3. Click desired flag.

Sort Contacts
1. Click View tab.
2. Click View Settings button in Current View group.
3. Click Sort button.
4. Define sort fields.
5. Click OK two times.

Filter Contacts
1. Click View tab.
2. Click View Settings button in Current View group.
3. Click Filter button.
4. Define filter criterion.
5. Click OK two times.

Assign a Color Category to a Contact
1. Select contact in Content pane.
2. Click Categorize button in Tags group on Home tab.
3. Click desired color category.

Find a Contact Using the *Search People* Box
1. Click in *Search People* box.
2. Type name or partial name.

Find a Contact Using the *Search Contacts* Box
1. Click in *Search Contacts* box.
2. Type name, partial name, or other search text.
3. Refine search as needed.
4. Click Close Search button.

Locate a Contact Using the Advanced Find Dialog Box
1. Click in or type search word in *Search Contacts* box.
2. Click Search Tools button in Options group on Search tab.
3. Click *Advanced Find*.
4. Enter search criterion.
5. Click Find Now button.
6. Close dialog box when finished.
7. If necessary, click Close Search button.

Send an Email Message to a Contact
1. Select contact or open Contact window.
2. Click Email button in Reading pane or in Communicate group on Home tab or Contact tab.
3. Type subject and message text.
4. Click Send button.

Schedule a Meeting with a Contact

1. Select contact or open Contact window.
2. Click Meeting button in Communicate group on Home tab or Contact tab.
3. Enter meeting details.
4. Click Send button.

Create a Contact Group from Contacts

1. Click New Contact Group button in New group on Home tab.
2. Type name in *Name* text box.
3. Click Add Members button.
4. Click *From Outlook Contacts*.
5. Double-click names to add to group.
6. Click OK.
7. Click Save & Close button.

Create a Task in the Task Window

1. Click New Task button in New group on Home tab.
2. Type subject text.
3. Change other options as required.
4. Click Save & Close button.

Create a Recurring Task

1. Click New Task button in New group on Home tab.
2. Type subject text.
3. Click Recurrence button in Recurrence group on Task tab.
4. Choose recurrence options.
5. Click OK.
6. Click Save & Close button.